The Mādhyamika Mind

The Mādhyamika Mind

HARSH NARAIN

MOTILAL BANARSIDASS PUBLISHERS
PRIVATE LIMITED • DELHI

First Edition: Delhi, 1997

ISBN: 81-208-1202-0

Also available at:

MOTILAL BANARSIDASS

41 U.A. Bungalow Road, Jawahar Nagar, Delhi 110 007
8, Mahalaxmi Chamber, Warden Road, Mumbai 400 026
120 Royapettah High Road, Mylapore, Chennai 600 004
Sanas Plaza, Subhash Nagar, Pune 411 002
16 St. Mark's Road, Bangalore 560 001
8 Camac Street, Calcutta 700 017
Ashok Rajpath, Patna 800 004
Chowk, Varanasi 221 001

PRINTED IN INDIA
BY JAINENDRA PRAKASH JAIN AT SHRI JAINENDRA PRESS,
A-45 NARAINA, PHASE I, NEW DELHI 110 028
AND PUBLISHED BY NARENDRA PRAKASH JAIN FOR
MOTILAL BANARSIDASS PUBLISHERS PRIVATE LIMITED,
BUNGALOW ROAD, DELHI 110 007

For
my daughter Dr. Muktāvalī

Contents

Preface *ix*

1. INTRODUCTION **1**

2. THE BUDDHA'S MIND **7**
   The Categorical, the Allegorical, and the Equivocal in the Buddha 7
   Wooing and Jilting Metaphysics 9
   The Conflicting Thrusts of the Metaphysical in the Buddha 11

3. LOGICAL DEVELOPMENTS **29**
   Realism Culminating in Destructed Nihilism 29
   Reaction to Realism Culminating in Absolute Nihilism 31
   Tension between Absolute Nihilism and Absolutism in the Mādhyamika 33
   Idealism, Absolutism, Docetism 36
   Theo-Buddhism 37
   The Soul's Hideouts 41
   The Buddhist Mind Divided against Itself 43

4. CONFLICTING INTERPRETATIONS **49**
   The Nihilistic Interpretation 49
   The Metaphysical-Absolutistic Interpretation 50
   The Soteriological-Absolutistic Interpretation 53
   The Linguistic-Analytic Interpretation 54
   Harking Back to the non-Mādhyamika Traditions 55
   The Mādhyamika's Confession 57

5. GERMS OF NIHILISM IN NON-BUDDHIST TRADITIONS **67**
   The Vedic '*Asat*' 67

The Nyāya-Vaiśeṣika *Asat-Kārya* 68
The Lokāyata Negativism 69
Pre-Buddhistic Upholders of Four-Cornered Negation 70

6. EVOLUTION OF THE MEANING OF ŚŪNYA/ ŚŪNYATĀ **73**
The Pāli Canon 73
Non-Canonical Pāli Buddhism 76
Sanskrit Hīnayāna Buddhism 77
Mahāyāna Buddhism 78

7. THE MĀDHYAMIKA AS ŚŪNYAVĀDA **85**
Graduated Teaching of the *Śūnyatā* Doctrine 86
(1) *Śūnyatā* as Relative Being 86
(2) *Śūnyatā* as Essenceless Being 88
(3) *Śūnyatā* as Non-Being 89
(4) *Śūnyatā* as Neither Being nor Non-Being 90
(5) *Śūnyatā* of *Śūnyatā* 93
Śūnyatā and *Prajñāpāramitā* 95

8. THE MĀDHYAMIKA DIALECTIC AND ITS SIGNIFICANCE **107**
From Bypassing Metaphysics through Its Outright Rejection to Its Total Transcendence 107
The Mādhyamika Rejects Metaphysics 107
An Omnibus Five-Member Dialectic 110
Nihilistic Significance of the Dialectic 111
The Logico-Linguistic Dilemma 115
Total Transcendence of Metaphysics 117

9. NIHILISM AND ABSOLUTISM **123**
'Tattva', Dharmatā, Tathatā, Bhūtakoṭi 123
Meaning of Absolute 129
Nihilism and Advaitism 132

10. RÈSUMÈ AND REVIEW **143**

ABBREVIATIONS 151

BIBLIOGRAPHY 153

INDEX 163

Preface

What do the Mādhyamikas really mean? After due scrutiny of their primary sources as well as of those of their rivals, coupled with a careful consideration of new-fangled interpretations by modern Mādhyamikologists, the present author essays in this work the task of demonstrating with due documentation that it is difficult to resist the conclusion that, far from being an Absolutism or Absolutistic Monism as commonly held in responsible circles today, Mādhyamika philosophy, styled *Śūnyavāda*, is, as held by the classics, Universal, Total, or Absolute Nihilism/Illusionism, indeed so Absolute a Nihilism/Illusionism that it leaves absolutely no room for religion and mysticism to which the Mādhyamikas do in their aphilosophical mood feel committed, a fact brought into focus by the present writer for the first time.

This author is indebted to the editors of the *Philosophy East and West*, the *Mādhyamika Dialectic and the Philosophy of Nāgārjuna*, and the *Prajñāloka: Journal of the Nāgārjuna Buddhist Foundation* for their permission to use papers published by them.

This work is the result of a project made available to the author by the University Grants Commission, to whom his thanks are due.

The author is also beholden to Messrs Motilal Banarsidass Publishers Private Limited who have made publication of this work possible with such promptitude.

Lucknow
March 31, 1993

Harsh Narain

CHAPTER 1

Introduction

The Mādhyamika system belongs to the Mahāyāna tradition of Buddhism, yet, as I see it, its Nihilism marks a departure therefrom. To my mind, Vijñānavāda idealism-Absolutism is more Mahāyānic than the Mādhyamika Nihilism. The Mādhyamika is caught rather unawares in the rigmarole of universal, all-embracing, absolute Nihilism to such an extent that he fails to harness it to his religion and mysticism. All this we shall see in the sequel. Interiorization of Buddhism is the hallmark of Mahāyāna, and the Mādhyamika is out to strike at the very distinction of exterior and interior adjudging both to be equally void. Attempts at contrary interpretations by our contemporaries notwithstanding, there is no alternative but to equate the Mādhyamika's *Śūnya* with the *Tuccha/Alīka* of Advaita Vedānta and *Atyantābhāva* of the Naiyāyika, illustrated by the son of a barren woman, skyflower, and the like.

This being the case, there is little room for the grant of even empirical reality to life and the world in the Mādhyamika system as presented by its first systematizer, viz. Nāgārjuna, and interpreted by Buddhapālita and Candrakīrti, even though they maintain a distinction between the ultimate and the empirical truths in their own way.

As if in order to restore empirical reality to life and the world, Bhāvaviveka, a follower of Nāgārjuna, had to strike his own line of thought, trying to contrive positive arguments to establish *Śūnyatā*. A schism in the Mādhyamika was the result.

Buddhapālita and Candrakīrti are called *Prāsaṅgikas* and their method is designated as *Prasaṅga (reductio ad absurdum)*, whereas Bhāvaviveka is called *Svātantrika* and his method, *Svatantrānumāna* (independent, positive reasoning). This Svātantrika school came later to be subdivided into Yogācārā-Svātantrika-Mādhyamika and Sautrāntika-Svātantrika-Mādhyamika, the one maintaining self-awareness *(svasaṁvedana)* while rejecting the external world and the other rejecting self-awareness and admitting external objects established through their particulars (*svalakṣaṇas*). The first sub-school is represented by Śāntarakṣita and Kamalaśīla, while the second, by Bhāvaviveka himself.[1]

It is the Prāsaṅgika school of Buddhapālita and Candrakīrti which has held its sway over the other school all along, to the extent of being treated as *the* Mādhyamika system proper, not only by the Prāsaṅgikas themselves but by the opponents of the Mādhyamika system as well.

I have confined my research to the Prāsaṅgika school. Though certain studies of the Svātantrika school have of late appeared in English, the bulk of its primary sources is far from available in Sanskrit original or English translation.

Nāgārjuna is credited with the authorship of six treatises, out of which the *Madhyamakaśāstra*, the *Vigrahavyāvartanī*, the *Ratnāvalī*, and the *Catuḥstava* are more important. His auto-commentary *Akutobhayā* and Buddhapālita's *Mādhyamikavṛtti*, though lost in their Sanskrit original yet of late reconstructed into Sanskrit from the Tibetan translations,[2] have been clouded by Candrakīrti's great commentary, *Madhyamakavṛtti* generally known as *Prasannapadā*. The last known representatives of the Prāsaṅgika school are Śāntideva and his commentator Prajñākaramati. The ninth chapter of Śāntideva's *Bodhicaryāvatāra* is entirely devoted to Mādhyamika Nihilism and breathes the same spirit as Nāgārjuna's. Another great Mādhyamika who follows Nāgārjuna in approach and method and helps consolidate the system against not only the Ābhidharmika school but also the Sāṅkhya and the Vaiśeṣika, is his chief disciple Āryadeva, author of the *Catuḥśataka,* which is only partly extant in its Sanskrit original, and the *Śataśāstra,* which is found only in Chinese translation and for some time past in English translation from the latter. Some of his smaller tracts are also extant.

To T.R.V. Murti, "The Mādhyamika system seems to have been perfected at one stroke by the genius of its founder—Nāgārjuna."[3] No doubt, Nāgārjuna is its first systematizer. Yet there can be no denying the fact that all his basic ideas are found scattered in the Prajñāpāramitā texts, which happen to be a mine of all of Mahāyāna doctrines, especially the Mādhyamika. While we are concentrating in this work upon Nāgārjuna and the Prāsaṅgika school, we are not ignoring the Prajñāpāramitā texts.

Except for their failure on the front of certain radical issues—such as their reckless use of *Śūnyatā, Pratītya-samutpāda,* etc., which we shall notice in the sequel—coupled with that on the front of reconciliation of their philosophy with their religion and mysticism brought into focus for the first time in this work—,the Mādhyamikas may be viewed as the most clear-headed group of Indian philosophers. But, for all their clear-headedness, they happen to be the most misunderstood of them today. A careful scrutiny of their primary sources, as also of those of their rivals, confirms the classical interpretation that their philosophy, styled *Śūnyavāda,* is absolute Nihilism rather than an Absolutism or Absolutistic monism, as commonly believed in responsible circles. The burden of this work is to bring to light the modern mistakes of regarding *Śūnyavāda* as an Absolutism and to throw into bold relief its real, Nihilistic character.

Nihilism is exclusively an Indian and typically a heterodox, especially Buddhist, development, without a parallel in foreign philosophical traditions. Finding it conspicuous by its absence in the Western philosophical tradition, many scholars seem to proceed on the tacit assumption that it is an impossibility of thought and that, therefore, Mādhyamika philosophy could be anything but total Nihilism, which it is traditionally made out to be. It is seldom appreciated in such circles that in the Indian tradition Nihilism has been in the air from Buddhist, rather pre-Buddhist times, to even slightly post-Mādhyamika times.

There are certain interpretations of the Mādhyamika philosophy which merit rejection out of hand. The authors of *Ṣaḍdarśanasamuccaya* (of Rājaśekhara), *Vivekavilāsa*, and *Sarvadarśanasaṅgraha* take it that the Mādhyamikas postulated the existence of what is called formless, pure, higher consciousness (*nirākāra-buddhi* or *svacchā parā saṁvid*),[4] whereas Candrakīrti comes out with a definite criticism of such consciousness.[5] Another example: An exponent of Nāgārjuna cites the latter to say that 'he has no position of his own' without quoting his actual words and then proceeds to construe the expression to mean that 'this basic truth, which he lays bare, is not anything exclusively his own but is in the possession of every self-conscious individual.'[6] On the contrary, Nāgārjuna has to say, 'I have no position whatever, . . . for the simple reason that I find nothing whatever.'[7] The unwary reader is bound to be misled by the patently false exposition.

Our finding in this work is that Nihilism has been not a mere fiction but a hard fact in the history of Indian philosophy, pre-Mādhyamika as well as post-Mādhyamika, and that, therefore, the nihilistic interpretation of *Śūnyavāda* cannot be dismissed summarily on the ground that no such philosophy is possible.

We are inclined to believe that the classics are nearer the truth about the Mādhyamika's position than the moderns. Philosophical *Śūnyavāda* is a form of illusionism and nihilism: it is absolute ontological nihilism as distinguished from the destructed nihilism of Harivarman; the soteriological nihilism of Arthur Schopenhauer and Eduard vön Hartmann; and the critical nihilism of Jayarāśi Bhaṭṭa, author of the *Tattvopaplavasiṁha*, the only extant work of the Lokāyata school. Again, the Hindu, Jaina, and Lokāyata schools of philosophy (barring of course Jayarāśi Bhaṭṭa) on the one hand and Mahāyāna and certain forms of Hīnayāna like the schools of the Sāmmitīyas and Vātsīputrīyas on the other, are noumenalists; the bulk of realist and idealist schools of Buddhism are phenomenalists; and the Mādhyamika school is illusionist and nihilist.

REFERENCES

1. Shotaro Lida, *Reason and Emptiness*, p. 30.
2. See Raghunath Pandeya, *The Madhyamakaśāstram of Nāgārjuna* with Nāgārjuna's *Akutobhayā*, Buddhapālita's *Madhyamakavṛtti*, Bhāvaviveka's *Prajñāpradīpavṛtti*, and Candrakīrti's *Prasannapadāvṛtti*, critically reconstructed, in two volumes.
3. T.R.V. Murti, *The Central Philosophy of Buddhism*, p. 87.
4. Rājaśekhara Sūri, *Ṣaḍdarśanasamuccaya*, Bauddhamata 45; Jinadatta Sūri, *Vivekavilāsa* 43; Mādhava, *Sarvadarśanasaṅgraha*, Bauddhadarśana.
5. *MŚP* 1.3, pp. 21ff.
6. K. Venkata Ramnan, *Nāgārjuna's Philosophy* As Presented in the *Mahāprajñāpāramitāśāstra*, pp. 41-42.
7. *VV* 29-30.

school. Again, the [illegible] and [illegible] schools of philosophy (barring of certain [illegible]) Bhartṛhari on the one hand and Mādhyamika and certain forms of Hīnayāna like the schools of the [illegible] and [illegible] on the other, are non-dualists; the bulk of realist and idealist schools of Buddhism are phenomenalists and the Mādhyamika school is illusionist and nihilist.[6]

REFERENCES

1. [illegible], p. 37
2. See [illegible] [illegible] [illegible] [illegible] [illegible] [illegible] and [illegible] [illegible] supplied in two volumes.
3. T.R.V. Murti, The Central Philosophy of Buddhism, p. 7.
4. [illegible]
5. [illegible], pp. 221
6. K. Venkata Ramanan, Nāgārjuna's Philosophy as Presented in the [illegible], pp. 41-42
7. [illegible]

CHAPTER 2

The Buddha's Mind

The Buddha's language is multi-stranded and multi-faceted enough to involve on his part the risk of self-inconsistency or self-contradiction, express, implied, or seeming. This proves a real hurdle in understanding him aright. Let us go into the issue.

The Categorical, the Allegorical, and the Equivocal in the Buddha

The Buddha's statements can be grouped under three heads: the categorical, the allegorical, and the equivocal. His categorical statements are either negative or positive. His negative statements pertain to denial of personal God, of personal ego, of the authority of the Vedas, of bloody sacrifice, and the like. His positive statements pertain to postulation of the Four Noble Truths, of heaven and hell, of gods and demons, of metempsychosis, and the like.

Certain statements of the Buddha are more allegorical than categorical. *Nibbāna/Nirvāṇa,* for example, is dearest to his heart, on which he waxes much more enthusiastic than others do on their *summum bonum.* Yet he chooses the path of allegorizing about it, which often leaves us in the lurch as to the real import of his utterances on the issue. Indeed, there is no teaching of the Buddha more controversial than *Nibbāna.*

Well, certain utterances of the Buddha on *Nibbāna* sound equivocal as well. Most of his equivocal statements pertain, however, to what he chooses to call *Abyākaṭāni*, the unspeakables/imponderables, ten in number, listed below:

1. The world is eternal.
2. The world is not eternal.
3. The world is finite.
4. The world is infinite.
5. The soul is identical with the body.
6. The soul is different from the body.
7. The Tathāgata exists after death.
8. The Tathāgata does not exist after death.
9. The Tathāgata does and does not exist after death.
10. The Tathāgata neither exists nor does not exist after death.

The Mahāsāṅghikas added the following four unspeakables to the list:

1. The world is eternal and not eternal.
2. The world is neither eternal nor not eternal.
3. The world is finite and infinite.
4. The world is neither finite nor infinite.

About these propositions, the Buddha is found often to make equivocal statements. To illustrate the point: Asked whether on leaving his body at death the saint who has attained the goal ceases to exist or exists eternally, the Buddha answers that such a saint is without measure, that he does not have that with which one can speak of him, and that on cessation of all the elements all description has ceased also.[1]

The lists of the allegorical and the equivocal are not mutually exclusive, however, several items being common to both. For instance, both kinds of statements are discernible in the Pāli canon in regard to *Nibbāna*.

Such being the case, to many the Buddha sounds obscure, ambiguous, or paradoxical, often to such an extent that he is adjudged a sceptic, an agnostic, or a pragmatist, masking his real self for fear of adverse public opinion. On the other hand, he is, more often than not, represented as a believer in the existence of the personal self and repudiator only of the personal ego. Sometimes, he is taken to posit a universal Self on the pattern of the Upaniṣads and to deny the existence of personal selves.

Wooing and Jilting Metaphysics

The Buddha begins his spiritual career with wooing metaphysics, but, when he sees metaphysics draw too near, he jilts it remorselessly.

His cardinal doctrine of Suffering (*duḥkha*) appears to be rooted in a metaphysical view of existence. Consider the following fundamental pairs of opposite attitudes to existence:

1. Existence has a permanent foundation.
   Existence is impermanent to the core.
2. Existence is meaningful, teleological.
   Existence is meaningless, mechanistic.
3. Existence is a good, a value, a boon.
   Existence is an evil, a disvalue, a curse.
4. Existence is at bottom of all happiness, joy, delight.
   Existence is actually or potentially all misery, sorrow, suffering.

At first sight, the Buddha appears to grant the second member of each of these pairs, summed up in his three Seals (*mudrās*), as the Tibetans would put these: 'All is impermanent', 'All is soulless/substanceless', and 'All is Suffering'. This is not all, however. He has a fourth Seal, 'Nibbāna is quiescent', which either represents the culmination of the first three Seals or serves to offset their thrust effectively, depending upon its interpretation.

Again, the Buddha claims to have discovered or realized the Four Noble Truths (*ariya saccāni*), which are:

1. Universal Suffering.
2. Cause of Suffering, which is *Paṭiccasamuppāda.*
3. Cessation of Suffering, which is *Nibbāna.*
4. Way to the cessation, which is the Noble Eightfold Path.

Thus, Suffering is not the whole truth. The whole truth is that Suffering is beginningless but not endless. It is universal or all-encompassing only till it is contained or eliminated altogether. This all is intensely metaphysical.

Besides, the Buddha on occasion postulates the existence of gods and recommends their worship. He is usually depicted as a staunch upholder of the no-soul doctrine, yet he is sometimes found to assert that at the highest level of truth and reality there is neither the soul (*attā*) nor the not-soul (*nir-attā*).[2] What is this if not metaphysics, pure and simple?

Indeed, examples of the Buddha's wooing metaphysics can be multiplied indefinitely.

But, when it comes to committing himself to specific metaphysical propositions like the ones listed under the unspeakables, the Buddha is found to jilt metaphysics without remorse. To use a mundane simile, he flirts with metaphysics without reserve, but, when metaphysics proposes to him, he shies away.

The ten unspeakables listed before constitute specific queries on ultimate, penultimate, or antepenultimate issues of metaphysics, without taking which seriously, little headway is possible in the realm of radical thought in soteriology. The Buddha dissuades his followers from such queries on two counts: first, they are irrelevant to the ideals of spiritual life preached by him and, second, they are unanswerable in the very nature of things. But humanity cannot rest content with indefinite postponement, shelving, or side-tracking such fundamental queries. No wonder, therefore, that his followers ignored the master in this behalf and persuaded themselves to found well-knit metaphysical systems. In the absence of clear guidelines from him, these systems were constantly at war with each other, so much so that it is difficult to decide what the Buddha actually means where he waxes metaphysical or where he discourages metaphysics.

The Conflicting Thrusts of the Metaphysical in the Buddha

Despite his disclaimer of commitment to ultimate questions of metaphysics, the Buddha does indeed have metaphysics and metaphysics to his credit. If we analyze his statements carefully, we shall discover two dominant thrusts therein, totally irreconcilable with each other. These are:

1. Realism pregnant with Nihilism
2. Idealism culminating in Absolutism

The Buddha begins as a realist par excellence. He analyzes existence into '*dharmas*', meaning elements or rather sense-data, which are presented as objective phenomena, usually. He grants full reality to the non-material alongside of the material. Out of the five aggregates (*khandhas*) all but form (*rūpa*) and out of the six elements (*dhātus*) psyche (*viññāṇa*) are clearly non-material/non-physical/psychical. Both the orders of reality are irreducible ones, whereby the Buddha deserves to be called a dualist. With a difference, however. On the question of the relation between the two orders of reality, they are said to be somehow interdependent, in the sense that the one constitutes the necessary and sufficient condition for emergence of the other and vice versa,[3] and life goes on.

The *dharmas* are said to bear three characteristics: non-duration (*anicca*), unrest (*dukkha*), and non-substantiality (*anattā*).[4] Stcherbatsky suggests a fourth characteristic also, final deliverance (*śānta*). It is evident, therefore, that the Buddha is a phenomenalist, in the simple sense that, according to him, the world consists of phenomena without noumena.

That the *dharmas* are objective appears to have been assumed in the Pāli canon almost throughout. An interesting statement of the Buddha merits quotation in this connection: "Whether the Tathāgata were to arise or whether the Tathāgata were not to arise, the nature and way of the *dhammas* remains."[5]

Now, if the *dhammas* are non-enduring or permanent, wherefrom do they spring into existence? We fail to get clear guidance from the Buddha. He observes: "Inexistent, the *dhammas* come into existence; existent, (they) pass into inexistence" (*dhammā ahutvā sambhonti, hutvā paṭiyenti*).[6] The later Buddhists came to be divided over the source of the *dhammas*. A section of the Sarvāstivādins postulated an unchanging substratum (*svabhāva, dravya*) underlying the changing *dharmas*, as if in open defiance of the Buddha's doctrine of non-substantiality. Another section of the Sarvāstivādins, Buddhaghoṣa and later Theravādins, and the Sautrāntikas formulated a theory of immediate contiguity (*samānāntara*), ascribing causal efficiency (*arthakriyākāritva, paccayatā*) to the immediately preceding *dhammas*. This, too, however, militates against the Buddha's theory of impermanence (*anicca*), which does not commit him to any doctrine of momentariness (*kṣaṇa-vāda, kṣaṇabhaṅga-vāda*). Such a statement of the Buddha as the following rather contradicts this doctrine: "This physical body made up of the four primary elements lasts for one year, lasts for two years, lasts for three years, lasts for four years, lasts for five years, lasts for ten years, lasts for twenty years, lasts for thirty years, lasts for forty years, lasts for fifty years, lasts for a hundred years, (and) lasts for more years also. What they call the sensorium, the mind, the psyche arises as one thing and ceases as another by night and by day as well."[7]

Well, the later Buddhists cannot be blamed for the contradictions in which they came to be involved. It is simply to explain the problem of continuity of the discrete, impermanent, non-substantial *dhammas* postulated by the Buddha as well as system in their emergence and disappearance that they had to wander about in the realm of imagination and thought in search of a satisfactory alternative.

Compelled by the logic of his own postulates, the Buddha often found himself on the road to self-contradiction and obscurity. We do not propose to recall in this connection his doctrine of *Nibbāna*, the obscurity of which still persists. We would do well to take the nature of the *dhammas* themselves as an example. We have seen that the tenor of the Buddha's teachings in general is in favour of realism of the sense-data called the *dhammas*. The *dhammas* are conceived by him as so substanceless and fleeting that he is sometimes led to declare them ephemeral and illusory. "Form is comparable to foam, sensation to bubbles, perception to mirage, disposition to plantain trunk, (and) psyche to illusion: so did the Buddha teach."[8]

Just see, the Buddha started, as is well known, by declaring the individual (*puggala*) as ephemeral and illusory and reducing it to sense-data (*dhammas*). Immediately after, he cut the ground, so to speak, from under the feet of the sense-data by declaring them non-substantial. Further, he rendered them fleeting, or, to put it otherwise, ever on their heels. And now he dismisses them as ephemeral and illusory, pure and simple, thereby paving the way to Nihilism. It is not for nothing that Candrakīrti quotes the statement verbatim, in its Sanskritized form.

And the doctrine of momentariness, born of his own metaphysical moorings, acts as a pointer to Nihilism in its own way. According to it, a *dhamma* vanishes immediately after its birth; in other words, its evanescence arises simultaneously with its emergence (*nāśasya tan-niṣpattāv eva niṣpannatvāt*).[9] Their simultaneity is so complete that "the momentary reality itself is called annihilation" (*yo hi bhāvaḥ kṣaṇasthāyī vināśa iti gīyate*).[10] Thus, the *dhammas* transpire to be no more real than unreal. This leads to a bi-way—one way towards idealism and the other towards Nihilism.

Of course, there are certain other indications of germs of Nihilism in the Buddha. He refers to an all-positivist/pan-positivist Lokāyata school, according to which 'all is' (*sabbaṁ atthi*) and an all-negativist/pan-negativist Lokāyata school, according to which 'all is not' (*sabbaṁ natthi*).[11] He also refers to all-believers who aver, 'I believe in all' (*sabbaṁ me khamati*) and all-believers who aver, 'I believe in nothing' (*sabbaṁ me na khamati*).[12] While referring to these, the Buddha preaches elimination (*paṭinissagga*) of all views/metaphysics/dogma (*diṭṭhīnāṁ*).[13] Is it not an anticipation of the Mādhyamika's exclusion of all views/metaphysics/dogma (*sarvadṛṣṭināṁ niḥsaraṇam*)[14] or removal of all views/metaphysics/dogma (*sarvadṛṣṭi-prahāṇa*)?[15]

Likewise, the Buddha preaches silence (*tuṇhīṁ-bhāva*) as the cessation of all speculation and thought (*vitakka-vicārānaṁ vūpasamā*).[16] Candrakīrti appears simply to follow suit when he describes the ultimate truth (*paramārtha*) as silence (*tūṣṇīṁ-bhāva*).[17] In fact, the Mādhyamika's distinction of *Paramārtha-Satya* and *Saṁvṛti-Satya* (conventional truth) is also anticipated in the Buddha's *Paramattha-Sacca* and *Sammuti-Sacca.*[18] In the same way, the Buddha's distinction of *Nītattha-Sutta* and *Neyattha-Sutta,* statements/teachings of direct meaning and indirect meaning, duly anticipates the Mādhyamika's *Nītārtha-Sūtra* and *Neyārtha-Sūtra.*[19]

Needless to mention that the Mādhyamika's tetralemma (*catuṣkoṭi*) of being, non-being, both, and neither is already employed by the Buddha *vis-á-vis* the Tathāgata.[20]

Now, the realist thesis came to such a pass that it took a turn to idealism. Idealism is often found on the look-out for an Absolute to sustain or generate the procession of ideas in a fixed order. Buddhist idealism was no exception, as we shall see in the next chapter. According to many, indeed, if fleeting sense-data stand in need of a substratum, a noumenon, subjacent to them, fleeting ideas stand in such a need also.

Buddhist thought has all along been marked by certain perennial tensions, such as *Saṁsāra* and *Nirvāṇa/Nibbāna,* Nihilationism (*uccheda-vāda*) and Eternalism (*sassata-vāda*), no-soul doctrine and near-soul doctrine, and atheism and theism. The Buddha was all for cessation of *Saṁsāra* and attainment of *Nibbāna.* The way of the one was to him basically opposed to the way of the other, although he claimed to strike a middle path to overcome the tensions between the two. Opposed as he was to wanton living, he discouraged painful, self-torturing austerities and penances.

The Buddha talks so much of the no-soul (*anattā*) that he has come to be regarded as an advocate of a no-soul doctrine second only to Cārvāka. But to say that he was out and out a repudiator of the existence of soul does not appear to be the whole truth, despite all avowals to that effect on the part of the bulk of his followers and modern Buddhologists. It has been noted by certain competent scholars that such an absolute statement as 'there is no soul' or 'the soul does not exist' is conspicuous by its absence in the Pāli canon. On the other hand, what occurs therein, and frequently, is that the body is not the *attā,*[21] the senses are not the *attā,*[22] the sense-objects are not the *attā,*[23] the five aggregates are not the *attā,*[24] and so forth. In fact, the Buddha appears to lament the fact that the aggregates are usually mistaken for the soul and to approve of detachment therefrom: "O Bhikkhus! matter/form is non-eternal, what is non-eternal is suffering, what is suffering is no-soul (*anattā*), what is no-soul should be viewed as such after duly realizing 'this is not mine, this is not me, it is not my soul'" (*netaṁ mama, neso'ham asmi, na me so attā*).[25] This statement is repeated in respect of the other aggregates as well. It is also added to the first statement, the one *vis-á-vis* matter/form, that so realizing, mind stands fully detached and liberated. Another statement is: "O Bhikkhus! matter/form is *anattā*. . . . feeling is *anattā*. . . . idea is *anattā*. . . . volition is *anattā*. . . . sensation is *anattā*."[26]

In such contexts, the target of attack seems to be not the theory of soul but various types of materialism. Śaṅkara refers to such materialists thus: "Some materialists take the body to be the soul,. . . . some other materialists take the senses to be the soul, still other materialists take the mind to be the soul, many other materialists take the intellect to be the soul, and there are certain materialists who take to be the soul the unmanifest within the intellect identifiable with Ignorance."[27] Here, too, one may read a repudiation of each one of the five aggregates on the one hand and each one of the five sheaths listed in the *Taittirīya Upaniṣad* from matter to intellect on the other, being regarded as the soul.[28] Thus, it is not the existence of the soul which is denied in the Pāli canon or by the Buddha but the identification of the non-soul with the soul. The Buddha exhorts us to have this attitude towards the three *lakkhaṇas* (*khandhas*, *dhātus*, and *āyatanas*): It is not mine, it is not me, it is not my soul (*netaṁ mama, neso 'ham asmi, na me so attā*).[29]

On G.C. Pande's computation, there is only one reference to the idea of the continuum in all the Nikāyas (discounting semi-commentarial works included in the fifth Nikāya), under the name *viññāṇa-sota*.[30]

Besides, there are quite a number of indirect indications in the Pāli canon which create a strong presumption in favour of the view that the Buddha did acknowledge the existence of an *ātman*. What survives in *Nibbāna*? *Viññāṇa* cleansed and purified (*Athāparaṁ viññāṇaṁ yeva avasissati parisuddhaṁ pariyodātam*),[31] luminous and infinite (*viññāṇam anidassanam anantaṁ sabbatopabham*).[32] Sometimes it is asserted in the Pāli cannon that *viññāṇa*, being variable, cannot be taken to be the soul (*attā*).[33] It appears that *viññāṇa* has two aspects, empirical and transcendental, the one being defiled by impurities and the other released from them.[34] It has been convincingly demonstrated by certain scholars that originally man was analyzed in Buddhism into body (*kāyā*) and mind (*viññāṇa/citta*) and that it was much later that *viññāṇa* became one of the five aggregates composing human personality.[35]

The *Mahāvagga* contains a significant remark, seldom noticed: It is that the doctrine of the conquest of self is taught not to destroy the souls of man but to preserve them.[36]

A ticklish statement of the Buddha is that, even as the word 'chariot' is a name given to the aggregate of its parts (even though there is no one entity like the chariot), the name 'soul' is given to the five aggregates taken together (even though there is no one entity like the soul).[37] Mrs. Rhys Davids has shown that the *Khandha* theory is a later development.[38] Hence the above passage cannot be pressed against the thesis maintained by us.

It is well known that the Buddha studiously avoided questions directly put to him regarding the existence of the soul or *attā* as also regarding the relation between soul and body.[39] On the question of survival of the Tathāgata, too, he chose to keep silent.[40] Does this not indicate the existence of some serious tension on his part in this regard? Indeed, after all has been said this way or that, it must be acknowledged that one can never be sure as to what he actually meant.

As a matter of fact, belief in some sort of survival is a necessary constituent of religion. If this life is all, there can be no hunger and thirst for the transcendent, indeed even for righteousness. That is why Cārvāka is not a religion. A religionist is an *Āstika* and a non-religionist a *Nāstika* in Pāṇinian parlance, according to which an *Āstika* is one who believes in the transcendent order (*para-loka*) and a *Nāstika* is one who disbelieves in the transcendent order (*para-loka*)—*'Asti, nāsti, diṣṭaṁ matiḥ'*.[41] There is no denying the fact that Buddhism has never questioned the belief in the transcendent. The Buddha might not have seen his way to commit himself this way or that on the issue of survival, but he nowhere disfavours the idea of survival. He upholds the doctrine of reincarnation or transmigration. Besides, survival of a salvific sort does enter Buddhism through its doctrine of *Nibbāna/Nirvāṇa.*

The question is: If the Buddha does not deny the existence of soul, why does he not state it in so many words? He rests content with the remark that the body is not the soul, the sense-organs are not the soul, and so on. Why so much emphasis on negative formulation? The position appears to be that his so-called no-soul doctrine is directed towards inculcating egolessness upon his audience. Dharmakīrti outlines the evils of belief in the self thus: One who believes in the self develops permanent love for one's ego. This leads to craving for pleasures. This leads to the feeling of *nēum* (and *tūum*) on our part. This inflates our ego. This leads to a series of rebirths. Besides, the 'I'-feeling gives rise to the 'thou'-feeling, the feeling of otherness. This leads to attachment and aversion respectively, which are responsible for all our evils.[42] He elsewhere observes that the no-soul view leads to the destruction of desire.[43] Here one is tempted to recall Sureśvara's proposition that the upshot of all scriptural commands is motivation towards renunciation and self-abnegation.[44]

In his zeal for inculcating upon the people a spirit of detachment from the world and narrow egoity, the Buddha was led to condemn the world as impermanent and evanescent and the self, too, as such. About the self, however, he was almost always cautious that the absolute self remains immune to his attack.

The Buddha seems to be obsessed with the idea that, unless the conceit of, 'I' and 'mine', is eradicated, salvation will not be possible. Even so, he nowhere seems to commit himself to the view that the self does not exist at all. He seems to take it that by denying the self he will be responsible for leading the masses into the abyss of what he calls nihilationism/materialism and by positing the self, in to that of eternalism which will only reinforce the conceit of 'I' and 'mine'. Pointedly asked by the wandering Vacchagotta whether the self is (*atthattā'ti*) or the self is not (*natthattā 'ti*), the Buddha keeps silent (*Bhagavā tuṇhī ahosi*).[45] When, after Vacchagotta's departure, Ānanda wants to know why the Buddha chose to remain silent, the Buddha says that, in the event of his affirming the existence of the self, Vacchagotta would have fallen into the error of eternalism, and that, in the event of his denying the existence of the self, he would have fallen into the error of nihilationism.[46] He appears to think that eternalism involves clinging to the conceit of 'I' and 'mine', while nihilationism involves indifference to *Nibbāna.* Hence he did not feel like preaching either of the two doctrines. This ambivalent attitude of his has been responsible for many a confusion in the history of Buddhist thought.

As a matter of fact, the Buddha's doctrine of *Nibbāna* presupposes the existence of the self and life everlasting. Otherwise, who will experience *Nibbāna,* whose *Nibbāna*? It appears that what is held by the bulk of the Buddhologists to be denied by the Buddha is accepted by him at this stage at any rate.

To us it appears that, though omniscience was thrust upon him soon after, the Buddha originally laid claim to have discovered only the Four Noble Truths, especially the way to *Nibbāna.* He had to steer clear of the labyrinth of the controversies raging round the concepts of soul, God, creation and destruction of the world, etc. He might have imagined that, if people were involved in such controversies, they would be far flung from the way of *Nibbāna.* Besides, on many issues, he might himself not have been clear in his mind. For these reasons, he thought it fit to observe silence on ticklish and Nibbānically irrelevant issues. On such issues, he preferred to parry questions asked by the commonalty but open out before the deserving. He often claimed that he was not a close-fisted teacher, a teacher who withholds some of his teachings from his disciples, which means simply that he had told the deserving all that they needed or deserved to know about the Truths discovered by him. This serves to reconcile his disclaimer of non-closefistedness with his claim to infinite knowledge by way of the example of the *siṁsipā*-foliage.

While teaching the nature of *Nibbāna,* the Buddha emerges sometimes as a nihilist and sometimes as an Absolutist. There his ambivalence is most baffling. According to some, he preached total extinction in *Nibbāna,* while, according to some others, *Nibbāna* is a veritable Absolute akin to the *Nirguṇa-Brahman.* After collating the various utterances of the Buddha on the issue, we have come to the conclusion that the enthusiasm with which he talks about *Nibbāna* is far from reconcilable with the thought that *Nibbāna* is a synonym for total extinction like death as conceived by the Cārvāka. Though, in his polemical vein, the Cārvāka goes as far as to declare that his salvation is death, yet no Cārvāka can wax enthusiastic about such salvation. No Cārvāka is known to preach suicide. We are, therefore, inclined to believe that the Buddha's *Nibbāna* is far from identifiable with total extinction. To us, it appears to be a kind of merger in the *Brahman*, which is neither total extinction nor personal immortality, neither nihilation nor eternality. It is a kind of *Brahma-Nirvāṇa* taught by the *Bhagavad-Gītā.* This is the only way the Buddha's fear-psychosis in regard to nihilationism and eternalism can be explained. This appears also to be the only way his silence on the question about the survival of the Tathāgata can be explained.

Truly enough, the Buddha dreaded nihilationism and eternalism to the utmost. This dread is at the root of his obscure expressions as regards the nature of *Nibbāna.* His dread and abhorrence of both the extremes keep him vacillating between the two and render him incomprehensible in the long run, unless we interpret him as in the preceding paragraph.

Now about tension between atheism and theism. K.N. Jayatilleke asserts that 'the Buddha is an atheist and Buddhism in both its Theravāda and Mahāyāna form is atheism.'[47] The Buddha certainly denies the existence of a divine creator and world-ruler in unequivocal terms. He argues: "If God [*Issara*] designs the life of the entire world—prosperity and adversity, the good and the evil deeds—, man is (but) an instrument of his will and all responsibility lies on God."[48] Again, "If Brahman (masculine) is lord of the entire world and creator of the multitude of beings, why has he ordained misfortune in the world; why has he not made the entire world happy; why has he made the world full of deceit, falsehood, conceit, and unrighteousness?. . . . The lord of beings is unrighteous/evil, who ordained unrighteousness when there could have been righteousness."[49] The Buddha also ridicules theists according to whom the world was made by a good God (*bhaddakena Issareṇa nimmito*).[50] He derides Brahman (mas.)[51] holds God responsible for the faults of mankind,[52] and considers prayers to such God to be futile.[53]

Yet the Buddha postulates the existence of gods in clear terms. In reply to Saṅgārava's pointed query, are there gods?, the Buddha answers that there are.[54] Indeed, the Pāli canon is full of references to gods as real beings.[55] What is more significant, however, is the fact that it envisages monks' taking refuge in them if necessary.[56] Indeed, according to it, the Buddha favoured and directly or indirectly taught worship of the gods on occasion. Once, for example, he said to two ministers, his hosts: "Wherever a wise man has taken up his abode, there he brings gifts to the gods of the place. Respected and revered by him, the gods revere and respect him. They tremble for him as a mother trembles for her own son. He who enjoys the grace of the gods, sees only the good."[57] Elsewhere he observes: "The son of a good family uses his wealth to present gifts, and reveres the gods worthy of gifts (*bali-patiggāhikā*), respects and worships them. They in their turn are then gracious and say to him: 'Live long, attain a ripe old age.'[58] In a similar vein he avers: 'By right action, Visākhā! the impure mind is purified. And how, Visākhā! the impure mind is purified by right action. Herein the virtuous disciple calls to mind. . . . the gods: there are the gods of the four great kings, the gods of the thirty-three, the gods of Yama's realm, the happy gods, those that delight in creation, and those that control the creations of others, the gods of Brahman's (mas.) world, and still more. . . . As the disciple thus calls to mind. . . . the gods, his mind is calmed, joy arises, and what impurities of mind there are they vanish just as impure silver refined by right processing."[59] Another significant observation of his is: "As long as the Vajjians honour, respect, revere, and venerate the cult places (*cetiya*) within and outside (the towns), and do not deny them the customary oblations (*bali*), they may expect blessings only, and no decrease."[60] Besides, the Buddha prescribes six meditations (*anussati*, Skt. *anu-smṛti*), of which the meditation on the gods (*devatānussati*) is one, the others being meditation on the Buddha, the teacher, the community, the discipline, and the generosity in giving.[61] In meditation on the gods, the meditator calls to mind the virtues which have made them what they are, as also their power and glory. This frees his mind and heart from delusions and passions.[62]

One must not try to read the tendency of pandering to the masses in this behalf. The Buddha claims to have perceived, in his pre-enlightenment meditations, first the radiance of the gods and then the forms of the gods. At more advanced stages, he claims to have talked with them and finally known all about them.[63] Besides, the Buddha has left indications that he subscribed to a theory of the Absolute in his own way. He asserts that what is perishable (*mosa-dhamma*) is false and that only that is true which is imperishable (*a-mosadhamma*), which is *Nibbāna* (*taṁ hi Bhikkhu! musā yaṁ mosa-dhammaṁ, taṁ saccaṁ yaṁ amosa-dhammaṁ nibbānam*).[64] And *Nibbāna* is called permanent (*dhuva*), immortal (*amata*), and the like.[65] He also speaks of a *Viññāṇa* which is invisible, infinite, luminous on all sides and where water, earth, fire, and air find no place:

Viññāṇam anidassanam anantaṁ sabbatopabham
Ettha āpo ca pathavī tejo vāyo na gādhati.[66]

The clearest passages pointing to the Absolute is the one occurring in the *Udāna* and the *Itivuttaka* verbatim: " There is, O monks! the unborn, the unbecome, the uncreated, the unformed. Were not there, O monks! the unborn, the unbecome, the uncreated, the unformed, an escape from the born, the become, the created, and the formed could not be found. Since there is, O monks! the unborn, the unbecome, the uncreated, the unformed, an escape from the born, the become, the created, the formed can be found."[67] Another passage in the *Udāna* which is attracted here is: "Where water, earth, fire, and air do not enter, the stars do not gleam, the sun does not shine, the moon does not shine, darkness does not exist. When the Brāhmaṇa sage realizes his self by silent meditation, he becomes free from form and formlessness [or rather the material and the immaterial], happiness and suffering."[68] A third passage in the text also merits consideration: "There is a sphere, O monks! where there is neither earth, nor water, nor fire nor air, nor endless space, nor the endless sphere of *viññāṇa,* nor the endless sphere of nothing, nor the endless sphere of neither-awareness-nor-nonawareness, nor this world, neither the other world, neither of the moon and the sun. Hence, O monks! I say [that it is] neither coming nor going, nor staying, nor falling, nor arising; but that it is unstable, unchanging, supportless. This verily is the end of suffering."[69] Finally, take this passage from the *Saṁyutta-Nikāya*: "This is the *Nibbāna,* the uncompounded, the ultimate, free from defilements, the truth, the further shore, the subtle, very difficult to see, the unfading, the stable, the undecaying, the ineffable, the undifferentiated, the peaceful, the deathless, the excellent, the good, the security, the destruction of craving, the wonderful, the marvellous, free from ill, the state free from ill, the harmless, the passionless, the purity, the release, the non-attachment, the island, the cave, the protection, the refuge, and the goal which the Well-Accomplished One has taught."[70]

The Buddha makes his point foolproof in this behalf by using the words *Nibbāna, Dhamma* and *Brahman* interchangeably. He describes as *Brahma-bhūta* as one who has attained *Nibbāna.*[71] He had himself attained the *Brahman* (*Brahma-patta*).[72] He had *Dhamma* as his body, he had become *Dhamma,* he had become *Brahman.*[73] He is also credited with turning the wheel of *Brahman*[74] or of *Dhamma.*[75] The saint dwells in *Brahman*[76] or in *Dhamma.*[77] The noble eightfold path which is designed to lead to *Nibbāna* is characterized as

Brahma-yāna and/or *Dhamma-yāna*.[78] The *Kathā-vatthu* calls *Nibbāna* eternal (*nicca/sassata*), permanent (*dhuva*), imperishable (*a-vipariṇāma-dhamma*).[79]

REFERENCES

1. *Athaṅgatassa na pamāṇaṁ atthi yena naṁ vajjuṁ taṁ tassa natthi Sabbesu dhammesu samohatesu samūhatā vādapathā pi sabbe, Sn,* Pārāyana-Vagga 5, St. 101.
2. *Sn,* Aṭṭhaka-Vagga 4, St. 22, 93, 154; Pārāyana-Vagga 5, St . 123.
3. See, for example, *DN* II, Mahānidāna-Sutta 2, pp. 50-51; *MN* I, Sammādiṭṭhi-Sutta 9, p. 72; *SN* II, Nidāna-Saṁyutta 12, Nagara-Sutta 65, p. 89.
4. Cp.: '*Rūpaṁ bhikkhave! aniccaṁ, yad aniccaṁ taṁ dukkhaṁ, yaṁ dukkhaṁ tad anattā .... vedanā aniccā .... saṅkhārā .... viññānaṁ aniccaṁ, yad aniccaṁ taṁ dukkhaṁ, yaṁ dukkhaṁ tad anattā....*, *SN* III, Khandha-Saṁyutta 22, Anicca-Sutta 45, pp. 276-77.
5. *Uppādā vā tathāgatānam anuppādā vā tathāgatānaṁ, ṭhitā vā sā dhātu dhammaṭṭhitatā dhammaniyāmatā idappaccayatā. SN* II, Nidāna-Saṁyutta 12, Paccaya-Sutta 20, p.24. Cp.: *"Utpādād vā tathāgatānaṁ anutpādād vā tathāgatānāṁ sthitaivaiṣā dharmāṇāṁ dharmatā." MŚP* 1.3, p. 13.
6. *MN* III, Anupada-Sutta 11, pp. 88ff.
7. *SN* II, Nidāna-Saṁyutta 12, Assutavā-Sutta 61, p. 81.
8. *Pheṇapiṇḍūpamaṁ rūpaṁ, vedanā bubbulūpamā,*
   Marīcikūpamā saññā' saṅkhārā kadalūpamā,
   Māyūpamaṁ ca viññāṇaṁ desitādiccabandhunā.
   SN III, Khandha-Saṁyutta 22, Pheṇapiṇḍūpama-Sutta 95, p. 360.
9. *TSP* 376.
10. *TS* 375.
11. *SN* II, 12, Jāṇussoṇi-Sutta 47; Lokāyatika-Sutta 48, p. 65.
12. *MN* II, Dīghanakha-Sutta 24, pp. 193-95.
13. *Ibid.*, p. 195. Also see *Sn* 4, 13, pp. 407-10.
14. *MŚ* 13.8.
15. *Ibid.*, 27.30.
16. *SN* II, 21, Kolika-Sutta 1, p. 227.
17. *MŚP* 1.3, p. 19.
18. Cp. *Sn* 4, 13, p. 409; *Kathāvatthu* 5, 5, Sammutiñāṇa-Kathā, pp. 277-78; *Kathāvatthū Aṭṭhakathā*, p. 139, quoted in *Abhidhammattha-saṅgaha*, II, p. 796.
19. *MŚP* 1.3, pp. 13-14; *AN* II, Bāla-Vagga 3, p. 57.
20. *MN* II, Cūla-Mālukya-Sutta 13, pp. 107-12; Aggi-Vacchagotta-Sutta 22, pp. 177-79.
21. *MN* I, Cūla-Saccaka-Sutta 35, p. 280; *SN* IV, 35, Kāmabhū-Sutta 233,

p. 151; Udāyi-Sutta 234, pp. 151-52.

22. *SN* IV, Passim.
23. *Loc. cit.*
24. *MN* I, Cūla-Saccaka-Sutta 35, p. 280.
25. *Rūpaṁ bhikkhave! aniccaṁ, yad aniccaṁ taṁ dukkhaṁ, yaṁ dukkhaṁ tad anattā, yad anattā taṁ "netaṁ mama, neso 'haṁ asmi, na me so attā" ti evaṁ etaṁ yathābhūtaṁ sammappaññāya daṭṭhabbaṁ. Evaṁ etaṁ yathābhūtaṁ sammappaññāya passato cittaṁ virajati vimuccati anupādāya āsavehi. SN* III, Khandha-Saṁyutta 22, Anicca-Sutta 45, pp. 276-77.
26. *Mahāvagga,* Mahākhandhaka 1, Anatta-Pariyāya 8, p. 16.
27. Śaṅkara, *Bhagavadgītā-Bhāṣya* 18.50, p. 447.
28. Cp. the correspondence between the five sheaths and the five aggregates in K.N. Jayatilleke, *Early Buddhist Theory of Knowledge,* p. 220.
29. *MN* III, Dhātuvibhaṅga-Sutta 40, pp. 325ff.; *AN* III, Yodhājīva-Vagga 14, Yodhājīva-Sutta 1, p. 265.
30. G.C. Pande, *Studies in the Origins of Buddhism,* p. 504.
31. *MN* III, Dhātuvibhaṅga-Sutta 40, p. 327.
32. *MN* I, Brahmanimantanika-Sutta 49, p. 403; *DN* I, Kevaṭṭa-Sutta 11, p. 190.
33. *AN* I, Vaggas 5, 6.
34. Pande, pp. 494-96.
35. *Ibid.*, pp. 496ff. Vasubandhu's following statement is significant '*Ātmany asati katham ādhyātmikam? Bāhyaṁ vā? Ahaṅkāra sanniśrayatvāc cittam ātmety upacaryate—"Ātmanā hi sudāntena svargaṁ prāpnoti paṇḍitaḥ" ity uktam. Cittasya cānyatra damanam uktaṁ Bhagavatā—"cittasya damanaṁ sādhu, cittaṁ dāntaṁ sukhāvaham" iti.*' Vasubandhu, *Abhidharmakośa* I.39.
36. *Mahāvagga* 6.31.
37. *SN* I, Bhikkhunī-Saṁyutta 5, Vajirā-Sutta 10, p. 135.
38. Pande, pp. 497-98.
39. *SN* IV, Avyākata-Saṁyutta 44, Moggalāna-Sutta 7, pp. 335ff.
40. *Ibid.*, Avyākata-Saṁyutta 44, passim; *MN* II, Cūla-Mālukya-Sutta 15, pp. 109ff.
41. Pāṇini, *Aṣṭādhyāyī* 4.4.60, read with Patañjali, *Mahābhāṣya ad loc.*
42. Dharmakīrti, *Pramāṇavārtika* 1.219-22.
43. *Ibid.*, 1.138-39.
44. Sureśvara, *Sambandhavārtika* 3.4.405-9.
45. *SN* IV, Avyākata-Saṁyutta 44, Ānanda-Sutta 10, p. 343.
46. *Loc. cit.*
47. K.N. Jayatilleke, *Facets of Buddhist Thought,* p. 18.
48. *Jātaka* 18. 528.142.
49. *Ibid.*, 22. 543. 936-38.

50. *MN* III, Devadaha-Sutta 1, p. 19.
51. *DN* I, Brahmajāla-Sutta 1, pp. 17-18.
52. *AN* III, Mahāvagga 7, Titthāyatana-Sutta 1, p. 161.
53. *DN* I, Tevijja-Sutta 13, p. 206.
54. *MN* II, Saṅgārava-Sutta 50, p. 496.
55. See, for example, *DN* I, Kevaṭṭa-Sutta 11, pp. 186-90; Brahmajāla-Sutta 1, pp. 17-20, 26; II, Mahāsamaya-Sutta 7, pp. 55, 108, 156-88, 189 ff.; Sakkapañha-Sutta 8, pp. 197-216, 264-65; *AN* III, 7, Uposatha-Sutta 10, pp. 194-99; IV 13, Paṭhama-Nānākaraṇa-Sutta 3, pp. 132-33; Dutiya-Nānākaraṇa-Sutta 4, p. 134; Paṭhama-Metta-Sutta 5, pp. 134-35; Dutiya-Metta-Sutta 6, pp. 135-36; Paṭhama-Tathāgata-Acchariya-Sutta 7, pp. 136-38; V, 17, Bhaddaji-Sutta 10, p. 448; XI, 2, Paṭhama-Mahānāma-Sutta 2, pp. 375-77.
56. *DN* III, Ātānāṭiya-Sutta 9, pp. 157 ff.
57. *Yasmiṁ padese kappeti vāsaṁ paṇḍitajātiyo*
Sīlavantettha bhojetvā saññataṁ brahmacārayo
Yā tattha devatā āsuṁ tāsaṁ dakkhiṇamānase
Tā pūjitā pūjayanti, mānitā mānayanti naṁ.
Tato naṁ anukampanti mātā puttaṁ va aurasaṁ
Devatānukampito poso sadā bhadrāni passati.
DN II, Mahāparinibbāna-Sutta 3, p. 71; *Mahāvagga*, Bhesajja Khandhaka 6, Sunīdhavassakāra-Vatthu 15, p. 245. (For '*brahmacārayo*', the latter text has *brahmācarino/brahmacāriyo.*)
58. *AN* III.
59. *AN* III, Mahāvagga 7, Uposatha-Sutta 10, pp. 194ff.
60. *AN* VI, 3, Sārandada-Sutta 1, p. 164; *DN* II, Mahāparinibbāna-Sutta 3, p. 60.
61. *Buddhānussati, dhammānussati, saṅghānussati, sīlānussati, cāgānussati, devatānussati—ime cha dhammā bhāvetabba. DN* III, Dasuttara-Sutta 11, p. 219. Cp. *AN* I, Apara-Accharāsaṅghātā Vagga 18, p. 41.
62. *AN* III, Mahāvagga 7, Uposatha-Sutta 10, pp. 194 ff.
63. *AN.*
64. *MN,* III, Dhātuvibhaṅga-Sutta 40, p. 330.
65. *SN* IV, Asaṅkhata-Saṁyutta 43, Parāyana-Sutta 44, 320.
66. *DN* I, Kevaṭṭa-Sutta 11, p. 190.
67. *Atthi bhikkhave! ajātaṁ, abhūtaṁ, akataṁ asaṅkhataṁ. No cetaṁ bhikkhave! abhavissa ajātaṁ, abhūtaṁ, akataṁ, asaṅkhataṁ, nayidha jātassa, bhūtassa, katassa, saṅkhatassa nissaraṇaṁ paññāyetha. yasmā ca kho bhikkhave! atthi ajātaṁ, abhūtaṁ, akataṁ, asaṅkhataṁ, tasnā jātassa, bhūtassa, katassa, saṅkhatassa nissaraṇaṁ paññāyati ti. Udāna* 8.3; *Itivuttaka,* Duka-Nipāta 17.
68. *Yattha āpo ca, pathavī, tejo, vāyo na gādhati*
Na tattha sukkā jotanti, ādicco na ppakāsati.

Na tattha candimā bhāti, tamo tattha na vijjati.
Yadā ca attanāvedi muniṁ monena brāhmaṇo,
Atha rūpā arūpā ca sukhadukkhā pamuccati.
Udāna 1. 10

69. *Atthi bhikkhave! tad āyatanaṁ yattha neva paṭhavī, na āpo, na tejo, na vāyo, na ākāsānañcāyatanaṁ, na viññāṇañcāyatanaṁ, na ākiñcaññāyatanaṁ, na nevasaññānāsaññāyatanaṁ, nāyaṁ loko, na paraloko, na ubho candimasūriyā. Tatrāpāhaṁ bhikkhave! neva āgatiṁ vadāmi na gatiṁ na ṭhitiṁ, na cutiṁ, na upapattiṁ; appatiṭṭhaṁ appavattaṁ anārammaṇaṁ evetaṁ. Esevanto dukkhassā ti. Ibid.*, 8.1

70. *Asaṅkhataṁ, anantaṁ, anāsavaṁ saccaṁ ca, pāraṁ, nipuṇaṁ, sududdasaṁ,*
Ajajjaraṁ dhuvaṁ, apalokitaṁ, anidassannaṁ, nippapañcaṁ, santaṁ,
Amataṁ, paṇītaṁ ca, sivaṁ ca, khemaṁ, taṇhakkhayo, acchariyaṁ ca, abbhutaṁ
Anītikaṁ, anītikadhammaṁ, nibbānaṁ etaṁ sugatena desitaṁ,
Abyāpajjo, virāgo ca, suddhi, mutti, anālayo,
Dīpo leṇaṁ ca, tāṇaṁ ca, saraṇaṁ ca, parāyanaṁ ti.
SN IV, Asaṅkhata-Saṁyutta 43, Pārāyana-Sutta 44, p. 320.

71. *MN* II, Kandaraka-Sutta 1, p. 9.
72. *MN* II, Upāli-Sutta 6, p. 59.
73. *DN* III, Aggañña-Sutta 4, p. 66.
74. *SN* II, Nidāna-Saṁyutta 12, Dasabala-Sutta 21, p. 27.
75. *SN* V, Sacca-Saṁyutta 56, Dhammacakkapavattana-Sutta 11, p. 363.
76. *AN* III, Mahāvagga-7, Uposatha-Sutta 10, p. 192.
77. *Loc. cit.*
78. *SN* V, Magga-Saṁyutta 45, Jāṇussoṇibrāhmaṇa-Sutta 4, p. 6.
79. *Kathāvatthu*, Mahāvagga I, Sabbamatthīti-Kathā 6, p. 117.

CHAPTER 3

Logical Developments

Thanks to the innate ambiguities of the Buddha's teachings sampled in the preceding chapter, the Buddhist Saṅgha was divided into eighteen sects about two or three centuries after his *parinibbāna.* They were followed by the rise of conflicting schools of Buddhist philosophy, with which we are concerned in this chapter. They are all logical developments from the ambiguous positions emerging out of the master's discourses.

Realism Culminating in Destructed Nihilism

Thanks to the nihilistic overtones of some of the teachings of the Buddha referred to in the last chapter, the realist tradition of Buddhism gave birth to what is called 'destructed nihilism', after Junjiro Takakusu.[1] Such Nihilism comes to the fore in the voluminous *Satyasiddhiśāstra* by Harivarman (c. 250-350 A.D.) of the Bahuśrutīya school, a splinter group of the Mahāsāṅghikas, styled as the Jojitsu (*satyasiddhi,* completion of truth) in Japanese and long mistaken in China for a Mahāyāna sect akin to the Mādhyamika, ever since the time of translation of the treatise into Chinese by Kumārajīva in 411-12 A.D. The Bahuśrutīyas' existence in Andhra is attested by inscriptions from the third century A.D. at Nagarjunikond, and near Peshawar in the fifth century A.D.

Harivarman propounds the truth of extinction (*nirodha-satya*),[2] final extinction, *Nirvāṇa,* otherwise expressed as the void of the self (*pudgala-sūnyatā*) and of the elements (*sarva-*

dharma-sūnyatā), condescending to grant only ephemeral reality to the *dharmas*, eighty-four in number instead of the seventy-five of the Sarvāstivādins, grouped under five aggregates (*skandhas*). According to him, yogins and the adept experience only non-birth (*anutpāda*) and the void (*ākiñcanya*).[3] From this he concludes that all *dharmas* are void (*śūnya*).[4] His voidness (*śūnyatā*) is not only the voidness of self(*sattvaśūnyatā*) but voidness of *dharmas* (*dharma-śūnyatā*) as well.[5] By *śūnya* he means cessation/extinction (*nirodha*).[6]

Harivarman adopts a purely realistic method of arriving at his Nihilism. He analyzes the five aggregates into molecules, molecules into atoms, and atoms into the finest elements having an entirely different nature from the first objects. Going one step further, he attains the Void. His words are: "There is no cognition of a whole (*avayavin*) over and above the *dharmas*. Hence all *dharmas* are incognizable and, being incognizable, non-existent . . . . Owing to the non-existence of the whole, parts are non-existent, too . . . . [One can show even otherwise that] all parts are non-existent. How? Being analyzed again and again, all the parts [of a whole] come to be reduced to atoms, which, too, being broken, attain non-existence pure and simple. All things culminate necessarily in the idea of *Śūnyatā*."[7]

We are inclined to the view that Harivarman's Nihilism is quite akin to Nāgārjuna's. (We shall be dealing with Nāgārjuna and his school in the rest of the chapters.) Junjiro Takakusu has sought, however, to make a fine distinction between the two thus: "Analyzing those five objects the school [Satyasiddhi school] reduces them to molecules, and further reduces them to even finer atoms, and by thus repeating the process the school finally attains the finest element which has an entirely different nature from the first objects. Going one step further, the school attains the Void. Thus the nihilism of this school is a 'destructed' or abstract Void. In other words, the non-entity asserted in this school is simply an abstraction from entity, or merely an antithetic Void as against existence. And this is not the synthetic Void or transcendental Void advanced by the Sanron [Mādhyamika] School."[8] Takakusu's distinction does not really hold good in sum and substance. The process by which he says Harivarman reaches his Void is nothing peculiar to him. It is shared by the Mādhyamikas as well. Śāntideva has urged it as an argument against the reality of *dharmas*.[9] Āryadeva employs a similar argument in refutation of the atom.[10] According to Advayavajra, such an argument is to be met with in 'western' Vaibhāṣikas as well.[11] It is suggested in the *Laṅkāvatārasūtra,* too.[12] Besides, the recurrent recourse in the Mādhyamika literature to likening reality to a banana tree, which, when all its skins are peeled off, has nothing left as its kernel, indicates a similar frame of reference.[13] In fact, Jñānaśrīmitra appears to breathe a Mādhyamika temper when he argues out *Śūnyatā* like this: Things are either partite or impartite. If the former, they are beset with the same difficulties as the wholes [which can be analyzed away as shown by Harivarman]; if the latter, they are beset with the same difficulties as the atom; and there is no third kind of existence. Thus, *Śūnyatā* is all-encompassing, universal.[14]

Of course, however, while Buddhism in general and the Satyasiddhi school in particular tend to make approximations to *Śūnyavāda* by means of the foregoing argumentation, it is the Mādhyamika alone who enjoys the credit of presenting *Śūnyavāda* as a systematic philosophy.

The momentarians (*kṣaṇabhaṅgavādins* maintain that all comes out of nothing and relapses into nothing; Harivarman contends that, if all comes out of nothing and relapses into nothing, all is nothing; the Mādhyamika argues that, if things are not there, nothing is not there also, because absence of one member of the pair of opposites is bound to mean absence of the other member as well. This is the gulf which divides Harivarman and the Mādhyamika.

Reaction to Realism Culminating in Absolute Nihilism

Human mind cannot rest satisfied with stark realism. It must penetrate beyond the phenomena and venture to transcend the dry data of our sensation. Such reaction to realism took place in the Buddhist tradition particularly in Mahāyāna. Nāgārjuna, the first and foremost philosopher of the Mādhyamika school, arrives at his *Śūnyatā* by examining the various categories postulated by the realist schools of Buddhism. These categories are: causality (*pratyaya*); motion and rest (*gatāgata*); perception (*cakṣurādīndriya*); matter (*skandha,* in fact causality again); space; being (*bhāva*) and non-being (*a-bhāva*); quality and the qualified (*rāga-rakta*); the conditioned (*saṁskṛta*) and the unconditioned (*a-saṁskṛta*); light and darkness; action and actor (*karma-kāraka*); soul; substance; fire and fuel (*agnīndhana*) and through these relativity, with a side-glance at soul; temporal sequence (*purvāparakoṭī*); suffering (*duḥkha*); change of essence (*saṁskāra*); relation (*saṁsarga*); essence (*svabhāva*) and change; bondage and liberation (*bandha-mokṣa*); deed and dessert (*karma-phala*); soul proper (*ātman*); time (*kāla*); Tathāgata; morals; Noble Truths; *Nirvāṇa; Pratītyasamutpāda*; and metaphysics (*dṛṣṭi*).

Nāgārjuna finds them all riddled with contradictions and hence rejects them to make room for *Śūnyatā.* According to him, there is nothing subjacent to phenomena and, thanks to their self-contradictory character, phenomena themselves are unreal. Therefore, there is nothing whatsoever. All is void, absolute void.

Relative void is comparatively easy to grasp, not so the absolute void. It is something inexpressible. Absolute void should not be confused with the Absolute, however. It is at best an apology for one, a negative void, so to speak. On this ground, the Mādhyamika deserves to be called not only a Nihilist but an absolute Nihilist, an advocate of pure nothing. If pure nothing can be styled an Absolute, however, the Mādhyamika is an Absolutist, but his Absolute would be merely a negative Absolute.

It is true that the Mādhyamika's truth is twofold: conventional (*saṁvṛti*) and transcendental (*paramārtha*), with possibly infinite gradations in between. But the duality of truth must not be confused with duality of reality. The Mādhyamika posits no reality, unless his absolute void is called a reality.

Tension between Absolute Nihilism and Absolutism in the Mādhyamika

But the Mādhyamika school is such, philosophically speaking. It seems to posit a three-tier hierarchy of religion, philosophy, and mysticism/gnosis/*Prajñāpāramitā.* As Mahāyānists, the Mādhyamikas happen to be as positivist, dogmatic, and devotional in religion as devotees of any other faith. They are second to none in their religious fervour. The canonical injunctions to worship *Prajñāpāramitā* as a goddess with flowers, incenses, garlands, unguents, aromatic powders, cloths, umbrellas, flags, buntings, bells, illuminations, etc.[15] and Nāgārjuna's prayer to *Prajñāpāramitā* [16] are instances in point.

As philosophers, the Mādhyamikas are second to none in their readiness to go to the logical extreme of their philosophical method and outlook, even at the cost of their religious outlook. And as mystics, they seem to have a kind of experience which is at the farthest conceivable remove from language and thought and absolutely incommunicable. As religionists, they are positivists and realists; as philosophers, negativists and nihilists; but heaven knows what they are as mystics. As philosophers, they posit nothing but they at least initiate a dialogue negating everything. But as mystics, they cease to do even that, they simply sink into silence.

The Mādhyamika seems to tend to relegate religion to the realm of conventional truth (*saṁvṛti-satya*). The issue is found posed, more or less pointedly, in the twenty-fourth chapter of the *Madhyamakaśāstra* of Nāgārjuna. The question in brief is: If all is *Śūnya,* void, pure and simple, all religious theory and practice would be rendered void. The reply proposed is something like this: There are two truths, conventional and transcendental, and the latter is never taught independently of the former.[17] Candrakīrti explains that, even as we have to have a container before we have water, we must have conventional truth before we have the transcendental, for the simple reason that the container and conventional truth are means to water and transcendental truth respectively.[18] It appears to be clearly suggested here that religious theory and practice belong to the order of conventional truth, which is nevertheless a means to the transcendental truth set out in the text under reference. Further, Nāgārjuna adds that, at the conventional level, *Śūnyatā* is to be viewed not as void as such but as relative being (*pratītyasamutpāda*), which does vouch for and conduce to religious theory and practice.[19] The upshot of Nāgārjuna's contentions in the chapter under consideration appears to be this: While considering the import of *Śūnyatā,* it must be borne in mind that the Buddha teaches two types of truth, relative and absolute, which are taught together, with reference to each other, rather than each separately. Corresponding to the distinction between relative and absolute truth, *Śūnyatā,* too, has two aspects, relative and absolute. In its absolute aspect, it is not meant for the laity, to whom its relative or pragmatic aspect alone can have any meaning. In this respect, *Śūnyatā* is nothing but the theory of origination of things through causes and conditions. It is evident that such *Śūnyatā* does not mar or nullify religious endeavour, it rather conduces to it. Religion aims at a change for the better, and according to the Buddhists in general what has not originated through causes and conditions will not change. Therefore, it is not such *Śūnyatā* but the denial of it which is likely to serve to mar or nullify religious endeavour. Denial of *Śūnyatā* would mean denial of the truth that things arise through causes and conditions, which is tantamount to the belief in the eternity and immutability of things. And, if things are regarded as immutable, it would be difficult to see how the Four Noble Truths can have any meaning. The kernel of the Four Noble Truths is that suffering arises through causes and conditions and has got to be eliminated. And this presupposes the mutability of things and their interdependence.

At the level of religion and lower philosophy, the Mādhyamika tends to grant a clear distinction between the immediate and the ultimate, appearance and reality, the conditioned and the unconditioned, the relative and the absolute, the world and the Tathāgata, *Śaṁsāra* and *Nirvāṇa aŚūnya* and *Śūnya,* ignorance (*avidyā*) and enlightenment (*bodhi*),[20] absence (*avidyamānatā*) and presence (*vidyamānatā*), non-apprehension (*an-upalambha*) and apprehension (*upalambha*),[21] absence of contemplation (*bhāvanānupalambha*) and contemplation (*bhāvanā*), absence of attainment (*Pratilambhānupalambha*) and attainment (*pratilam-bha*),[22] but at the level of higher philosophy, he would repudiate and iron out such distinctions in unequivocal terms and, as we shall see at the proper place in the sequel, advocate a complete equipollency between the two members of each pair of the opposites.[23] What is *Saṁsāra* from the standpoint of *pratītyasamutpāda, sub-specie temporis,* is *Nirvāṇa* from the standpoint of the ultimate truth, that is *Śūnyatā, sub-specie aeternitatis,* so to speak.[24] This is comparable more or less to the Advaitin's contention that there is at bottom neither birth nor cessation, neither bound nor wayfarer, neither an aspirant for liberation nor liberated.[25] There is a marked difference, however. In Advaitism, there is a what may be called levelling up the Brahman and the world, whereas in Mādhyamika thought there is a levelling down of *Nirvāṇa* and *Saṁsāra.* The Brahman and the world are one because all is Brahman at bottom, whereas *Nirvāṇa* and *Saṁsāra* are one because all is *Śūnya.* It is significant that, while equating the Tathāgata and the world, the ground given is the essencelessness (*niḥsvabhāvatva*) of both.[26] The Mādhyamika's categorical assertion is that there is not the slightest difference between *Saṁsāra* and *Nirvāṇa,*[27] which should be an eye-opener to those who are given to interpreting *Śūnyavāda* on Advaitic lines.

All the same, however, neither the Mādhyamika nor the Advaitin seem to succeed in reconciling the immediate with the ultimate or in deriving the one from the other. There is in evidence a marked vacillation on their part between the two orders of truth and reality, which is the greatest stumbling block in the way of correct appreciation of their position. While contemplating the empirical, the Mādhyamika seems to take the distinction of the devotee and the deity for granted; but, while contemplating the transcendental, he is inclined to dismiss all as illusory, not excluding the Tathāgata and *Nirvāṇa,* the very objects of his devotional endeavour.[28] The discontinuity between theory and practice in Buddhism is ridiculed by Jayanta Bhaṭṭa, the great Naiyāyika. Thus, the Buddhists contend that there is no soul, yet they worship for the attainment of paradise. They contend that all is momentary, yet they erect lasting Vihāras. They maintain that all is *Śūnya,* yet they preach offering of gifts to the preceptor. This all, says Jayanta, is a case of pure hypocrisy on the part of Buddhists.[29]

Such a bifurcation of religion and philosophy appears to have a close parallel in Advaitism, according to which the Brahman is the sole reality. Obviously, an insight into this truth of truths should obviate the necessity of worship and devotion, for worship and devotion presuppose a wide enough gap between the deity and the devotee to whom devotion is deemed due. But even the great Śaṅkara did not hesitate to worship gods and goddesses, like ordinary mortals, as is evident from his hymns, such as the *Dakṣiṇāmūrti-Stotra,* whose authenticity is beyond question, for the simple reason that Sureśvara, his direct disciple, has bequeathed to us a commentary on it. Again, the truth of the Advaitin is that *Mokṣa* is a desideratum, something to be striven for, but its truth of truths is that it is already achieved.

Idealism, Absolutism, Docetism

Another imposing logical development from the Buddha's ambiguities and silence is what is called Yogācāra-Vijñānavāda, an idealism culminating in Absolutism. The putative father of this school is Maitreyanātha, though out of his many treatises at least two—*Uttaratantra* and *Abhisamayālaṅkāra*, breathe a Mādhyamika spirit. To Asaṅga and his younger brother Vasubandhu belongs the credit of developing the school into a well-knit system.

Besides, there are several Mahāyāna Sutras, particularly the *Ārya-Sandhinirmocana-Sūtra* and *Laṅkāvatāra-Sūtra* which constitute the canonical source books of Buddhist idealism in general.

It is noteworthy that Buddhist idealism invariably culminates in Absolutism. Therefore, both have to be dealt with together. Our purpose being limited, however, we can take only passing notice of this development.

Well, Buddhist idealism starts with reducing all external phenomena or rather the whole of the external world to the status of figments of constructive ideation like dreams and ends up with postulating an eternal principle of pure consciousness described variously as *Vijñaptimātratā*, *Cittamātratā*, and the like. It is an idealism to begin with but Absolutism pure and simple in the long run.

Vijñaptimātratā, is called ineffable (*acintya*), changeless (*dhruva*), bliss (*sukha*), as well as the Buddha's *Dharmakāya*.[30] It is the source or ground of the evolving cosmic consciousness called *Ālayavijñāna*, of which all external as well as internal phenomena, including individual centres of consciousness, are mere transformations.

Besides, the *Tathatā* postulated in the *Mahāyāna-śraddhotpādaśāstra* ascribed to Aśvaghoṣa, the *Laṅkāvatāra-Sūtra*, and the writings of Maitreyanātha, Asaṅga, and Vasubandhu is nothing but the Absolute, pure and simple.

Theo-Buddhism

In later Buddhism, the original Buddhist pantheon came to be enriched increasingly. In Mahāyāna and its later offshoots, a number of gods and goddesses began to be worshipped formally, which is common knowledge by now. Sometimes, however, dissenting notes are heard in this regard. For example, Nāgārjuna writes:

The Gods are all eternal scoundrels,
Incapable of dissolving the suffering of impermanence.
Those who serve them and venerate them
May even in this world sink into a sea of sorrow.
Those who despise them and blaspheme
May in this world enjoy all kinds of fortune.
We know the gods are false and have no concrete being;
Therefore the wise man believes them not.
The fate of the world depends upon causes and conditions;
Therefore the wise man does not rely on gods.[31]

The Buddha had dispensed with God the Creator but, if the Pāli canon truly records his utterances on the subject, he felt the need of filling the vacuum by superhumanizing himself and installing himself above the highest of the gods, indeed even above Mahā-Brahman, the supreme deity of his time, and Śakra (Indra), the Lord of the gods. He became the Lord of the gods (*devātideva*), omnipotent and omniscient, at whose birth, enlightenment, and death, the various gods paid their homage. Brahman (mas.) and Śakra dance attendance on him. He is himself reported to have said: "I have no teacher, none is like me; in the world of men and gods none is my equal." He prescribes pilgrimage of four holy places (*dassanīyāni saṁvejaniyāni ṭhānāni*), which are: where he was born, where he attained enlightenment, where he started the turning of the *dhamma*-wheel, and where he attained *Parinibbāna/Nibbāna*.[32] He foretold Ānanda that even great Kṣatriyas and Brāhmaṇas and householders would worship his body or its relics (*sarīra-pūjaṁ*).[33] He enjoined upon his disciples to install his *stūpas* at crossroads and worship these with wreaths, fumigation, and fragrant powder.[34] He ruled that *stūpas* should be erected to preserve the relics of the body of the Tathāgata, Paccekasambuddha, Arhat, and the world-ruler (*rājā cakkavattī*).[35]

Well, Sāriputta declares before the Buddha: "I have such

conviction in the Exalted One that I think that there never was nor would ever be nor is now a recluse or Brāhmaṇa who may excel the Exalted One in respect of knowledge." Further, Sāriputta compared the highest state of knowledge with a king's fortress having only one door (*eka-dvāraṁ*) so that anyone entering it must follow one and the same route. The Buddha approved of the statement with the remark that, "in speaking thus, you will be reporting me properly and not misinterpreting me". Sāriputta adds that the past and future Enlightened Ones were and would be equal to the Buddha in knowledge, but in the present there can be none, for two perfectly Enlightened Ones cannot possibly be born in the same cosmos at the same time. This statement, too, is fully endorsed by the Buddha.[36] One may be tempted to hark back to a similar controversy raging in Islam round the concept of finality of prophethood, particularly round the concept of one last prophet in one cosmos. This we have tried to deal with elsewhere.[37]

The Buddha's followers gave his words the status of Divine revelation after installing him into a veritable Godhead, omnipresent, omnipotent, omniscient, infinitely good, and eternal. In emulation of the Veda-based schools of philosophy, they too, began to ascribe eternity to their revelation. Kumārila, the leading Pūrva-Mīmāṁsā philosopher, sardonically remarks that, in their zeal to have an eternal revelation like the Mīmāṁsakas', the Buddhists have also begun to claim eternity for their revelation at the expense of their doctrine of momentariness.[38] Dharmakīrti devotes a sizable portion of his magnum opus to demonstrating the absolute authoritativeness of the Buddha.[39] Prajñākaragupta, his commentator, devotes 19 pages to the refutation of the existence of God and 7 pages to the refutation of the authority of the Vedas but as many as 117 pages to the demonstration of the authority of the Buddha.[40] Harivarman goes to the extent of ruling, "The Buddha's teachings must not be judged. Why? If the Venerable One has himself judged, what is there to judge? If on the other hand, the Venerable One has not judged, others, too, cannot judge."[41]

In fact, in the Pāli canon itself, the Buddha is viewed not only superhumanly and transcendentally[42] but also as an inscrutable being, incomprehensible (*an-upalabbhiyamāna*) even while actually present.[43] According to a certain statement in the Pāli canon, it is wrong to suppose that the Buddha did any preaching: all preaching was done by Ānanda.[44]

In Mahāyāna, the Buddha rises to the dignity of a God, rather a Super-God. The Ādi-Buddha is *Svaymbhū* (self-born, or rather self-existent) and the Creator of the cosmos.[45] According to another text, Avalokiteśvara, a lesser divinity, is the Creator of the cosmos.[46] According to the Hwa-yāna school, the Buddha is infinite, all-pervading, omnipresent, filling the entire universe with himself alone. All is from him, through him, in him. Thus, he becomes a 'pantheistic' God, so to speak.[47] Nāgārjuna says: "If one hears even the name of the Amitābha Buddha, one would attain salvation."[48]

Mahāyāna also developed a kind of Docetism culminating in its own species of Absolutism. After a number of vicissitudes the doctrine had to undergo, it was finally settled that the Buddha had three bodies: *Dharma-kāya, Sambhoga-kāya* and *Nirmāṇa-kāya.* The first body is the Absolute, described in the *Trikāya-stava* (before 1000 A.D.) as neither one nor many, neither being nor non-being, homogeneous and indeterminate like space, changeless, omnipresent, beyond thought and speech, and so on.[49] The second body has a supramundane form invisible to the naked eye and inhabiting in the *Sukhāvatī-vyūha* or *Tuṣita-loka,* the Buddhist counterpart of *Svarga.* The human Buddha is the *Nirmāṇa-kāya.* The second body lasts till *Nirvāṇa.* The first body is akin to the *Nirguṇa-Brahman,* the second to the *Saguṇa-Brahman/ Saccidānanda/*Viṣṇu, and the third to human incarnations of Viṣṇu.

Religion serves to orient our life and thought towards, anchor our ego in, and stretch our vision on to the transcendent conceived as the ground and goal of existence or its centre of gravity. The transcendent is usually but not necessarily personified, the personification admitting of differing levels and degrees. As we have seen, the Buddha gives to the laity a non-cosmogonic polytheistic model, which is the transcendent for them and which came to occupy the foremost place amongst the Buddhist laity and to be increasingly enriched with the spread of Buddhism all over Asia. In Mahāyāna, Buddhism soon develops into transpoly-theistic monotheism as well as Absolutism. Incidentally, this Absolutism seems to have cast its shadow over the Mahāsāṅghikas, who are credited with propounding the doctrine of beginningless and endless pure mind (*anādi-ananta-vimala-citta)* possessed by all human beings, which is the germ of Buddhahood. And, significantly enough, the *Mahāyāna-Parinirvāṇa-Sūtra* uses the trilogy of *nitya, sukha,* and *ātman* (permanent, happiness, and self) as opposed to *anitya, duḥkha,* and *anātman* (impermanent, suffering, and no-soul).[50]

The Soul's Hideouts

Driven out by the bulk of the early Buddhists, the soul sought refuge in the Puggalavādins (the Vātsiputrīyas of the *Abhidharmakośa,* the Āryasammtīyas of the *Abhidharmakośa-Bhāṣya,* and the Vajjiputtakas of Buddhaghoṣa). All other early Buddhists have all along been suffering from fear-psychosis *vis-á-vis* the theory of soul. However, in spite of their vociferous repudiation of the charge of eternalism on this score, which could be brought against them by their adversaries, they do on occasion fall into the trap of acknowledging the permanent entity of the soul. The *Laṅkāvatāra-Sūtra,* for example, admits unequivocally that the *ātman* or *'pudgala'* is hidden within the aggregates like melody within musical instruments, gems, etc. within the earth, embryo within the pregnant woman, essence within medicinal herbs, fire within fuel. If the *ātman* did not exist, there would be no stages (of enlightenment), no self-mastery, no psychic power, no anointment of the highest order, no excellent *Samādhi.* If the nihilationist (*vaināśika*) comes and asks, 'If the soul exists, show me', he should be answered, 'Show me your own doubt (*vikalpa*)'. Those who preach soullessness (*Nairātmya-vādinaḥ*) are opponents of the Buddha's teaching, for they advocate either 'it is' or 'it is not'.[51] D.T. Suzuki maintains that this startling passage refers to the higher self, the larger self, and not to the lower, individual self.

Incidentally, the Buddha once asserted that at the highest level of truth and reality there is neither *attā* nor *nir-attā* (not-self).[52] The Mādhyamika is sometimes overtaken by a realist temper and displays a robust sense of reality. He asserts that he is not out to negate what is seen, heard, and known.[53] He repudiates the charge of his being a *Nāstika* (repudiator of being) on the ground that he acknowledges being on the empirical plane.[54] He goes to the extent of castigating those who reject the eternal in favour of the non-eternal (*anitya*).[55] In his puzzlingly realistic moods, he upholds the Nyāya theory of the quadruplicity of the ways of knowing as against their duality proposed by the Diṅnāga school called the Sautrāntika-Yogācāra school of Buddhism,[56] setting aside into the bargain the latter's distinction of *svalakṣaṇa* (pure, momentary self-characterized uniques/ point-instants) and *sāmānya-lakṣaṇa* (universal constructs), postulated as the objects of the two ways of knowing respectively;[57] the Vaiśeṣika distinction of substance and attribute as against the rejection of substance by the Buddhist realists;[58] the soul theory of the non-Buddhist as against its total rejection by other schools of Buddhism,[59] the realist theory of object-directed consciousness (*ālambane sati cittam utpadyate*) as against the Buddhist idealist theory of contentless consciousness (*sva-saṁvitti*).[60]

In this connection, it would be pertinent to point out that the *Laṅkāvatāra-Sūtra* contains a peculiar statement, which is: "All this is unborn. But it is not that things do not exist. Things do exist, but they do so without sufficient reason, like *fata morgana*, dream, and illusion."[61]

The Buddhist Mind Divided against Itself

Human mind abhors vacuum. It abhorred metaphysical vacuum not long after Muḥammad had warned his people against metaphysical speculations and discussions. In default of a metaphysics of their own, they soon began to lean on Greek metaphysics. The Buddha, too, had often to compromise his stand against metaphysics and make commitments of a metaphysical sort. Even so, he kept practical interest steadily in view, and endeavoured to get away with ad hoc, hurriedly framed negative propositions. This tendency is particularly pronounced in his propositions about the self. He did not feel called upon to give a disquisition on the self on its own. He felt, it appears, that, whatever be the nature of the self, people's belief in the self or rather in the not-self as the self was responsible for rendering them selfish, egoistic, and overattached to things mundane, without renouncing which they could not hope to attain *Nibbāna.* His negative statements about the self are, therefore, intended, so it seems, to inculcate upon people the spirit of self-abnegation and self-effacement. Unless people forgot their narrow self or ego, he thought, they would not remember *Nibbāna.* So, without bothering about the metaphysics of the self, he went on discoursing on the not-self, even at the risk of misunderstanding on the score of metaphysics. That is why, when asked pointedly whether the self does or does not exist, he chose to keep silent. He feared both nihilationism and eternalism. He felt concerned not with the validity or invalidity of such propositions but with their utility or non-utility for the attainment of *Nibbāna.*

This is the secret of the Buddha's unspeakables (*avyākaṭāni*). We have seen how he occasionally transgressed the limits of the speakables and entered into the realm of the unspeakables. But later Buddhist schools of philosophy are in pretty open revolt from the unspeakables, on each of which they have to speak volumes. Nevertheless, they must maintain the dignity of the master, with the result that they soon begin to contradict themselves, remedy the contradiction, and finally sink into silence (*tūṣṇīṁbhāva*). The Unspeakables up in arms again! Nevertheless, emphases and preferences of the various Buddhist schools are as clear as broad daylight.

We are inclined to the view that, if we scrutinize the sayings of the Buddha carefully, we shall find that he was hard put to keep the skirts of his garments unsoiled by the dreaded nihilationism and eternalism. Same is the case with his followers. They kept oscillating and vacillating between the two extremes, swinging now towards the one and then towards the other, with the result that nihilationism and eternalism are found to recur in Buddhism again and again without reconciliation or outright rejection in a consistent manner.

The gulf dividing early Buddhism, the Mādhyamika, and Yogācāra-Vijñānavāda is so yawning that their scriptures, too, are radically different. It is a unique phenomenon in the history of religion. Every religion tends to suffer schism sooner or later, but sects or schools of philosophy usually remain committed to a common scripture. There is seldom any difference in scripture ascribable to one and the same human agency, the difference that comes to develop is in the approach to the common scripture, in interpretation thereof, to be precise. But the Buddhists have three sets of scriptures. According to Mahāyāna, the Buddha delivered three sets of sermons to three different sets of audience differing in spiritual competence, thereby giving each of the three broad divisions of his church a scripture of its own.

After enlightenment, the Buddha is believed to have delivered his first sermon at Isipattana Migadāva (Sārnāth), where he taught realism, viz. objective reality of things. This was meant for the laity. He delivered the second sermon on the Gijjhakūta hills at Rājagaha (Gṛdhrakūṭa hills at Rājagṛha), where he taught Nihilism or the essencelessness of all *dharmas* without exception. This was meant for more competent audience. He delivered the last sermon at Vesālī and certain other places, where he taught essencelessness of one species of *dharmas* and essentiality of another.

The Mādhyamikas and the Vijñānavādins agree on one point, and it is this that the first sermon belongs to a lower order and was designed for a lower category of audience. That sermon is compiled into the Pāli canon. But they differ as regards the value of the second and third sermons. According to the Mādhyamikas, the second sermon is the highest sermon, meant for the highest category of audience. It is compiled mainly into the Prajñāpāramitā Sūtras, on which Mādhyamika philosophy is based. The Mādhyamikas contend that the Buddha revealed the final truth in his second sermon, but that, finding it terrifying to many advanced souls even toned it down and delivered it in the third sermon. On the contrary, the Vijñānavādins contend that, in order to highlight the limitations of the first sermon for advanced souls, the Buddha thought it fit to present an antithesis, and, when he found that the antithesis had done its job of turning the audience's attention from the first sermon completely, he revealed the full and final truth in the third sermon which lies midway between Realism and Nihilism and is known as Idealism-cum-Absolutism. The primary scripture of Idealism-cum-Absolutism is *Ārya-Sandhi-nirmocana-Sūtra* extant in Chinese only.

In short, the Buddhist mind is divided against itself on more than one point and in more than one respect.

REFERENCES

1. Junjiro Takakusu, *The Essentials of Buddhist Philosophy,* p. 78.
2. Harivarman, *Satyasiddhiśāstra,* p. 377.
3. *Ibid.,* pp. 378-79.
4. *Ibid.,* p. 379.
5. *Loc. cit.*
6. *Śūnya eva nirodha ity ucyate. Ibid.,* p. 386.
7. *Na hy asti dharmāṇām avayavī grāhyaḥ. Ataḥ sarve dharmā agrāhyāḥ. Agrāhyād abhāvātmakāḥ. . . . Avayavino 'bhāvād avayavā api na santi. . . . Sarve cāvayavā abhāvātmakāḥ. Kasmāt? Aṇuśo bhidyamānā atyantābhāvatāṁ sarveṣāṁ dharmāṇāṁ niṣṭhā śūnyatābuddhi jananam avaśyam. Ibid.,* pp. 367-68.

8. Takakusu, *op. cit.*, p. 78.
9. *BCA* 9.86-87.
10. *CS* with *CSV* 13.5-6; *Hastavālaprakaraṇa* 1, 3.
11. *Advayavajrasaṅgraha,* p. 15.
12. *Laṅkāvatārasūtra,* Gāthā 523.
13. See, for example, *Ratnāvalī* 2.1; *BCA* 9.151.
14. *Sāṁśe 'vayavivad doṣo, niraṁśe paramāṇuvat.*
Nāparaṁ vastu cāstīha, sarvagrāsā hi śūnyatā.
Jñānaśrīmitra, Sākārasiddhiśāstra, in *Jñānaśrīmitra-Nibandhāvalī,* p. 430.
15. *Aṣṭasāhasrikā-Prajñāpāramitā,* p. 46. Cp. p. 50.
16. Nāgārjuna, *Prajñāpāramitā-Stuti,* containing 21 couplets and prefixed to the *Aṣṭasāhasrikā-Prajñāpāramitā,* ed. cit.
17. *MŚ* 24.8.
18. *Tasmān nirvāṇādhigamopāyatvād avaśyam eva yathāvasthitā saṁvṛtir ādāv evābhyupeyā, bhājanam iva salilārthineti. MŚP* 24.10.
19. *MŚ* 24.18.
20. As in Asaṅga, *Mahāyānasūtrālaṅkāra* 13.12.
21. *Ibid.,* 9.78.
22. *Ibid.,* 9.79.
23. *MŚ* 7.33; 16.4, 10; 22.16; 25.9, 19, 20; etc.
24. *MŚ* 25.9; *Jñānaśrīmitra Sākārasiddhiśāstra,* p. 464; *Sākārasaṅgrahaśūtra,* p. 555.
25. *Brahmabindū-Upaniṣad* 10; Gauḍapāda, *Māṇḍūkyakārikā*, 2.32.
26. *MŚ* 22.16.
27. *MŚ* 25.19-20; Jñānaśrīmitra, *op. cit.*, pp. 464, 555.
28. *Aṣṭasāhasrikā-Prajñāpāramitā,* p. 20.
29. Jayanta Bhaṭṭa, *Nyāyamañjarī,* Prameya-Prakaraṇa, p. 39.
30. *Sa evānāsravo dhātur acintyaḥ, kuśalo, dhruvaḥ,*
Sukho, vimuktikāyo 'sau dharmākhyo 'yaṁ mahāmuneḥ.
Vasubandhu, *Triṁśika-Vijñaptimātratā* 30.
31. Nāgārjuna, *Mahāprajñāpāramitā-Śāstra,* quoted in Helmuth von Glasenapp, *Buddhism—A Non-Theistic Religion,* p. 31.
32. *DN* II, *Mahāparinibbāna-Sutta* 3, p. 109.
33. *Loc. cit.*
34. *Ibid.*, p. 110; *Kathāvatthu* 17.1.
35. *DN, loc. cit.*
36. *Āyasmā Sāriputto Bhagavantaṁ etad avoca—'Na cāhu, na ca bhavissati, na cetarahi vijjati añño samaṇo vā brāhmaṇo vā Bhagavatā bhiyyo bhiññataro yad idaṁ sambodhiyaṃ' ti. 'Uḷārā kho te ayaṁ Sāriputta! āsabhī vācā bhāsitā. Ekaṁso gahito. Sīhanādo nādito, Ibid.*, p. 66; *'Aṭṭhānaṁ etaṁ anavakāso yaṁ ekissā lokadhātuyā dve arahanto sammāsambuddhā apubbaṁ acarimaṁ uppajjeyyuṁ netaṁ ṭhānaṁ vijjati' ti. DN* III, Sampasādanīya-Sutta 5, p. 89; *'Tagghaṁ tvaṁ*

Sāriputta! evaṁ puṭṭho evaṁ byākaramāno vuttavādī ceva me hosi, na ca maṁ ābbhācikkhasi, dhammassa cānudhammaṁ byākarosi, na ca koci sahadhammiko vādānuvādo gārayhaṁ ṭhānaṁ āgacchati' ti. Loc. cit.

37. Harsh Narain, 'Feasibility of a Dialogue between Hinduism and Islam', *Islam and the Modern Age,* VI, 4 (November, 1975), pp. 80-82.
38. Kumārila, *Tantrāvartika* 1.3.12, p. 162.
39. Dharmakīrti, *Pramāṇavārtika* 1.31-33, 34-36, 136, 141-44, 147-48, 285-86; 3.216; 4.108.
40. Prajñākaragupta, *Pramānavārtika-Bhāṣya,* pp. 50-166.
41. *Na kartavyo Buddhapravacanavicāraḥ. Kasmāt? Yadi Bhagavatā svayaṁ vicāritaṁ, kim asti vicārāya? Yadi Bhagavatā na vicāritaṁ, anye 'pi vicārayituṁ na śaknuyuḥ. Kasmāt? Sarvajñābhiprāyo hi duravagāhaḥ.* Harivarman, *Satyasiddhiśāstra,* p. 38.
42. For instance:

    Isisattamassa, akuhassa, tevijjassa, Brahmapattassa,
    Nhātakassa, padakassa, passaddhassa, viditavedassa,
    Purindadassa, Sakkassa, Bhagavato tassa sāvako 'haṁ asmi.
    MN II, Upāli-Sutta 6, p. 59.
43. *Diṭṭheva dhamme saccato thetato Tathāgato anupalabbhiyamāno . . .* . . *SN* III, Khandha-Saṁyutta 22, Yamaka-Sutta 85, p. 334; Anurādha-Sutta 86, p. 340.
44. *Na vattabbaṁ, 'Buddhena Bhagavatā dhammo desito' ti. 'Amanta. Kena desito? 'ti. 'Āyasmā Ānandena desito' ti. Kathāvatthu* 18.179 (2).3, p. 483.
45. *Padyakāraṇḍavyūha-Sūtra,* quoted in Narendra Deva, *Bauddha-Dharma-Darśana,* pp. 149-50.
46. *Guṇakāraṇḍavyūha-Sūtra,* in *Mahāyāna-Sūtra-Saṅgraha,* Vol. I, p. 265.
47. Wm. Theodore de Bary (ed.), *The Buddhist Tradition,* pp. 166-96. Also see Takakusu, pp. 108-25.
48. Nāgārjuna, *Prajñāpāramitā-Śāstra,* quoted in Ryukan Kimura, *A Historical Study of the Terms Hīnayāna and Mahāyāna and the Origin of Mahāyāna Buddhism,* p. 20.
49. *Yo naiko nāpy aneko, svaparahitamahāsampadādhābhūto,*
    Naivābhāvo na bhāvaḥ, kham iva samaraso nirvibhāvasvabhāvaḥ.
    Nirlepaṁ, nirvikāraṁ, śivaṁ, asamasamaṁ, vyāpinaṁ, niṣprapañcam,
    Vande pratyātmavedyaṁ, tam aham anupamaṁ, dharmakāyaṁ jinānām. Nāgārjuna, *Trikāya-Stava,* quoted in Narendra Deva, p. 116.
50. Kimura, p. 139.
51. *Laṅkāvatāra-Sūtra (Sagāthaka)* 10.757-58, 760-61, 763-65.
52. *Sn,* Aṭṭhaka-Vagga 4, Duṭṭhaṭṭhaka-Sutta 3, St. 8; Purābheda-Sutta 10, St. 11; Tuvaṭaka-Sutta 14, St. 5; Pārāyana-Vagga 5, Jatukaṇṇimāṇava-Pucchā 12, St. 3.

53. *Yathā dṛṣṭaṁ, śrutaṁ, Jñātam naiveha pratiṣdhyate. BCA* 9.26.
54. *Samvṛtyā Mādhyamikair astitvenābhyupagamān [nāstikena saha] na tulyatā. MŚP* 18.7, p. 157; *Kiṁ khalv eṣa viṣayaparicchedaḥ sarvathā nāsti? Na nāstīti, niḥsvabhāvasya bhāvasya vidyamānatvāt. CŚV* 13.51, p. 105.
55. *Anitye nityam ity evaṁ yadi grāho viparyayaḥ,*
Anityam ity api grāhaḥ śūnye kiṁ na viparyayaḥ? MŚ 23.14.
56. *MŚP* 1.3, p. 25.
57. *Ibid.*, pp. 20ff.
58. *Ibid.*, pp. 21-24; *CS* 14.14.
59. *Varaṁ khalu Kāśyapa! Sumerumātrā pudgaladṛṣṭir āśritā, na tvevābhāvābhiniveśikasya śūnyatādṛṣṭiḥ.* Quoted in *MŚP* 13.8, p. 108, as the Lord's words. Cp. *'Yadi jñānaṁ karaṇaṁ viṣayasya paricchede, kaḥ kartā? Na ca kartāram antareṇāsti karaṇādīnāṁ sambhavaḥ. Ibid.*, 1.3.
60. *Ibid.*, 1.3, pp. 21ff; *BCA* 9.15-27.
61. *Anutpannam idaṁ sarvaṁ, na ca bhāvā na santi ca.*
Gandharva-svapna-māyākhyā bhāvā vidyanty ahetukāḥ. LS, Gāthās 581-82, p. 145.

CHAPTER 4

Conflicting Interpretations

A careful scrutiny of the primary sources of Mādhyamika philosophy, as also of those of its rival systems, leads the present writer to the irresistible conclusion that it is *Śūnyavāda* in its true significance, is Absolute Nihilism rather than Absolutism or monism, metaphysical, soteriological, or linguistic, as has come to be held currently. Let us examine the different approaches to Mādhyamika philosophy or *Śūnyavāda.*

The Nihilistic Interpretation

In the early days of Buddhist studies, scholars were unanimously of the opinion that *Śūnyavāda* was rank nihilism or negativism, that it countenanced a view of reality as pure void. Burnouf appears to be the first to strike the nihilistic chord. He described the doctrine as a nihilistic scholasticism.[1] According to H. Kern, *Śūnyavāda* is 'complete and pure nihilism', and, according to M. Walleser, 'negativism which radically empties existence up to the last consequences of negation'. H. Jacobi takes it that on the Mādhyamika view 'all our ideas are based upon a non-entity or upon the Void'. A.B. Keith holds that the Mādhyamika's reality is 'absolute nothingness'. I. Wach characterizes him as the most radical nihilist that ever existed.[2]

This school of interpretation is not very popular today. Of the very few scholars adhering to the way of nihilistic interpretation, S.N. Dasgupta regards *Śūnyavāda* as "neither idealism nor realism nor absolutism, but blank phenomenalism which only accepts the phenomenal world as it is but which would not, for a moment, tolerate any kind of essence, ground or reality behind it."[3] In three of his published papers, the present writer has tried to argue out the case for the nihilistic interpretation, with a difference, however, rather more meticulously. These papers constitute the first major contribution to this way of interpreting the Mādhyamika's position, culminating in the present work.

Another contribution in this direction worthy of mention is a book in Hindi entitled *Nāgārjuna-kṛta Madhyamakaśāstra aur Vigrahavyāvartanī* by Yasha Deva Shalya, published in 1991. Mr. Shalya follows the present writer's line of interpretation on the whole. His chief contribution lies in his incisive examination of Nāgārjuna's refutation of the various categories of Buddhist realism, seldom attempted in any other quarter.

The Metaphysical-Absolutistic Interpretation

Later scholars, from D.T. Suzuki, F.Th. Stcherbatsky, and S. Schayer to C.D. Sharma and T.R.V. Murti, find in *Śūnyavāda* an Absolutism more or less akin to that of *Vijñānavāda* or even the Vedānta. This revolutionary change in the approach to *Śūnyavāda* came about through the discovery and rediscovery of Tibetan, Chinese, and Japanese Buddhism.

S. Schayer asserts that the Mādhyamika is, after all, for an absolute essence beyond every particular manifestation.

F.Th. Stcherbatsky translates *Śūnyatā* as relative or contingent.[4] He hastens to add, however, that it "means not something void, but something 'devoid' of independent reality (*svabhāvaśūnya*), with the implication that nothing short of the whole possesses independent reality, and with the further implication that the whole forbids every formulation by concept or speech (*niṣprapañca*) since they can only bifurcate (*vikalpa*) reality and never directly seize it."[5] Taking a positive, holistic-absolutistic view of Mahāyāna he contends, "in Mahāyāna all parts or elements are unreal (*śunya*), and only the whole, i.e. the Whole of the wholes (*dharmatā* = *dharma-kāya*) is real."[6] He sums up the Mādhyamika position thus: "The universe viewed as a whole is the Absolute, viewed as a process it is the Phenomenal."[7] In his criticism of Schayer, however, he seems to have deviated from this path, inasmuch as he was led to maintain that the Mādhyamika denied the possibility of an Absolute Reality.[8]

Louis de La Vallée-Poussin, another great Buddhologist, "was disinclined to accept this interpretation [of Stcherbatsky on metaphysical-holistic-absolutistic lines] but in a short note, published after his death, he pronounced himself without ambiguity [in its favour]. . . ."[9]

D.T. Suzuki observes that *Śūnyatā* is threefold:

1. Absence, such as the absence of the hare's horn,
2. Extinction, such as the extinction of a burning fire, and
3. Unoccupancy, such as in the sentence. There is a table that side of the wall, while there is nothing that side.

According to him, the Mādhyamika's *Śūnyatā* refuses to fall under any of these categories: it is totally transcendent,[10] it is experiential. Edward Conze also has it that Śūnyatā is experiential-intuitional and that raising questions of being and non-being in regard to it is nonsense.[11]

In his *Central Philosophy of Buddhism*, T.R.V. Murti asserts that the terms *Śūnya* and *Śūnyatā* are applied to phenomena as well as to the Absolute: to phenomena because, being dependent upon and relative to each other, they are devoid of essence; to the Absolute because it is devoid of conceptual distinctions.[12] According to him, the Mādhyamika denies not the real but doctrines about the real.[13] He regards *Śūnyavāda* as "a very consistent form of absolutism".[14]

It is evident that Murti's approach can well be treated as a variety of metaphysical Absolutism, pure and simple. But in the "Buddhism and Śūnyatā", his last contribution to the subject, he seems to have shifted his position to some extent or other. Here he begins to sense 'genuine difficulties about conceding Absolutism to the Mādhyamika'.[15] He does concede, however, that *Śūnyavāda* can "be called an absolutism because it is an uncompromising absolute stand".[16] And this in the face of his own statement: "Nor does it mean that no other philosophy except that of the Mādhyamika could lead to *Mokṣa.* There may be other equally effective and valid ways of *Mokṣa,* like that of the Advaita Vedānta, etc. But the Śūnyatā is certainly one way, a certain way."[17] Then again: "In all the three absolutisms (Mādhyamika, Vijñānavāda and Advaita Vedānta) the highest knowledge is conceived as Intuition beyond all traces of duality. A distinction must, however, be made between the *advaya* of the Mādhyamika and the *advaita* of the Vedānta, although in the end it may turn out to be one of emphasis of approach."[18] The shift of emphasis in his stand, howsoever slight, cannot elude the discerning eye.

C.D. Sharma is the foremost amongst the Vedāntizers of Mādhyamika philosophy. According to him, "Śhūnya essentially means Indescribable (avāchya or anabhilāpya) as it is beyond the four categories of intellect (chatuṣkoṭi-vinirmukta).... The world is Indescribable because it is neither existent nor non-existent; the Absolute is Indescribable because it is transcendental and no category of intellect can adequately describe it."[19] Again, "Nāgārjuna himself in his Ratnāvalī (I, 45 and 60) identifies Reality with Pure Consciousness or Bodhi or Jñāna. Āryadeva also identifies Reality with the Pure Self or the Chitta. (Cittaviśuddhi-prakaraṇa, 27, 28, 74). Shāntideva in much-inspired verses praises the only Reality, Bodhi-Chitta or the True Self which is Pure Consciousness. (Bodhi charyāvatāra I, 8, 10, etc.) If the Bodhi or Nāgārjuna, the Chitta or Āryadeva, and the Bodhi-Chitta of Shāntideva are not the self-luminous Self, which is Pure Consciousness, what else on earth can they be?"[20] Sharma continues: "The only difference between Shūnyavāda and Vedānta, therefore, is the difference of emphasis.... Shūnyavāda represents the earlier stage while Vedānta represents the later stage of the development of the same thought."[21]

This account will remain incomplete without a reference to the view of the great modern seer Sri Aurobindo. He identifies the Mādhyamika's Śūnya with *Asat*, literally non-being, of the Vedic-Upaniṣadic texts, which (*Asat*) gave birth to *Sat*, literally being.[22] "Asat is a zero", he observes, "which is all or an indefinable Infinite which appears to the mind a blank, because mind grasps only finite constructions, but is in fact the only true Existence".[23] He takes "Non-Being in the sense, not of an inexistent Nihil but an *X* which exceeds our idea or experience of existence, a sense applicable to the Absolute Brahman of the Advaita as well as the void or zero of the Buddhists."[24]

This is undoubtedly a most luminous explanation of the Vedic-Upaniṣadic *Asat*. It may also be conceded that, as we saw in the preceding chapter, some of the Mahāyāna masters deserve to be credited with a kindered experience of the Absolute. But it must be granted, as indicated there and will be clear from the next chapter onwards, that the philosophical expression given to the experience in the Mādhyamika texts leaves little or no room for such an Absolutistic interpretation.

The Soteriological-Absolutistic Interpretation

There is another assertive section of scholars, who maintain that the Mādhyamika's Śūnyatā must be interpreted not metaphysically or ontologically but soteriologically. That is to say, Śūnyatā is not a metaphysical doctrine supposed to report about the world, not indeed a descriptive term at all. It is a soteriological device, a way to end suffering, a path of salvation. This is supposed to be precisely the approach of the Chinese San-lun school of Buddhism, which believes in emptying the mind of all metaphysical speculation for the final denouement called salvation or *Nirvāṇa*.

Most of the advocates of Absolutistic interpretation along with certain others are found to subscribe to this approach. D.T. Suzuki writes: "Emptiness is not to be confounded with nothing-ness nor is one to imagine that there is an object of thought to be designated as emptiness, for this idea goes directly contrary to the nature of emptiness itself."[25]

Frederick J. Streng also emphasizes the epistemological character of the Mādhyamika's *Śūnyatā* thus: "This dialectic, however, is not simply a destructive force which clears the ground for a constructive formulation of truth, nor even a dissipation of the fog surrounding an essence of truth or reality. The dialectic itself provides a positive apprehension, not of a 'Thing' but of the insight that there is no independent and absolute thing which exists eternally, not a 'Thing' which can be constructed."[26]

The Linguistic-Analytic Interpretation

R.C. Pandeya regards *Śūnyavāda* as a species of philosophical analysis and opposes its characterization as dialectical absolutism. Dialectic, he contends, is a synthetic thought-process, whereas the whole procedure of the Mādhyamika is analytical. The Mādhyamika stops after analyzing concepts and does not proceed towards synthesis. According to Pandeya, the analytic activity of the Mādhyamika is confined to analysis of concepts and propositions and has nothing to do with factual analysis. It is meant not to analyze the whole into parts but to throw into relief the self-contradictoriness of the whole. In fact, according to the Mādhyamika, there is nothing like a whole. Hence it has to be treated as a negative analyticism. As a matter of fact, observes Pandeya, there is no appropriate term for Mādhyamika philosophy. He proposes, therefore, that it be either not given any name at all or called 'analytic zeroism', bearing it in mind, however, that here zero does not mean pure void.[27]

A.K. Chatterjee asserts that Mādhyamika philosophy is metaphilosophy and its language metalanguage as distinguished from object-language.[28] He also observes that "*Śūnyatā* is the total rejection of the pretensions of language to mirror reality. Language cannot describe; it can only distort or falsify."[29]

The question is, Is there a reality at all for language to mirror, describe, distort, or falsify, or not to? Neither Chatterjee nor Pandeya seem to be interested in this question. They lead us nowhere as to the question whether or not the Mādhyamika has a metaphysical commitment after all and, if not, how it is possible to rest satisfied with evading questions regarding the world around us. Chatterjee has not gone beyond the Mādhyamika's method, which we have occasion to examine somewhere in the sequel.

Harking Back to the non-Mādhyamika Traditions

The Nihilistic view of *Śūnyavāda* finds ample support from the Indian tradition. The consensus of Brahmanical opinion is in favour of regarding *Śūnyavāda* as pure Nihilism.[30] Certain Brāhmaṇa philosophers also find in it an outright repudiation of all the four conceivable categories of reality—viz., is, is-not, both, and neither—and hold it to be thesisless through and through.[31] It will be shown in the sequel that it is nothing but Nihilism in its extremist form.

It is true, however, that certain later Upaniṣads[32] and such Vedāntic classics as the *Yogavāsiṣṭha*[33] and Gauḍapāda[34] are found to appropriate the Mādhyamika's *Śūnya* and charge it with an absolutistic meaning associating and identifying it with the Absolute, the Brahman, and certain later compendia[35] seem to interpret *Śūnya* as pure consciousness. But they seem to be actuated by the desire to effect a synthesis between the Vedānta and Buddhism or rather Vedāntize Buddhism rather than interpret the Mādhyamika system in a disinterested spirit.

Jaina writers endorse the nihilistic view of *Śūnyavāda* taken by the Brāhmaṇical tradition.[36]

A much more significant fact is that even the Yogācāra school of Buddhism subscribes to the same view of *Śūnyavāda*. The *Sarvasiddhāntasaṅgraha*, ascribed to Śaṅkara, quotes the Yogācāra as criticizing *Śūnyavāda* on the score of its being total Nihilism.[37] Against the Mādhyamika, the Yogācāra argues thus: "Since you maintain the thesis of all void, your *pramāṇa* (proof), too, is void. Hence you have no right to a debate with others. Such stalwarts of the Yogācāra-Vijñānavāda school as Asaṅga, Vasubandhu, and Sthiramati, too, proclaim "*Śūnyavāda* to be a doctrine of absolute nothingness."[38]

The *Abhidharmadīpa* belonging to the Vaibhāṣika school lists four theses: all is (*sarvam asti*), some are (*pradeśo 'sti*), all is not (*sarvaṁ nāsti*), and all is inexpressible (*avyākṛtāstivādin*).[39] The *Vibhāṣāprabhā-Vṛtti* commentary thereon identifies the third thesis with that of the Vaitulika Ayoga-Śūnyatāvādin[40] clubbing him with the Vaināśika (nihilationist).[41] The *Abhidharmadīpa* also refers to a doctrine to the effect that what originates dependently does not exist (*yat-pratītya-samutpannaṁ tat svabhāvān na vidyate*),[42] is sure to remind one of the Mādhyamika verse of more or less similar wording and to the same effect: *Tat tat prāpya yad utpannaṁ notpannaṁ tat svabhāvataḥ.*[43]

In all likelihood, *ayoga-śūnyatā* means denial of causal relation and can, therefore, be construed to cover both the Mādhyamika and Vijñānavāda standpoints.[44] Yet the commentator observes that the verse quoted above belongs to the Vaitulika (*Vaitulikaḥ kalpayati*)[45] and interprets it like this: Being essenceless like the firebrand, all *dharmas* are ephemeral (*alātacakravan niḥsvabhāvatvāt sarvadharmā nirātmānaḥ*).[46] And this reasoning the commentator calls idle dialectic (*brahmodya*).[47]

There is little doubt, therefore, that both author and the commentator hold the Mādhyamika to be a Nihilist.

Unlike the Vijñanavādins in general, Jñānaśrīmitra explores the possibility of reconciling the Mādhyamika and the Yogācāra standpoints.[48] According to him, the real (*śuddha*) Mādhyamika does not differ from the Yogācāra. What is the Mādhyamika's middle path (*madhyamā*)? Freedom from positing and negating, from *Śūnya* and *Aśūnya*, from existence and non-existence. Hence nothing is lost. The Buddha's endeavours have been rendered ineffectual by interpreting his *Śūnya* to mean non-being (*abhāva*).[49]

On the grounds of the all-negating attitude of the *Tattavasaṅgraha*, authorship of a clearly Mādhyamika text entitled *Mādhyamikālaṅkāra-Kārikā* with its *Vṛtti* (gloss), and testimony of Tibetan historians, it is held, and rightly, that Śāntarakṣita is a Yogācāra-Mādhyamika-Svātantrika. There are other such syncretisms,[50] which afford to be ignored here.

The Mādhyamika's Confession

By far the most significant, however, is the fact that the Mādhyamikas themselves refer to Yogācāra-Vijñānavādins and others as taking their Nihilism for granted and yet let them go without any disclaimer from their (the Mādhyamikas') side. Even while answering the charge of Absolute Nihilism brought or imagined to be brought against him, the Mādhyamika never pleads not guilty. This serves to cast rather a decisive shadow of doubt on the modern absolutistic interpretation of *Śūnyavāda.*

The whole of Nāgārjuna's *Vigrahvyāvartanī* seems to accord tacit approval to the critic's ascription of Nihilism to him. The imaginary critic in the work proceeds on the assumption that, if all is void, the Mādhyamika's proposition that all is void is itself void and hence devoid of validity.[51] This argument is developed in 20 out of the 72-stanza work. It is strange that, this work, small in size but great in merit, has received scant consideration by those favouring an Absolutistic interpretation of *Śūnyavāda.* In this work, Nāgārjuna nowhere disfavours the ascription of Nihilism to him. Instead, his reply that he does not find any reality whatsoever to postulate or deny,[52] serves to confirm the truth of the ascription.

Such implicit confirmation of the ascription of Nihilism to the Mādhyamika way of thinking is not lacking in the later Mādhyamika literature as well. Bhāvaviveka's reference to the Yogācāras ascribing Nihilism to Mādhyamika philosophy without the least concern on his part to correct them is an instance in point.[53] He also considers the question, as raised in the *Vigrahavyāvartanī*, that, if all is void, the very proposition that all is void is itself void and hence devoid of sense.[54]

Chapter X of Āryadeva's *Śataśāstra* is devoted exclusively to this problem. In his *Catuḥśaṭaka*, too, the problem is raised at one place.[55] The *Laṅkāvatāra-Sūtra* contains the remark: "The essence of all entities is unreal, and this proposition is unreal, too." [56]

Śāntideva discusses the question of universal nihility *vis-à-vis* the question of validity of the means of knowledge (*pramāṇa*) thus: "If the means of knowledge (*pramāṇa*) is false then what is known by it is false, and hence the essential non-being of entities fails to be established."[57] He purports to say that on the Mādhyamika view the means of knowledge, being *Śūnya* or false, no longer remains true means of knowledge, and, in the absence of any valid means of knowledge, the knowledge that all is *Śūnya* or false is itself false. His reply to this question is not much to the point, and so we ignore it here. We have adverted to this question, first, to bring home to the reader the significant fact that, in whatever context the imaginary objector raises objections to the thesis of *Śūnyatā*, he proceeds on the assumption that *Śūnyatā* is nothing but pure Void, and, second, to note that the Mādhyamika nowhere takes exception to the assumption.

The Mādhyamika invokes what in the sequel we have chosen to call his thesis of thesislessness to meet such arguments.[58] That, however, this thesislessness springs from the consciousness of absolute void or, what is the same thing, the non-apprehension of anything whatever, is made abundantly clear by Nāgārjuna, Āryadeva, and Candrakīrti.[59] Indeed, as we shall demonstrate in the sequel, the Mādhyamika thesis of thesislessness is nothing but Absolute Nihilism in disguise.

In the 24th chapter of the *Madhyamaka-Śāstra*, Nāgārjuna examines an imaginary objection: If all is *Śūnya*, there is neither origination nor decay, and negation of the Four Noble Truths will become unavoidable.[60] And so on. His rejoinder is a detailed one, but there is no suggestion therein that the charge of Nihilism is unfounded. This issue has occurred above briefly in chapter 3 (*supra*).

Full details eminently deserve to be given here. By the Absolutist interpreter of Mādhyamika philosophy, much is made of Nāgārjuna's rejoinder to the (imaginary) objection: "If all this is *Śūnya*, there is neither origination nor decay, and the negation of the Four Noble Truths will become chargeable against you."[61] On behalf of the objector, Nāgārjuna refers to the chain of negation which will follow of themselves in the wake of the negation of the Four Noble Truths, and concludes that such a state of affairs will lead to chaos. His reply is: "To this we rejoin: You do not appreciate the purpose of *Śūnyatā*, *Śūnyatā* [itself], and the meaning of *Śūnyatā*. That is why you raise this objection. The Buddhas preach the *dharma* with reference to two truths, the empirical truth and the ultimate truth. Those who do not know the division of the two truths do not know the great truth in the Buddha's teaching. The ultimate is not taught save *vis-à-vis* the empirical, and *Nirvāṇa* is not attained without recourse to the ultimate. Misapprehended, *Śūnyatā* destroys the unintelligent, even as a wrongly caught serpent or wrongly practised science. . . If, then, you criticise *Śūnyatā*, it is not our fault, for the criticism does not apply to the *Śūnya*."[62]

That is to say, according to Nāgārjuna, *Śūnyatā* has two levels, one for the initiated and one for the laity, and the latter must be taught to adhere to the Four Noble Truths as also to all other canons of righteousness taught by the Buddha. According to Āryadeva, Truth is taught in three steps: In the first step, the seeker is told that there is such a thing as sin which attaches to and pollutes the self and that, therefore, one must beware of sin. In the second step, he is told that not only the sin but the self itself does not exist. In the third and final step, it is revealed to him that all is nothing, void.[63]

Candrakīrti expounds the idea of Nāgārjuna thus: "*Śūnyatā* is taught with a view to putting an end to all speech; therefore, the purpose of *Śūnyatā* is cessation of all speech. You, on the other hand, who construe *Śūnyatā* to mean non-being (*nāstitva*) and thereby only enlarge the net of speech do not know the purpose of *Śūnyatā* . . . Hence, how can there be non-being in *Śūnyatā* which is of the nature of cessation of all speech? So, you do not know even *Śūnyatā* . . ."[64] We take it that Candrakīrti purports to say that *Śūnyatā* is neither being, nor non-being, nor both, nor neither; that it would therefore be incorrect to equate or identify it with non-being; and that it is only this wrong identification that gives rise to the objection that it will strike at the root of all practice, all righteousness.

In this connection, Nāgārjuna makes another observation which deserves notice. He says, "All fares well with him with whom *Śūnyatā* fares well; nothing fares well with him with whom *Śūnyatā* does not so fare."[65] Candrakīrti tries to bring out the idea of this pithy remark thus: "With him with whom this *Śūnyatā* fares well, *Pratītya-samutpāda,* too, fares well; with him with whom *Pratītya-samutpāda,* fares well, the Four Noble Truths fare well. How so? Because suffering is phenomenal (*pratītya-samutpanna*), not non-phenomenal. And, being essenceless, it is *Śūnya.* Suffering being there, its origination, its cessation, and the way leading to its cessation fare well with him."[66]

Well, Nāgārjuna goes on: "By seeking to lay four [own] faults at our doors, you have forgotten the very horse you are riding. If you regard objects as essentially existent, then, by doing so, you see objects [emerging] without causes and conditions. Thereby you fail to explain effect, cause, doer, means, action, origination, cessation, and consequence. It is *Pratītya-samutpāda* which we call *Śūnyatā.* It is relative being, it is the very Middle Path. There is no irrelative [or uncaused] *dharma* (thing); therefore, there is nothing non-*Śūnya.* If all this is non-*Śūnya,* there is neither origination nor decay, and denial of the Four Noble Truths becomes chargeable against you.

How can there be uncaused suffering? For suffering is

said to be non-eternal, which would not be possible if it had essence. If it is existent by nature, then what is there to originate? Therefore, there is no origination for one who rejects *Śūnyatā*. If suffering exists, it will not cease. By upholding its essence, you speak against its cessation."[67] Thereafter, Nāgārjuna recounts the teachings of the Buddha which will lose their significance on the non-*Śūnyatā* view, and thereby lays the same charges at the doors of the opponent as the latter sought to do at his.

It is obvious that here Nāgārjuna purports to define *Śūnyatā* in its empirical aspect alone. Candrakīrti has it that in the present context *Pratītya-samutpāda* means emergence of things through causes and conditions *(hetu-pratyayānapekṣya prādurbhāvaḥ)* or, coversely, non-emergence of things without causes and conditions, of themselves (*svabhāvenānutpadaḥ)*.[68] So, the denial of *Śūnyatā* in its empirical aspect is tantamount to the belief in the immutability of things, thereby rendering the doctrine of the Four Noble Truths altogether meaningless. Therefore, *Śūnyatā* in its empirical aspect alone can be said to be in question here.

Nāgārjuna has elsewhere, too, held that belief in the being of things is tantamount to belief in their eternity. He has, accordingly, characterized the realist as an eternalist in these words: "If there were being in the nature of things, it would not be non-existent; for the negation of nature cannot be proved."[69] According to him, "To say '[it] is' is eternalism, to say '[it] is not' is nihilationism. Therefore, the wise must not brook either isness or non-isness (*astitvanāstitve*)."[70]

But Nāgārjuna deserves to be held guilty of prevarication, and on two counts. First, the imaginary objector is concerned to know what *Śūnyatā* actually is rather than what it is understood to be empirically, conventionally, or pragmatically. And Nāgārjuna's rejoinder is confined to the empirical truth about *Śūnyatā* and with such a vengeance that the ultimate truth about it tends to recede into the background. Second, Nāgārjuna and its followers have all along been creating the impression that Mādhyamika philosophy is a philosophy of Absolute Void/*Alīka/Tuccha/Nityanivṛtti.* Says Candrakīrti, "That is *Śūnya* which by nature is not" (*Tatra Śūnyam ucyate yat svabhāvena nāsti*).[71] And the Mādhyamika examples of son of a barren woman, skyflower, etc. are well known. If such is the case, *Śūnyatā* cannot be empirically relevant.

As a matter of fact, in another text, too, Nāgārjuna identifies *Śūnyatā* with *Pratītya-samutpāda.*[72] But, as if to make amends for the fault of the prevarication, he hastens to add that the negation by *Śūnyatā* is like a phantom man (created by a magician or thaumaturgist) prohibiting another phantom man (from a certain course of conduct).[73]

It appears that the reckless use of the words '*Śūnyatā*' and '*Pratītya-samutpāda*' in Mādhyamika literature in any and every context is partly responsible for the misinterpretation of *Śūnyavāda* and for the harking back to the Absolute. Overuse of a fine concept tends to have a blunting effect on our sensibility, even as overaddiction to drug or drink has on our nerves. Take the case of *Pratītya-samutpāda.* By the Mādhyamika, it is construed to mean sometimes as causality,[74] sometimes again as non-causality,[75] sometimes still again as relativity,[76] and sometimes, finally, as the ineffable.[77] If this is the case, nothing is gained by describing *Śūnyatā* as *Pratītya-samutpāda.* Moreover, *Śūnyatā* itself is interpreted in as many ways, which makes the confusion worse confounded.

As a matter of fact, the tradition of nihilistic interpretation of the Mādhyamika's position is so overwhelming, unanimous, and unexceptionable that one should think a thousand and one times before daring to sound a note of dissent. Faulting those who are inclined to read the Upaniṣad's Self into the Buddha's doctrine, Murti sardonically remarks: "Either the monks were too stupid to grasp the master's basic teaching, or they were so clever that they fabricated and foisted on him an opposite doctrine. . .*Prima facie,* those systems and schools of thought which owe their allegiance to the founder of this religion have greater claim to understand Buddhism than the moderns who are removed from him by centuries of time as well as distance of culture and outlook."[78] And he concludes: "The entire development of Buddhist philosophy and religion is proof of the correctness of our nairātmya interpretation of Buddhism."[79] It is an irony of the situation to find the same scholar throwing the unbroken tradition to the winds and putting an entirely new-fangled interpretation upon Mādhyamika philosophy, in unison with certain other scholars.

REFERENCES

1. J.W. de Jong, 'Emptiness', *Journal of Indian Philosophy*, 2 (1972),7.
2. For all these references, see F.Th. Stcherbatsky, *The Conception of Buddhist Nirvāṇa* (Leningrad, 1927), p. 37.
3. S.N. Dasgupta, *Indian Idealism*, p. 79.
4. Stcherbatsky, *op. cit.*, p. 42.
5. *Ibid.*, p. 43.
6. *Ibid.*, p. 41.
7. *Ibid.*, p. 48.
8. de Jong, *loc. cit.*
9. *Loc. cit.*
10. D.T. Suzuki, *On Indian Mahāyāna Buddhism*, p. 270.
11. Edward Conze, *Thirty Years of Buddhist Studies*, p. 22.
12. T.R.V. Murti, *The Central Philosophy of Buddhism*, p. 142, n. 1.
13. *Ibid.*, p. 218.
14. *Ibid.*, p. 234.
15. Murti, 'Buddhism and Śūnyatā', *The Nava Nalanda Mahavihara Publication*, Vol. IV, p. 95.
16. *Ibid.*, p. 113.
17. *Ibid.*, p. 115.
18. *Ibid.*, p. 112.
19. C.D. Sharma, *A Critical Survey of Indian Philosophy*, p. 86.
20. *Ibid.*, p. 321.
21. *Ibid.*, pp. 321-22.
22. Sri Aurobindo, *The Life Divine*, I, p. 35.
23. *Loc. cit.*
24. *Loc. cit.*
25. D.T. Suzuki, *op. cit.*, p. 49.
26. Frederick J. Streng, *'Emptiness'*, p. 148.
27. R.C. Pandeya, 'The Mādhyamika Philosophy: A New Approach', p. 20.
28. A.K. Chatterjee, *Facets of Buddhist Thought*, p. 23.

29. *Ibid.*, p. 27.
30. See, for example, *Nyāya-Sūtra*, with glosses and scholia thereon; Kumārila, *Mīmāṁsā-Ślokavārtika* 1.1.5, Nirālambanavāda, st. 14; Śaṅkara, *Śārīraka-Bhāṣya* 2.2.31 and *Bṛhadāraṇyaka-Upaniṣad-Bhāṣya* 4.3.7; Rāmānuja, *Śrī-Bhāṣya* 2.2.30; *Sāṅkhyapravacana Sūtra* 1.44.47, and Vijñānabhikṣu's *Bhāṣya* thereon; Mādhava, *Sarvadarśanasaṅgraha*, Bauddha-Darśana.
31. See, for example, *'Nāstiko Mādhyamikādiḥ. Anena hi parapakṣo 'bhyupagamyate, na punaḥ parapakṣpratiṣedho 'bhyupagamyate ity arthaḥ. Tad idam uktam—parapakṣaniṣedhamātraprayuktaḥ pravartata iti. Tathā hi—nedaṁ jagad asti bādhyamānatvān, nāpi nāsti pratīyamānatvān, nāpi sadasadrūpaṁ virodhān, nāpy anubhayarūpaṁ virodhād eva pratīteś ceti. Udayana, Nyāyavārtikatātparyapariśuddhi* 1.1.1, p. 291.
32. *Bhāvābhāvavihīno 'smi, bhāsāhīno 'smi bhāsmy aham, Śūnyāśūnyaprabhāvo 'smi, śobhanāśobhano 'smy aham. Maitreyī-Upaniṣad* 3.5.
Śūnyātmā, sūkṣmarūpātmā, viśvātmā, viśvahīnakaḥ, Devātmā, devahīnātma, meyātmā, meyavarjitaḥ.
Tejobindū-Upaniṣad 4.43.
Mūle śūnyaṁ vijānīyāt. Śūnyaṁ vai Parabrahma.
Ganeśapūrvatāpinī-Upaniṣad 3.1.
33. *Yaḥ śūnyavādināṁ śūnyo, bhāsako yo 'rkatejasāṁ,*
Vaktā, mantā, ṛtaṁ, bhoktā, draṣṭā, kartā, sadaiva saḥ.
Yogavāsiṣṭha 3.5.7.
34. *Astināstyastināstiti, nāstināstīti vā punaḥ,*
Calasthitobhayābhavair āvṛṇoty eva bālisaḥ.
Kotyaś catasra etās tu grahair yāsāṁ sadā 'vṛtaḥ
Bhagavān ābhir aspṛṣṭo, yena dṛṣṭaḥ sa sarvadṛk.
Gauḍapāda, *Māṇḍūkya-Kārikā* (also known as *Āgamaśāstra*) 4.83-84
35. Mādhava, *op. cit.*, *loc. cit.*; Rājaśekhara, *Ṣaḍdarśanasamuccaya*, Bauddha-Mata 45.
36. See, for example, Prabhācandra, *Prameyakamalamārtaṇḍa*, pp. 96-98; Hemacandra, *Anyayogavyavaccheda-Dvātriṁśikā* 17, with Mallisena, *Syādvādamañjarī*, pp. 115-22, thereon.
37. *Iti Mādhyamikenoktaṁ śūnyatvaṁ śūnyavādinā*
Nirālambanavādī tu Yogācāro nirsasyate—
Tvayoktasarvaśūnyatve pramāṇaṁ śūnyam eva tat,
'Ato vāde 'dhikāras te na pareṇopapadyate.
Svapakṣasthāpanaṁ tadvat parapakṣasya duṣaṇam
'Kathaṁ karoty atrabhavān? viparītaṁ vaden na kim?
Śaṅkara, *Sarvasiddhāntasaṅgraha*, p. 12.
38. For example, *'Kecid virundhanti—sarvadharmāḥ sarvathā niḥsvabhāvāḥ śaśaviṣāṇavad'—iti. Ataḥ sarvāpavādapratiṣedhārtham āha—Abhūtaparikālpo 'stiti* Sthiramati, *Madhyāntavibhāgabhāṣyaṭīkā*

1.2, p. 9
39. *Sarvam asti, pradeśo 'sti, sarvaṁ nāstīti cāparaḥ, Avyākṛtāstivādīti—catvāro vādinaḥ smṛtāḥ. Abhidharmadīpa* 5.41 (or st. 299 of the all-book stanza series)
40. *Vibhāṣāprabhāvṛtti,* ad loc., pp. 257-58.
41. *Ibid.*, 300, p. 259.
42. *Abhidharmadīpa* 315.
43. See *MŚP* 1.1, p. 3.
44. *Abhidharmadīpa* with *Vibhāṣāprabhā-Vṛtti,* Padmanabha S. Jaini's Introduction, p. 124.
45. *Vibhāṣāprabhā-Vṛtti,* 315, p. 276.
46. *Loc. cit.*
47. *Ibid.*, p. 277.
48. Jñānaśrīmitra, *Sākārasaṅgrahasūtra* 3.45-53, 140.
49. *Ibid.*, 3.45-53.
50. T.R.V. Murti, *The Central Philosophy of Buddhism,* pp. 102-3.
51. *VV* 1.
52. *VV* 30.
53. See, for example, *'Yogācārā evam āhuḥ: Bhavān sādhayati tattvataḥ saṁskṛtāh śūnyā—iti. Yac ca śūnyaṁ...yadīdam asat, tadā nocchedo nirodho vā; kiṁ kena śūnyaṁ bhaviṣyati?'* Bhāvaviveka, *Karatalaratna,* pp. 56-57.
54. *Ibid.*, pp. 45-63, *passim.*
55. *CŚ* with *CŚV* 8.9.
56. *Sarvabhāvasvabhāvo 'san, vacanaṁ hi tathā 'py asat. Laṅkāvatāra-Sūtra,* Gāthā 265, p. 300. Cp. *'Uktaṁ ca Hevajre: svabhāvaś caivādyanutpannaṁ, na satyaṁ na mṛṣeti ca.' Advayavajrasaṅgraha,* p. 26.
57. *Pramāṇam aprāmaṇaṁ cen, nanu tatpramitaṁ mṛṣā. Tattvataḥ śūnyatā tasmād bhāvānaṁ nopapadyate. BCA* 9, 139.
58. *VV* 29.
59. *VV* 30; *CŚ* 16.25; *MŚP* 1.1, pp. 44, 55-58.
60. *MŚ* 24.1.
61. *Yadi śūnyam idaṁ sarvam, udayo nāsti na vyayaḥ. Caturṇām āryasatyānām abhavas te prasajyate. MŚ* 24.1.
62. *Ibid.*, 24.7-10, 11, 13.
63. *Vāraṇaṁ prāg apuṇyasya, madhye vāraṇam ātmanaḥ, Sarvasya vāraṇaṁ paścād yo jānāti sa buddhimān. CŚ* 8.15
64. *MŚP* 24.7.
65. *Sarvaṁ ca yujyate tasya śūnyatā yasya yujyate. Sarvaṁ na yujyate tasya śūnyaṃ yasya na yujyate. MŚ* 24.14.
66. *MŚP, ad ibid.*
67. *MŚ* 24.15-23.
68. *MŚP* 24.18.

69. *Yady astitvaṁ prakṛtyā syān, na bhaved asya nāstitā.*
Prakṛter anyathābhāvo na hi jātūpapadyate. MŚ 15.8.
70. *Ibid.*, 15.8.11. Also see *CST* 3.21. Elsewhere, however, Nāgārjuna remarks: "Isness without birth and death is simply unthinkable" *(prasajyetāstibhāvo hi na jarā maranaṁ vinā). MŚ* 25.4. At a third place, again, he remarks: "Being is either eternal or non-eternal" *(...bhāvo hi 'nityo 'nityo 'thavā bhavet). Ibid.*, 21.14. It is difficult to reconcile the three statements.
71. *MŚP* 20.18.
72. *Yaś ca pratītya bhāvo bhāvānāṁ śūnyateti sā hy uktā.*
Yaś ca pratītya bhāvo bhavati hi tasyāvābhāvatvam. VV 22.
73. *Nirmitako nirmitakaṁ māyāpurusaḥ svamāyayā sṛṣṭam*
Pratiṣedhayeta yadvat pratiṣedho 'yaṁ tathaiva syāt. VV 23.
P.L. Vaidya gives '*pratiṣedhayase'*, which is wrong. I have followed S. Mookerjee.
74. *MŚ* 24.16-40.
75. *Ibid.*, 1.1.
76. *Sā prajñaptir upādāya pratipat saiva madhyamā.* 24.18.
77. *Yaḥ pratītyasamutpādaṁ prapañcopaśamaṁ śivam*
Deśayāmāsa Sambuddhas taṁ vande vadatāṁ varam. Ibid., 1.2.
78. Murti, p. 25
79. *Ibid.*, p. 26.

CHAPTER 5

Germs of Nihilism in non-Buddhist Traditions

A close scrutiny of certain non-Buddhist, indeed even pre-Buddhist, texts reveals conscious or unconscious nihilistic tendencies, which serve to render it preposterous to adjudge our nihilistic interpretation of *Śūnyavāda* impossible on the ground that nihilism itself is impossible, that nihilism is a figment of imagination rather than a fact in history of philosophy, and that it is impossible to think of a real philosopher maintaining nihilism seriously. This appears to be a common, preconceived notion at the back of the mind of the Mādhyamikologists of other persuasions, which must be taken care of before proceeding further.

The Vedic 'Asat'

The *Ṛg-Veda* and the *Taittirīya-Upaniṣad* prefix *'Asat'*, literally non-being, to *'Sat'*, literally being. Says the former, "In times older than the gods, being came out of non-being."[1] And the latter. "In the beginning [of creation] it was all non-being.,"[2] The *Ṛg-Veda* elsewhere maintains: "Then [=before creation] there was neither non-being nor being, neither the stars nor the yonder sky."[3] It adds, a verse later: "Then there was neither death nor the deathless (*amṛta*). . ."[4] It was a state of total chaos, beyond description as being or non-being.

The idea of birth of being from non-being came in for criticism at the hands of the *Chāndogya-Upaniṣad* thus: "How could being arise out of non-being?"[5] The *Gītā* echoes it when it declares: "Of non-being there is no becoming: of being there is no un-becoming."[6]

Here is a theory, here again is a criticism of the theory, that the cosmos or being was preceded by a state of total chaos or pure non-being without a beginning. This is a theory describable as the theory of un-beginning but ending Void.

The Nyāya-Vaiśeṣika Asat-Kārya

The Vedic *'Asat'* came to acquire philosophical relevance at the hands of the Nyāya-Vaiśeṣika school in the form of their theory of *Asat-Kārya* (non-preexistence of the effect) as opposed to the Sāṅkhya-Yoga theory of *Sat-Kārya* (pre-existence of the effect) confirmatory of the position of the *Chāndogya-Upaniṣad* and the *Gītā.* According to the Nyāya-Vaiśeṣika position, the pot, prior to its coming into being, did not exist in the clay. It is totally a new entity out of nothing though, of course, the clay, which is only its inherent (*samavāyin*) cause. The effect comes into being upon the destruction of the cause, albeit not without residue, the residue consisting in the parts (*avayavas*) which are the abiding stuff "through which the essence of the cause is transferred to its effect". This idea of nihilation of the cause with residue (*sānvaya-vināśa*), even though distinguished from the nihilation of the cause without residue (*niranvaya-vināśa*), appears to hark back to the possibility of nihilism of some form or other.

Also, the *Nyāya-Sūtra* examines a view of the origin of things from non-being pure and simple in five Sūtras constituting what Vācaspati Miśra calls *'Śūnyatopādāna-Prakaraṇa'* (examination of the view that things come out of the Void).[7]

In a later section entitled by Vācaspati as '*Sarvaśūnyatā-nirākaraṇa-Prakaraṇa*' (refutation of total nihilism), the *Nyāya-Sūtra* states and refutes a certain view akin to nihilism.[8]

This nihilism is likely to be pre-Mādhyamika. There is reason to believe that the *Nyāya-Sūtra* is pre-Mādhyamika.

Nāgārjuna's *Vaidalya-Sūtra* is devoted exclusively to the refutation of the sixteen categories dealt with in the opening chapter of the *Nyāya-Sūtra.* Since the extant text of the *Vaidalya-Sūtra* has no colophon, it is possible that it is part of a larger work, presumably covering the other parts of the *Nyāya-Sūtra,* and that the rest of the work is lost. In fact, even the extant text discloses knowledge of at least the section dealing with the validity of the instruments of knowledge (*pramāṇas*),[9] much of which finds place in the objection-part (*pūrva-pakṣa*) of Nāgārjuna's text, explicitly or implicitly.[10] Besides, many Sūtras of the *Nyāya-Sūtra* are found quoted in the *Śataśāstra* of Āryadeva, a junior contemporary of Nāgārjuna.[11] Indeed, even in his *Vigrahavyāvartanī,* Nāgārjuna seems to be having in mind the Nyāya epistemology and to try and meet the objections raised by the Naiyāyika against the former's nihilism.

The Lokāyata Negativism

Kayyaṭa refers to repudiators of perception (*pratyakṣāpalāpinam*), to ward off whose objection to inference based on perception, according to him, Patañjali uses deductive reasoning (*sāmānyato-dṛṣṭam anumānam*) in a particular context.[12]

Who could have been the repudiators of perception? The Mādhyamikas do repudiate perception at the trans-empirical level, but along with all other sources of knowledge. Same is the case with Jayarāśi Bhaṭṭa, a Lokāyata philosopher of eighth century A.D., whose *Tattvopaplavasiṁha* is devoted exclusively to the refutation of all the popular sources of knowledge (*pramāṇas*).

Jayarāśi argues that validity of the sources of knowledge cannot be established, nor, in the absence of valid sources of knowledge, the reality of things. Hence nothing whatsoever can be established, in the ultimate analysis (*paramārtha*), howsoever real things may appear empirically (*vyavahāra*).[13] It is either downright scepticism or pure nihilism.

Pre-Buddhistic Upholders of Four-Cornered Negation

During the Buddha's time, rather even before him, there were certain philosophers called *Amarāvikkhepikā* (eel-wrigglers), who are said to be fighting shy of committing themselves to any specific position and, therefore, tried to dodge all queries with the remark: I do not not-say so *(evaṁ ti pi me no)*, I do not say that (*tathā ti pi me no*), I do not say otherwise (*aññathā ti pi me no*), I do not not-say (*no ti pi me no*), it is not not that I do not-say (*no no ti pi me no ti*).[14] The Buddha's rather senior contemporary, Sañjaya Velaṭṭhiputta, used exactly the same language in speaking about the other world.[15]

Again, in the Pāli canon itself, we find a reference to a philosopher named Dīghanakha, who used to proclaim, "I approve of no (view)" (*sabbaṁ me na khamati*).[16] This has a ring of the exclusion of all views (*sarvadṛṣṭiprahāṇa*) emphasized by the Mādhyamika, even as the Amarāvikkhepikā's negativism described above has a ring of the four-cornered negation emphasized by the Mādhyamika, as we shall see in the sequel at the proper place. Besides, the Buddha also refers to a view according to which "All is nothing" (*sabbaṁ natthi*), attributing it to a class of Lokāyata philosophers.[17]

REFERENCES

1. *Ṛg-Veda* 10.72.
2. *Taittirīya-Upaniṣad* 2.7.
3. *Ṛg-Veda* 10.129.1.
4. *Ibid.*, 10.129.2.
5. *Chāndogya-Upaniṣad* 6.2.1-2.
6. *Bhagavad-Gītā* 2.16.
7. *Nyāya-Sūtra* 4.1.14-18.
8. *Ibid.*, 4.1.37-40.
9. *Ibid.*, 2.1.8-20.
10. Nāgārjuna, *Vaidalya-Sūtra* 2-19.
11. Giuseppe Tucci (ed.), *Pre-Diṅnāga Buddhist Texts on Logic from Chinese Sources*, pp. xxvii-xxviii.
12. *Pratyakṣāpalāpinaṁ prati pratyakṣapūrvakānumānāsambhavāt sāmānyatodṛṣṭam anumānam upanyasyate—oṣadhivanaspatīnām iti.* Kayyaṭa, *Mahābhāṣya-Pradīpa* 5.11.119.5.

13. Jayarāśi Bhaṭṭa, *Tattvopaplavasiṁha*, pp. 1, 125.
14. *DN* I, Brahmajāla-Sutta 1, pp. 23-26; *MN* II, Sandaka-Sutta 26, pp. 219-20.
15. *DN* I, Sāmaññaphala-Sutta 2, p. 51.
16. *MN* II, Dīghanakha-Sutta 24, pp. 193-95.
17. *SN* II, Nidāna-Saṁyutta 12, Kaccānagotta-Sutta 15, p. 17; *Jāṇusoṇi-Sutta* 47, p. 65; Lokāyatika-Sutta 48, p. 65.

CHAPTER 6

Evolution of the Meaning of Śūnya/Śūnyatā

Suñña/Śūnya and *Suññatā/Śūnyatā* happen to belong to the key-terminology of Buddhism in all its branches. And it is the be-all and end-all of the Mādhyamika system. It is likely, therefore, to be a fruitful enterprise to trace the evolution of the meaning of the term in the entire career of Buddhism. We have naturally to begin with the Pāli canon.

The Pāli Canon

According to the Pāṇinian as well as non-Pāṇinian grammatical tradition, the word *śūnya* means "deserted for the dog" (*śune kukkurāya hitam*), but, according to Bhāgīrathaprasād Tripāṭhī, "left for the air" (*śunāya vāyave hitam*), i.e. empty, like space.[1] In the Pāli canon, '*suñña*' means empty, desolate, vacant, lonely, absent, and the like, non-technically speaking. Thus, *suññaṁ Brahma-vimānam*[2] means empty world of Brahman (the masculine). Likewise, in the passage, "He sees a *suñña* village. Whichever house he enters he finds it empty *(ritta)*, void (*tuccha*), *suñña*,"[3] the first *suñña* appears to mean lonely and the second, desolate or deserted. Again, when the state called freedom of mind (*ceto-vimutti*) is described as *suñña* of desire, defect, delusion,[4] *suñña* appears to stand for the void or devoid.

Another significant passage in this connection is the one concerning what is called *suññatā-vihāra* or the order of planes of existence on which the Buddha dwelt, as set out in the Cūla-Suññatā-Sutta of the *Majjhima-Nikāya*.[5] The planes are:

1. Consciousness of humanity (*manussa-saññā*)
2. Consciousness of forest *(arañña-saññā)*
3. Consciousness of the earth *(pathavī-saññā)*
4. Consciousness of the infinity of space (*ākāsānañcāyatana-saññā)*
5. Consciousness of the infinity of ideation (*viññāṇañcāyatana-saññā*)
6. Consciousness of nothingness (*ākiñcaññāyatana-saññā*)
7. Consciousness of neither-consciousness-nor-unconsciousness (*nevasaññānāsaññāyatana-saññā*)
8. Objectless cessation of consciousness (*animittacetosamādhi*)
9. The supreme, ultimate Void *(paramānuttarā suññatā)*

The whole thing is explained thus: the monastery is devoid (*suñña*) of monks, etc. One dwelling in forest may find it devoid of the village and men but undevoid of the forest itself. Similarly, one meditating upon the earth, upon the infinite consciousness, upon the state of nothingness, and upon the state of neither-consciousness-nor-unconsciousness remains devoid of all else than the meditated objects. Finally, while meditating upon the state of objectlessness (*animittacetosamādhi*), one finds it, too, impermanent and thereby gets rid of the three impurities of thirst, rebirth, and ignorance. At this stage, *Suñña/Suññatā* performs a positive, internal function. This stage, however, remains undevoid of the body-sense till the end of one's life. Thereafter, one enters what is called pure ultimate unsurpassable *Suññatā* (*parisuddha-paramānuttara-suññatā*).[6]

That the Buddha analyzed the whole of reality into a fivefold scheme of point-instants or elements or rather sense-data called *dharmas* is common knowledge; that he occasionally preached their ultimate unreality, so as to prompt not only Nāgārjuna[7] and Gauḍapāda[8] but the *Kathāvatthu,*[9] too, to claim that he preached no *dharmas* at all, is unknown to many. Of the five *dharmas,* he likens senses (*rūpa*) to dots of foam, feeling (*vedanā*) to bubbles, perception (*saññā*) to mirage, impression (*saṁskāra*) to banana tree, and awareness or ideation (*viññaṇa*) to illusion (*māyā*).[10] Here the tendency to Nihilism is clear. A clearer Nihilistic teaching, however, is: "Depending upon the oil and the wick does the light of the lamp burn; it is neither in the one nor in the other, not is it anything in itself; phenomena are, likewise, nothing in themselves. All things are unreal; they are deceptions; *Nibbāna* is the only truth."[11] The rejection by the Buddha of both the existence view (*bhava-diṭṭhi*) and non-existence view (*vibhava-diṭṭhi*) of reality,[12] too, serves to align him with the Nihilistic Śūnyavādins, broadly speaking.

The Mādhyamika seeks to reconcile the Buddha's realistic, *dharma*-positing, with nihilistic, *dharma*-denying, sermons by declaring the former as of a secondary or empirical import and the latter as of primary or absolute import.[13] Indeed, there are suggestions in the Buddha himself that the latter is a higher teaching than the former.[14]

As will transpire in the sequel, it is the Mādhyamika's way to repudiate all views, all metaphysics, without exception. And it is significant that the Buddha himself preaches repudiation of all views to an ascetic, Dīghanakha, in no equivocal terms.[15] There are a good many such suggestions elsewhere, too.[16]

Candrakīrtī's verdict is that the absolute truth is silence (*paramārtho hy āryāṇāṁ tūṣṇīmbhāvaḥ*). Its significance will be worked out in the sequel. What is common, however, to the Buddha and the Mādhyamika both is an older tradition to this effect acknowledged in the Pāli canon. So, Mahāmoggalāna is represented there as referring to it as though it were a pre-existing doctrine.[17]

It all is tantamount to nihilism carried almost to its logical extreme.

Perhaps the first philosophical use of the term *Suñña* is discernible in the *Saṁyutta-Nikāya* passage determining the meaning of the expression *'suñño loko'* (the world is *Suñña*) thus: Since the world is devoid of the self (or substance) or anything of the self (or substance), they say, "the world is *Suñña*".[18] Here *'Suñña'* is translated as 'empty'. This innovation in the use of the term acquires enough popularity in later Buddhist texts.

Certain canonical texts mention *Suññatā-Samādhi* alongside of *Animitta-Samādhi* and *Appaṇihita-Samādhi.*[19] These are dealt with usually under three *Vimokkhas—Suññatā, Animitta,* and *Appaṇihita*—[20] and sometimes under the first two only,[21] sometimes again under *Vimokkha-Mukhas* (channels of emancipation) as well. *Suññatā-Vimokkha* dawns upon contemplation on the no-soul doctrine etc.[22] Here the mind becomes completely free from the three impurities (*āsavas*).

Another significant fact about *Suññatā* in the Pāli canon is that the Cūla-Suññata-Sutta of the *Majjhima-Nikāya* so philosophizes about the term as to qualify it by *yathābhucca* (veridical), *avipallattha* (changeless), *parisuddha* (pure), *paramānuttara* (supremely unsurpassable).[23] Besides, the *Saṁyutta-Nikāya* and the *Aṅguttara-Nikāya* declare the Buddha's discourses as profound and concerned with *Suññatā* (*ye te Suttantā Tathāgata-bhāsitā gambhīrā gambhīratthā lokuttarā Suññata-paṭisaṁyuttā*).[24]

Mahāyāna Buddhism mentions several kinds of *Śūnyatā.* The *Paṭisambhidāmagga,* however, surprises us by listing as many as twenty-five kinds of *Suññatā,* which need not detain us here.[25]

Non-Canonical Pāli Buddhism

That *Suññatā*-emancipation, the channel of *Suññatā*-emancipation, or *Suññatā* itself is attained by dwelling upon the no-soul idea is a recurring theme of many a post-canonical Pāli author, such as Nāgasena and Buddhaghoṣa.

Nāgasena speaks of "bringing to light the self-character of things which is supremely *Suñña,* free from willing and living, absolutely *Suñña.*"[26] Here *Suñña* seems to presuppose the thesis of *Niḥ-svabhāvatā* (essencelessness), so characteristic of Mādhyamika philosophy.

Buddhaghoṣa writes: "Even as a wooden machine is *Suñña* (being) devoid of soul and will and yet it walks and sits thanks to the fitting of wood and rope and behaves as if it were willing and living, this name-and-form (man), too, is *Suñña* (being) devoid of soul and will and yet it walks and sits thanks to the conglomeration of one (*dhamma*) with another and looks as if it were willing and living."[27] It is evident that *Suñña* is tantamount to soulless here. Elsewhere, too, Buddhaghoṣa equates insight into *Suññatā* with insight into soullessness.[28]

Buddhaghoṣa is inclined to view things as *Suñña* in various ways. Thus, one way *Suññatā* is called four-cornered (*catukoṭika*): (1) non-perception of soul in oneself, (2) non-perception of one's own soul elsewhere, (3) non-perception of any other soul anywhere, and (4) non-perception of anyone else's soul in oneself.[29] Another way, *Suññatā* is viewed in six forms: things are *Suñña* (devoid) of (1) soul/substance, (2) anything pertaining to the soul, (3) permanence, (4) eternality, (5) imperishability, and (6) everlastingness.[30] A third way, *Suññatā* is viewed in eight forms: things are *Suñña* of everlasting essence, enduring essence, essence of happiness, soul-essence, everlastingness, permanence, eternity, and imperishableness.[31] A fourth way, *Suññatā* is viewed in ten forms; a fifth way, in twelve forms; a sixth way, in forty-four forms.[32] We need not go into details in this connection. *Suññatā* here boils down to *Anattā* (soullessness).

Sanskrit Hīnayāna Buddhism

According to Pāli canon, things (*dhammas*) are characterized by impermanence (*anicca*), suffering (*dukkha*), and soullessness (*anattā*). The Sarvāstivādins added void (*suñña/ Śūnya*) to the list.[33] It is already anticipated, however, in the *Therīgāthā*, which adds two further characteristics, *agha* (sinful) and *vadha* (destructive) to the list of the four.[34] Harivarman, whom we have had occasion to notice in chapter 3, carries forward the tradition of characterizing things by impermanence, suffering, *Śūnya* and *Anātman*.[35]

What is the difference between *Śūnya* and *Anātman*? Three answers have come to our notice. According to Aśvaghoṣa, things are called *Śūnya* because they have neither a doer nor a knower in them.[36] That is to say, *Śūnya* means soulless, *Anātman*. And *Anātman* itself. According to Aśvaghoṣa, *Anātman* consists in the fact that the world is devoid of desire/will (*nirīha*), is unfree (*asvatantra*), and conditionally originated.[37] Yaśomitra appears to equate *Anātman* with the negation of *Ātma-dṛṣṭi* (soul-view) and *Śūnyatā* with the negation of *Ātmīya-dṛṣṭi* (view of things concerning the soul).[38] Harivarman maintains that *Śūnyatā* means emptiness. If a pot has no water, we say it is empty or devoid of water. In the present context, *Śūnyatā* represents the fact that there is no soul in the body (*pañcaskandheṣu pudgalo nāsti*). Whereas *Nairātmya* (soullessness/substancelessness) means *Naiḥsvābhāvya* (essencelessness) or negation of everything whatever.[39] In chapter 3, we have seen that Harivarman is a Nihilist in his own right and postulates two kinds of *Nairātmya/Śūnyatā*, viz. *Sattva-śūnyatā* and *Dharma-śūnyatā* closely corresponding respectively to *Pudgala-nairātmya* and *Dharma-nairātmya* of Mahāyāna Buddhism.[40]

Further, Ghoṣaka, Vasubandhu, and the *Vibhāṣāprabhā-vṛtti* are also unanimous in characterizing things under four aspects: impermanence, suffering, *Śūnya*, and *Anātman*.[41]

Mahāyāna Buddhism

According to Maitreyanātha, the founder of Yogācāra, the duality of object and subject is *Śūnya*, but the ground of the illusory duality is not *Śūnya*. This ground is Pure Consciousness,[42] variously described as *Tathatā*, *Bhūtakoṭi*, *Animitta*, *Paramārthatā*, and *Dharmadhātu*.[43] Another way *Śūnya* is used by him is the triplicity of *Abhāva-Śūnyatā*, *Atadbhāva-Śūnyatā*, and *Svabhāva-Śūnyatā*. He relates this triplicity with the triplicity of *Svabhāva* (essence): *Parikalpita-*, *Paratantra-*, and *Pariniṣpanna-Svabhāva*. Out of the three *Svabhāva*s, the first is simply not, in any way whatsoever, hence it represents *Abhāva-Śūnyatā*; the second is not such as it is imagined, hence it represents *Atadbhāva-Śūnyatā;* and the third is of the very essence of *Śūnyatā* (*Śūnyatā-svabhāva*), hence it represents *Svabhāva-Śūnyatā.*[44] A kindred distinction is made by him in the concept of *Nairātmya* (substancelessness).[45] Asaṅga also subscribes to this trilogy of *Śūnyatā.*[46]

What is the difference between *Śūnyatā* and *Nairātmya*? According to some, what lacks something is said to be *Śūnya* (empty) of that thing. According to Sthiramati, there is no difference in meaning. *Nairātmya* refers to *Niḥsvabhāvatā* (essencelessness), whereas *Śūnyatā* refers to *Aniṣpanna-svabhāvatā.*[47]

We have already referred to the distinction between the two terms made by Aśvaghoṣa in his *Saundarananda,* in the preceding section. In his *Mahāyānaśraddhotpādaśāstra,* he tries to interpret *Śūnyatā* in his own way. He observes that the Mahāyāna Sūtras declare the Tathāgata "in the end only vacuity like space". The unwary mistake the statement to mean that "Space or Emptiness itself is the Tathāgata". The right import of the statement, according to Aśvaghoṣa, is something else: it "was used in order to destroy belief in phenomena as real". He elucidates his point further: "Men are to understand that space is nothing. It has no existence and is not a reality. It is a term in opposition to reality. We only say this or that is visible in order that we might distinguish between things. All phenomena are only in the Mind and have really no outward form, therefore, as there is no form it is a mistake to think there is anything there. All phenomena only arise from false notions of the Mind. If the Mind is independent of these false ideas, then all phenomena disappear."[48] Thus, it appears, by *Śūnyatā,* Aśvaghoṣa means being void or devoid of phenomena.

According to Yogācāra-Vijñānavāda school in general, *Śūnyatā* means the negation not of all but of the duality of subject and object and the world infected thereby. Maitreyanātha enunciates the standpoint thus: "Constructive ideation (*abhūta-parikalpa*) or rather the ground of constructive ideation is. Duality (of subject and object) finds no place there. *Śūnyatā* does exist there, however. But the (ground of) constructive ideation, too, exists in it (in *Śūnyatā*)."[49] As stated by Vasubandhu in his comments on this couplet, *Śūnyatā* is nothing but the freedom of the ground of constructive ideation from the duality of subject and object.[50] The transcendent stream of consciousness is the ground, constructive ideation constitutes the phenomenal world, the *Parinispanna* is the transcendent consciousness as freed of the duality of subject and object, and *Śūnyatā* is the freedom itself.

From this account, it is apparent that, on the Vijñānavāda view, *Śūnyatā* is not pure, total negation (*prasajya-pratiṣedha*) but limited negation (*paryudāsa*), in the sense that it negates the duality of subject and object but leaves the transcendent stream of consciousness untouched. Sometimes, however, on the basis of couplet 27 of Vasubandhu's *Triṁśikā*,[51] it is claimed to be just the opposite, viz., tantamount to pure, total negation. The couplet says: 'Even when the wayfarer comes to realize that all is ideation pure and simple and that there is nothing besides it, it does not attain *Śūnyatā* till the ideation, too, disappears from the mind.' That is to say, negation of object is not enough; negation of subject has also to be attained. But is there nothing to transcend the subject-object duality? Vijñānavāda cannot reply in the negative: it does postulate the ground of the ideation called *Dharmakāya*, the Absolute.[52] Where is pure negation?

The Vijñānavādins sometimes begin to talk in the language of the Mādhyamika. For instance, Sthiramati equates *Śūnyatā* with exclusion of all views (*sarvadṛṣṭi-niḥsaraṇa*).[53] Asaṅga also seems to follow the Mādhyamika dialectic of four-cornered negation, viz., negation of being, non-being, both, and neither.[54] Likewise, he seems to follow in the footsteps of the Mādhyamika when he dismisses the difference between *Saṁsāra* and *Nirvāṇa* at the trans-empirical level.[55]

In fact, as suggested by Sthiramati, it is the burden of Vasubandhu's *Triṁśikā* to refute both the realist and the

Mādhyamika theses, respectively, of the reality of objects like the reality of consciousness and of the merely empirical reality of consciousness like the empirical reality of objects.[56]

Indeed, in Vijñānavāda literature, the distinction between idealism and nihilism gets blurred occasionally to the chagrin of the reader.

Apart from the Mādhyamika hangover discernible in the Vijñānavādin's notion of *Śūnyatā,* we can be assured that he has developed two principal meanings of *Śūnyatā*: negation of the duality of subject and object and, as an extension thereof, negation of the external world (*bāhyārtha-śūnyatā*). It is to be borne in mind, however, that the external world is sought to be negated *qua* external world and not *qua* ideational construct. Sthiramati contends that rope is said to be *Śūnya* as snake and not as rope.[57]

We have seen that *Śūnyatā* occupies an important place in Buddhism entire and that way it may be called *Śūnyavāda,* but only loosely, because, barring the Mādhyamika, all other schools of Buddhism postulate *Śūnyatā* on a limited scale only. The concept finds its culmination in Mādhyamika philosophy, which is rightly designated as *Śūnyavāda* proper. This issue we proceed to take up in the next chapter.

REFERENCES

1. Bhagīrathaprasāda Tripāṭhī, *'Śune Kukkurāya Hitam iti Śūnyam', Sārasvatī Suṣamā,* XXIV, 2 (Bhādrapada, 2026 Vik.), pp.141-45.
2. *DN* I, Brahmajāla-Sutta 1, p. 17.
3. *SN* IV, Saḍāyatana-Saṁyutta 35, Āsīvisopama-Sutta 238, p. 157.
4. *MN* I, Mahāvedalla-Sutta 43, p. 368.
5. *MN* III, Cūla-Suññata-Sutta 21, pp. 169-73.
6. *Ibid.*, pp. 168ff.
7. *MŚ* 25.24; *CSt.* 1.4.
8. Gauḍapāda, *Māṇḍukya-Kārikā* 4.99.
9. *Na vattabbaṁ—'Buddhena Bhagavatā dhammo desito' ti? Āmanta. 'Kena desito' ti. Āyasmatā Ānandena desito ti. Kathāvatthu* 18.179 (2), p. 483.
10. *Pheṇapiṇḍūpamaṁ rupaṁ, vedanā bubbulūpamā,*
    Maricikūpamā saññā, saṅkhārā kadalūpamā,
    Māyūpamaṁ ca viññāṇaṁ desitādiccabandhunā.
    SN III, Khandha-Saṁyutta 22, Pheṇapiṇḍūpama-Sutta 95, p. 360.

11. *MN* III, Dhātuvibhaṅga-Sutta 40, p. 330. Cp. *Sn.*, sts. 757-58.
12. *MN* I, Cūla-Sīhanāda-Sutta 11, p. 92.
13. *MŚP* 1.1, p. 13.
14. *MN* I, Alagaddūpama-Sutta 22, pp. 179-80, where *dharmas* are likened to a raft to be let off after crossing the stream.
15. *MN* II, Dīghnakha-Sutta 24, pp. 193-97.
16. *Sn.*, Aṭṭhaka-Vagga 4, Mahābyūha-Sutta 13, pp. 407ff.
17. *SN* II, Bhikkhu-Saṁyutta 21, Kolita-Sutta 1, p. 227.
18. *SN* IV, Saḍāyatana-Saṁyutta 35, Suññataloka-Sutta 85, pp. 50-51.
19. *DN* III, Saṅgīti-Sutta 10, p. 172; *SN* IV, Asaṅkhata-Saṁyutta 43, Suññatasamādhi-Sutta 4, p. 313; *AN* III, Rāgapeyyālam 18, p. 279; *Paṭisambhidāmagga*, Mahāvagga I, Ñāṇākathā I, p. 54.
20. *Paṭisambhidāmagga*, Mahāvagga I, Vimokkha-Kathā 5, p. 311.
21. *Dhammapada*, Arahanta-Vagga 7, Gāthā 92.
22. *Paṭisambhidāmagga*, Mahāvagga I, Vimokkha-Kathā 5, p. 311.
23. *MN* III, Cūla-Suññata-Sutta 21, pp. 169-73.
24. *SN* II, Opamma-Saṁyutta 20, Āṇi-Sutta 7, p. 222; *AN* II, Parisa-Vagga 5, p. 68.
25. *Paṭisambhidāmagga*, Yuganaddha-Vagga 2, Suñña-Kathā 10, p. 437.
26. *Saṅkhārānaṁ sabhāvaṁ paramasuññataṁ nirīha-nijjīvitaṁ accantaṁ suññataṁ ādiyitabbam.* Nāgasena, *Milindapañha*, Bombay University Series, p. 404.
27. Buddhaghoṣa, *Visuddhimagga* III, ch. 18, p. 1391.
28. *Ibid.*, ch. 20, p. 1482; ch. 21, pp. 1544ff.
29. *Ibid.*, ch. 21, pp. 1544-45.
30. *Ibid.*, p. 1546.
31. *Ibid.*, p. 1547.
32. *Ibid.*, pp. 1548-49.
33. *Sarvāstivāda-Pañcavastukaśāstra*, p. 10.
34. *Therīgāthā*, Talaputa's verse.
35. Harivarman, *Satyasiddhiśāstra*, pp. 354, 493.
36. Aśvaghoṣa, *Saundarananda* 17.20.
37. *Ibid.*, 17.21.
38. Yaśomitra, *Abhidharmakośa-Sphuṭārthā* 6.19, p. 911.
39. Harivarman, *Satyasiddhiśāstra*, pp. 317, 376-77, 505.
40. *Ibid.*, pp. 379, 535.
41. Ghoṣaka, *Abhidharmāmṛta*, p. 83; Vasubandhu, *Abhidharmakośa* 6.16; *Abhidharmadīpa-Vibhāṣāprabhāvṛtti* 384, pp. 316-17.
42. Maitreyanātha, *Madhyāntavibhāgaśāstra* 4.
43. *Ibid.*, 15.
44. *Ibid.*, 7.
45. *Ibid.*, 7-8.
46. Asaṅga, *Mahāyānasūtrālaṅkāra*, Avavādānuśāsanyadhikāra 14, 34.
47. Sthiramati, *Madhyāntavibhāgabhāṣyaṭīkā* 7-8, p. 90.

48. Aśvaghoṣa, *Mahāyānaśraddhotpādaśāstra*, tr. from the Chinese under the title *The Awakening of Faith*, p. 70.
49. Maitreyanātha, *Madhāntavibhāgaśāstra* 1.2.
50. Vasubandhu, *ad ibid.*
51. *Vijñaptimātram evedaṁ ity api hy upalambhataḥ Sthāpayan nagrataḥ kiñcid tanmātre nāvatiṣṭhate.* Vasubandhu, *Triṁśikā-Vijñaptimātratāsiddhi* 27.
52. *Ibid.*, 30.
53. Sthiramati, *Madhyāntavibhāgāṣyaṭīkā* 21. p. 47.
54. Asaṅga, *Mahāyānasūtrālaṅkāra* 6.1.
55. *Ibid.*, 6.5.
56. *Atha vā vijñānavad vijñeyam api dravyata eveti kecin manyante, vijñeyavad vijñānam api samvṛtita eva na paramārthata—ity asya dviprakārasyāpi ekāntavādasya pratiṣedhārthaḥ prakaraṇārambhaḥ.* Sthiramati, *Triṁśikābhāṣya.* Prefatory remarks, p. 93.
57. *Yathā śūnyā rajjuḥ sarpasvabhāvena...na tu rajjusvabhāvena, tathehāpi.* Sthiramati, *Madhyāntavibhāgabhāṣyaṭīkā* 2, p. 12.

CHAPTER 7

The Mādhyamika as Śūnyavāda

As we have seen, Pāli Buddhism postulates what came to be called *pudgala-nairātmya* or *pudgala-śūnyatā*. By *pudgala/puggala* Theravāda meant the individual soul (*attā*) and by *śūnyatā/suññatā*, soullessness (*anattā*). According to it all is soulless. The term *pudgala/puggala* soon underwent an extension of meaning and began to stand for the enduring reality, called substance, essence, or substratum, subjacent to the phenomena, as the realists in general would have it. Accordingly, from soullessness, *pudgala-śūnyatā* took a plunge into a wider meaning, substancelessness/noumenonlessness. This development gave a wider denotation to *pudgala-śūnyatā*, viz., negation of the individual soul as well as of the essence or substance of things, of the noumena behind the phenomena. The Vijñānavādin bade goodbye to the phenomena along with the noumena and the individual soul and retained only the transcendent stream of consciousness. The Mādhyamika did not think it fit to spare even that.

In order to drive his *Śūnyavāda* home, the Mādhyamika adopts a graduated scheme, which though seldom stated in so many words, appears to underlie the whole of his approach. But at the same time it has given rise to misconceptions in regard to the Mādhyamika's position. In the Mādhyamika works *Śūnyatā* is presented sometimes as relative being, sometimes again as essenceless being, often as non-being, equally often as neither being nor non-being, and finally as exclusion of all views. Those who fail to piece such statements together and connect them into a graduated whole tend to mistake some preparatory stage of the Mādhyamika's denouement as *the* grand finale. This is why some say that *Śūnyatā* is nothing but relativity, some others that it is mere essencelessness, still others that it is an Absolute beyond thought-categories of being and non-being, and so on. In what follows we proceed to try and present a complete picture of *Śūnyatā*.

Graduated Teaching of the Śūnyatā Doctrine

The various grades of the Mādhyamika teaching are found interspersed almost throughout the Mādhyamika works and it sometimes becomes difficult to disentangle them for systematization into a hierarchical order. The same we are out to do here according to our lights.

(1) *Śūnyatā as Relative Being:* Nāgārjuna emerges more often than not as a thoroughgoing relativist with a strong distaste for any kind of Absolute whatsoever barring, as it were, the Negative Absolute. He takes enormous pains to demonstrate that nothing possesses absolute being, that all is relative. All reality is characterized by interdependence. Nothing exists in its own right, independently of other things. The existence of each object is borrowed from its relationship with other objects. This may be called the doctrine of universal relativity. It rejects all thought of an Absolute as the ground of the realm of relativity. According to it, all is relative (*pratītya-samutpanna*). "No Absolute (*apratītya-samutpanna*) whatsoever is."[1] "There is no non-relative entity of anything anywhere any time."[2] Nāgārjuna also remarks that, since this world is non-existent, the other world is non-existent also.[3]

What we wish to drive at *vis-à-vis* the Mādhyamika's position is best illustrated by Nāgārjuna's interesting discussion of the relativity of the elements (*dharmas*) with reference to fire and fuel as follows: "If the fire is relative to the fuel, or the fuel is relative to the fire, which of the two came first, to which the fire [or] the fuel is relative? If an entity becomes possible in and through its relationship with that entity which itself owes its existence to its relationship with the former, which entity can exist on account of which? The entity which owes its existence to another is non-existent; how, then, can it need the latter? If, on the other hand, it so needs when it is existent, the question of needing simply does not arise."[4]

The doctrine of universal relativity (*pratītya-samutpāda*) is the stepping stone to the doctrine of *Śūnyatā*. The knowledge of the former at once leads to the knowledge of the latter. Their relation is so intimate that Nāgārjuna has no hesitation in identifying the two. He observes, "What is relativity we call *Śūnyatā*. It (*Śūnyatā*) is relative being *(upādāya prajñapti)*. It is the middle path."[5] This proposition is pregnant with implications. The Mādhyamika turned *pratītya-samutpāda*, literally and originally conditioned/dependent origination, into *pratītya-samutpāda* as dependent or relative being, as relativity. He had better replace the term with *pratītya-samupapāda*. In this sense, however, he expresses *pratītya-samutpāda* otherwise as *upādāya-prajñapti* (relative appearance, relative being, relativity). In fact, *pratītya-samutpāda*, which emerged in the Pāli canon as a theory of causation, became at the Mādhyamika's hands tantamount to a veritable denial of causation. Indeed, Nāgārjuna's verdict is that what has come into being through causes and conditions has in fact not come into being at all, and, since it has not come into being, it is *Śūnya*, void, pure and simple.[6] It is significant that Candrakīrti interprets *pratītya-samutpāda* to mean "non-origination by nature" (*svabhāvenānutpādaḥ*).[7]

Nāgārjuna's suggestion is that his denial of the world does not imply belief in another order of reality like the Absolute, immanent in or transcendent to phenomena. It is quite in conformity with the spirit of the Prajñāpāramitā texts, which refuse to set *Śūnyatā* over against the *dharmas* and to acknowledge positive knowledge of any such reality in the highest wisdom conceived by them. Nāgārjuna himself expresses the view that *Śūnyatā* is nothing other than existents and that there is no existent without *Śūnyatā.*[8] Advayavajra follows suit.[9] Prajñākaramati expresses himself categorically against the attempt to install *Śūnyatā* over against the realm of being: "*Śūnyatā* is not different from being, for being itself is of the nature of that; otherwise, in the event of *Śūnyatā's* being different from being, there would be no essencelessness of dharmas."[10]

This issue tends to crop up in the Mādhyamika works again and again, and it will surely recur in the sequel occasionally.

(2) *Śūnyatā as Essenceless Being:* Nāgārjuna unequivocally expresses the view that, being essenceless, things do not exist.[11] He contends, "Essencelessness of things is proved by the phenomenon of change. And there can be no object without essence. Hence the *Śūnyatā* of things."[12] According to him, the fact of change presents an insuperable problem, a veritable dilemma, to the realist. "If there be no essence, what would undergo change? If [again,] there be an essence, what would undergo change? The same object cannot undergo change (viz., cannot become another object), nor can another object do so; for the youth does not age, nor does the aged one age. If the same object becomes another, milk itself would become curd. [If you say that something else becomes curd,] what other then milk can become curd?"[13]

The Mādhyamikas are never tired of describing the world as pure illusion, but in doing so they never suggest that they see anything non-illusory behind it.[14]

The Mādhyamika system is an extension of the Buddha's theses of egolessness, universal evanescence, and quietude of *Nibbāna.* His doctrine of egolessness came later to develop into the doctrine of denial of substance or abiding reality, which led to denial of a reality subjacent to phenomena. From the position that the changing phenomena have no underlying, changeless reality, it was only a short step to the position that phenomena have no underlying reality at all. The former position made short work of the latter. The Naiyāyikas, Pūrva-Mīmāṁsakas, Sarvāstivādins, and Vaibhāsikas hold that appearances are real. The Advaita Vedānta and Vijñānavāda hold that appearances are unreal, and posit a reality underlying them. Early Buddhism dismissed substance, including the ego (*pudgala-nairātmya* or *pudgala-śūnyatā*), but postulated two orders of reals called *dharmas*, personal and impersonal, which come out of nothing, endure for a bare moment, and then relapse into nothing, thanks to the law of discontinuous continuity (*pratītya-samutpāda*). The Satyasiddhi and Mādhyamika schools went a step farther and dismissed the *dharmas* (*dharma-nairātmya* or *sarva-dharma-śūnyatā*), too. The Mādhyamika, in effect, calls appearances unreal without acknowledging a reality behind them. S.N. Dasgupta is right when he remarks that Mādhyamika philosophy "is, therefore, neither idealism nor realism nor absolutism, but blank phenomenalism which only accepts the phenomenal world as it is but which would not, for a moment, tolerate any kind of essence, ground or reality behind it."[15] It is, indeed, in this vein of blank phenomenalism that Nāgārjuna says: "This all is groundless, and groundless has it been called."[16] "This all is supportless, and supportless has it been called."[17]

(3) *Śūnyatā as Non-Being:* We have seen that the Mādhyamika does not believe in the reality of things, external as well as internal, and declares them empty (*śūnya*) of both existence and essence (*svabhāva*). The natural corollary is that his *Śūnyatā* can be equated with non-being. This is true in a severely limited sense. Postulation of non-being is a necessary stage in the Mādhyamika approach. In fact, he starts with the repudiation of being of all kinds: causality, motion, matter, space, qualificance and qualificand, light and darkness, soul, substance, time, morals and does not spare relativity and essence. What he seems to be concerned to drive at through his examination of such modes of being is to demonstrate that nothing can be said to be in any of the states conceivable by man, and that, this being the case,

nothing whatever exists.

According to Buddhism in general, reality is divisible into the conditioned (*saṅkhata/saṁskṛta*) and the unconditioned (*asaṅkhata/asaṁskṛta*). The Mādhyamika negates both. Nāgārjuna argues: "There being no proof of emergence, endurance, and extinction, the conditioned does not exist; and, in default of establishment of the conditioned, how can there be the unconditioned?"[18] The direct corollary is that, there being neither the conditioned nor the unconditioned, there is no reality whatever.

(4) *Śūnyatā as neither Being nor non-Being:* But this is just another stage in the movement of Mādhyamika thought. We have shown that the Mādhyamika is a repudiator of being. We shall see presently that he is concerned as much with repudiating non-being as with repudiating being. His repudiation of non-being has been a source of much distortion of his standpoint. Even responsible scholars tend sometimes to fall a victim to the thought that, since the Mādhyamika has no love for non-being, he must be an Absolutist. Which is far from being the case, as we shall notice at the proper place in the sequel.

Against the concept of non-being, Nāgārjuna argues like this: When there is no being, how can its non-being be conceived?[19] If being is not proved, non-being is not proved either; for what people call non-being is but the opposite of being.[20] The Buddha himself repudiates both being and non-being in the Kātyāyana dialogue. If existence is there by nature, its negation cannot be; for there can be no change in nature.[21] If there is no being, there can be no non-being either, for without one there can be no many.[22] Prajñākaramati argues against non-being in the same vein. According to him, non-being is something subjective and unreal. And, where there is nothing to deserve the name of non-being, it is foolish to talk of non-being as the negation of being.[23] Śāntideva contends: "When there is no being which could be negated, non-being becomes supportless. How can then be any presentation of it? When neither being nor non-being is presented to consciousness, there being no alternative, the intellect ceases to operate."[24] "Without positing a figment of imagination, its non-being cannot be grasped. Therefore, the non-being of being, which is false, is, evidently, itself false."[25] Thus, non-being is doubly unreal. Candrakīrti remarks in the same vein: " 'The son of a barren woman' is nothing but words. No objective counterpart of the expression is found of which positivity or negativity could be predicated. Therefore, how is it possible to think of, no-object in terms of being and non-being?"[26] He also observes: "If something existed, its repudiation would lead to negativism and hence to a false view. When we find nothing whatsoever, what can be stolen/lost/negated there? Non-being is nothing whatsoever . . ."[27]

The position is that being and non-being are correlatives, so that the one cannot be thought of save in relation to the other. If, therefore, there is no being, no object, how can there be non-being, no-object?

From the foregoing account it is evident that the Mādhyamika's denial of non-being is a semantical rather than an ontological proposition. He does not deny that all is reducible to non-being or that all is non-being; he simply demurs to calling the negation of being by the name of non-being.

The Buddha preaches that all comes out of nothing and relapses into nothing (empirically speaking, of course). Harivarman contends that, if that is the case, all is nothing. The Mādhyamika argues that his *Śūnyatā* does not stop short at nothing. When, however, the Mādhyamika expresses disapproval of the tendency to identify his *Śūnyatā* with non-being finally speaking, he means to say only that 'nothing' is meaningless without the duality of being and non-being, and that, since being is not there, nothing is not there also. So, between Harivarman and the Mādhyamika the issue is merely a semantic one rather than ontological. Compare Nietzsche: ". . . once rid of the conception of the 'true world', we have nothing against which to contrast the 'apparent world' and the latter concept, deriving its only significance from a spurious contrast, is thus itself a spurious concept: 'with the true world we have also gotten rid of the apparent world'."[28]

The burden of the Mādhyamika dialectic is to show that all is void, nothing. The Mādhyamika is not satisfied, however, with the words, 'void' and 'nothing'. 'Void' presupposes a filler thereof. Likewise, 'nothing' presupposes some 'thing'. Since he does not brook any presupposition whatsoever, he finds the terms inadequate to express what he actually means.

Thus, the Mādhyamika repudiates being as well as non-being, the former on ontological and the latter on semantic grounds. There is a third alternative, however, viz., both being and non-being rolled into one (*ubhaya-saṅkīrṇātmatā*), and a fourth one, viz., a category exclusive of both being and non-being (*ubhaya-pratiṣedha-svabhāvatā*).[29] What does the Mādhyamika have to say about these two categories? Prajñākaramati's reply is: "Not that, in the event of both being and non-being having been negated as shown above, the combination of both of them or negatedness of both is the real state of affairs. Since the idea of being is the ground of all ideation, after its repudiation all of these ideations stand repudiated with one stroke."[30] Out of the four categories (*Koṭis*) of reality that can be conceived by man, viz., being, non-being, both, and neither, the first two are basic or primary categories and the latter two, derivative of these. When the Mādhyamika proceeds to repudiate the primary categories, the derivative ones stand repudiated of themselves.

While the Mādhyamika tends initially to identify *Śūnyatā* with non-being, he distinguishes them at a higher stage,[31] which, as should be manifest from the foregoing account, is quite in keeping with his basic position.

In the Mādhyamika system, the negation of the world is so complete that it ceases to be mere negation and becomes the sole substitute for reality, so to speak. All naming is determination, and, when there is negation, pure and simple, with no existence beside it—that is to say, when there is indeterminate or absolute negation—even calling it negation is unwarranted, for the simple reason that it will turn determinate in the process of being named. Naming is intended to mark something out of its context, the group of its co-existents, and, when there is nothing but negation in the Mādhyamika's world, the question of marking it out by naming stands entirely ruled out.

(5) *Śūnyatā of Śūnyatā*: We have seen how Nāgārjuna rejects being and non-being, including their combination and negation. Now we shall see that he rejects *Śūnyatā* too. In the *Mādhyamaka-Śāstra*, Chapter XV, will be found self-essence, existence, and non-existence, all repudiated with the felicity characteristic of Nāgārjuna. We have shown that his rejection of non-being is semantic rather than ontological. Similarly, his rejection of *Śūnyatā*, too, is semantic rather than ontological. As regards the combination and negation of the two categories, too, the same position holds good.

Nāgārjuna avers, "Were there something non-*Śūnya*, there could be something *Śūnya*. But, since there is nothing non-*Śūnya*, how will the *Śūnya* be?"[32]

It is obvious that here Nāgārjuna has risen to a height of imagination at which he finds inadequate even the concept of *Śūnyatā*, not, however, on ontological but on purely semantic grounds, as was the case with his repudiation of non-being. What is left after negating everything conceivable is characterizable neither as non-being nor as *Śūnya*, for the simple reason that there is nothing in opposition to which these concepts could logically be framed. Nāgārjuna tries to make his point of view clearer by the important reservation: "The Buddhas preach *Śūnyatā* as the exclusion of all [ontological] views/theses. Incurable do we declare those who are inclined to erect *Śūnyatā* itself into a particular thesis."[33]

The residue after the negation of everything whatsoever is truly ineffable. All description proceeds by relating one thing to another. Without this process there can be no speech at all. And, when there is nothing at all in relation to which the so-called residue is to be described, it is nothing but ineffable or indescribable (*prapañcopaśama*), where language loses all its utility and efficiency. They who erect this *Śūnyatā* into a particular theory, or convert it into a real being, as is the case with those who read Absolutism into the Mādhyamika system, are far from curable. Candrakīrti remarks, "Those who see being even in *Śūnyatā* are not such as we talk with. He who, in reply to the observation, 'I shall give you no money, says, 'Well, let me have the no-money', cannot by any means be convinced of the non-existence of money."[34]

Our interpretation of Nāgārjuna's refutation of *Śūnyatā* is fully borne out by the following passage of Candrakīrti: "If there were something like *Śūnyatā* [over and above the objects], the essence of objects would depend upon it. But this is not the case. Here *Śūnyatā* is propounded as the generic characteristic of all reals. There is no non-*Śūnya* real, and non-*Śūnyatā* itself does not exist. [That is to say, all reals being *Śūnya,* there is no non-*Śūnya* real; and hence *Śūnyatā,* in default of its opposite, simply does not exist.] And, when there are no non-*Śūnya* objects and there is no non-*Śūnyatā,* it follows that, in the absence of its opposite, *Śūnyatā,* too, is not there like the garland of sky-flowers."[35]

As a matter of fact, there is hardly any real difference between non-being and *Śūnyatā.* By the former, the Mādhyamika seems to mean determinate negation, while, by the latter, indeterminate negation. Otherwise, both the terms denote one and the same fact. That is to say, when he speaks generally, he defines *Śūnyatā* such as in these statements: "That is called *Śūnyatā* which is non-existent by nature."[36] "*Śūnyatā* is the essencelessness of all reals, characterized by non-recognition."[37]

It must be evident by now that the Mādhyamika denies not negation, for denial itself is negation, but the first, the second, and, as will be thrown into bolder relief in the sequel, the third negation. The end-all of the system is exclusion of all views (*sarvadṛṣṭi-prahāṇa*), about which more in the sequel, is itself a negative activity.

Śūnyatā and Prajñāpāramitā

It is common knowledge that Mādhyamika philosophy is a development of the amorphous ideas of *Śūnyatā* characterizing the canonical Mahāyāna Sūtras, especially the Prajñāpāramitā texts, which came to be systematized and skilfully developed by Nāgārjuna into a full-fledged doctrine of *Śūnyatā*, into *Śūnyavāda*, to be precise, as it has come to be popularly known.[38] Let us, therefore, scrutinize these texts to find out what light they have to throw on the notion of *Śūnyatā*.

According to one of the texts, all *dharmas*, as well as the soul, are non-existent.[39] Elsewhere, all *dharmas* are described as illusory and dream-like. Indeed, the text goes to the length of proclaiming: "Even the All-Enlightened One (*Samyak-Sambuddha*) is illusory and dream-like; even All-Enlightened-One-Hood is illusory and dream-like."[40]

This interesting statement, which has been put into the mouth of Subhūti, who is shown as addressing the sons of gods, takes the latter aback, and they ask Subhūti if he really means what he says. Let us quote their own words: "Well, Revered Subhūti! do you say that even the All-Enlightened One is illusory and dream-like? Do you say that even All-Enlightened-One-Hood is illusory and dream-like?"[41] Subhūti, undeterred by the question, replies: "Sons of gods! even *Nirvāṇa* I declare illusory and dream-like, let alone any other *dharma*."[42] [The sons of gods are further confused. But Subhūti goes on:] "If there were any other, more distinguished (or superior) *dharma* than *Nirvāṇa*, that, too, I would declare illusory and dream-like."[43]

These and similar straightforward statements leave hardly any room for doubt about the fact that, according to the *Prajñāpāramitā* texts, all is pure void.

There are clear indications in the Prajñāpāramitā texts that *Śūnyatā* is not beyond but identical with *dharmas*. Lest someone, like those who read Absolutism into them, should construe *Śūnyatā* to mean something over and above the *dharmas*, these texts are never tired of repeatedly reminding the reader that *Śūnyatā* is non-different from the *dharmas*. Take, for example, the following: "Sensum is void (*śūnya*) of sensum. What is voidity (*śūnyatā*) of sensum is not sensum, nor is voidity other than sensum. Sensum itself is voidity; voidity itself is sensum. Feeling is void of feeling. What is voidity of feeling is not feeling, nor is voidity other than feeling. Feeling itself is voidity; voidity itself is feeling."[44] The same remarks have been made in the text as regards the remaining three complexes (*skandhas*), viz., perception (*saṁjñā*), impression (*saṁskāra)*, and awareness (*viññāṇa*). We have already seen that this view is fully shared by Nāgārjuna.

T.R.V. Murti is of the opinion that "*Prajñāpāramitā* as non-dual intuition is the Absolute."[45] The difficulty is determining the meaning of 'the Absolute' apart, which we will take up in the sequel, the statement is misleading. The definitions of *Prajñāpārmitā*—literally, the highest wisdom—available in the texts under consideration appear to lend full support to the Nihilistic interpretation of the Mādhyamika system. Says one of the texts: "What is non-apprehension of all *dharmas* is called *Prajñāpāramitā*. When there is no feeling, ego-consciousness, experience, practice, then there is *Prajñāpāramitā*—so it is said."[46]

A more emphatic assertion of the non-difference of *Śūnyatā* from the phenomenal world and, consequently, a repudiation of the non-Absolutistic character of *Prajñāpāramitā*, is contained in the same text a bit earlier, as follows: "*Prajñāpāramitā* should not be taken to be over and above the complexes, seats *(āyatanas*), and bases (*dhātus*). What is the reason for it? Because, Subhūti! that the complexes, seats, and bases themselves are void (*śūnya*), abstract (*vivikta*), and quiescent (*śānta*) is *Prajñāpāramitā*."[47] Here the significance of the emphasis represented by the expression 'themselves' (*eva*) cannot go unnoticed.

Elsewhere, All-Enlightenment is defined as "where nothing is cognized".[48] In elucidation of this remark of his, Subhūti says to the Buddha, without being refuted: "On account, Lord! of the voidity of all *dharmas*, there is no *dharma* which could be cognized. That is to say, Lord! all *dharmas* are *śūnya*. Those *dharmas*, Lord! for the cessation of which righteousness is preached are non-existent; likewise, he who experiences the ultimate All-Enlightenment, that which is to be experienced, he who knows, that which is to be known—all these *dharmas* are *śūnya*."[49]

These texts list many kinds of *Śūnyatā*, among which are included *Śūnyatā* of the conditioned, *Śūnyatā* of the unconditioned, transcendental *Śūnyatā*, absolute *Śūnyatā*, and *Śūnyatā* of *Śūnyatā*[50] which preclude all possibility of postulation of an Absolute at the hands of the Mādhyamika.

We shall find at the proper place in the sequel that the Mādhyamika's is at once a no-doctrine attitude to reality as well as, rather more primarily than that, a no-reality doctrine. This finds confirmation from such statements in other Mahāyāna Sūtras as the following: "This all is mere name, subsisting by name alone. The named as different from the name does not exist. Such *dharmas* as are designated by various names are simply not there. Such is the *dharma*-hood of the *dharmas*. Nameness is devoid of name, nor does name subsist by name. All *dharmas* are nameless though revealed by name. These *dharmas* are non-existent and are brought forth by ideation."[51] All *dharmas* are false . . . illusory . . . dream-like . . . watermoon-like . . ."[52]

As a matter of fact, at the level of *Prajñāpāramitā*, Mādhyamika philosophy tends to culminate in what is called the cessation/exclusion/vanishing of all viewing *(sarvadṛṣṭi-niḥsaraṇa/sarvadṛṣṭi-prahāṇa)*, the *Śūnyatā* view not excepted,[53] resulting ultimately in perfect silence/dumbness *(tūṣṇīṁbhāva)*.[54] The Mādhyamika system is for freeing/purging the mind of the web of concepts and views (*vikalpa-jāla)* and verbal syndrome (*prapañca*), so to speak. On that account, however, it must not be mistaken for something akin to Advaita, as will transpire in a later chapter.

Indeed, the Mādhyamika finds it extremely difficult to give us even the faintest idea of the deliverances of *Prajñāpāramitā* and can do little better than mutter that it is of the nature of silence (*tūṣṇīṁbhāva*), cessation of all expression (*prapañcopaśama*)[55] or rather outright unknowing (*anupalambha*).[56] It has no knowing whatever (*yatra jñānasyāpy apracāraḥ*).[57] This is of course a puzzling statement. In certain Chinese versions of the Mādhyamika teaching, Prajñāpāramitā is held to have no marks whatsoever and consequently no knowing, but it is maintained that "there is a markless knowing and an unknowing intuition", that there is such a thing as "the knowing of unknowing" to be termed "all-knowing (*sarvajñatā*)", that, therefore, "the holy man empties his mind and fills (makes real) his intuition", that "though he always knows, he never knows", that "thus he can muffle his brilliance and sheathe his light", that "because there is no knowing in Knowledge, he is able to intuit metaphysically outside of events."[58] Candrakīrti identifies such knowing unknowing with indeterminate, non-conceptual knowing (*nirvikalpaka*), which is free from conceptual thinking (*vikalpa*) or exercise of the mind (*citta-pracāra*).[59] A Chinese Mādhyamika text says, "Knowing while not knowing is not having determinate knowing."[60]

But what becomes of the Mādhyamika's refutation of contentless/formless consciousness (*sva-saṁvitti*)? Obviously, the two positions will have to be judged mutually contradictory, unless the "indeterminate knowing", "the knowing of unknowing", is clearly distinguished from contentless consciousness. We fail to imagine what *Prajñāpāramitā* can possibly reveal to us or even mean to us with all its capabilities of "the knowing of unknowing".

However, it would be preposterous on our part to read the Absolute into *Prajñāpāramitā,* as some scholars are tempted to do today. To read into it anything whatever would mean determining it, and all determination is negation on the Mādhyamika view. If in *Prajñāpāramitā* there be any knowing it would be pure, indeterminate knowing, distinguishable from pure unknowing. Such to our mind is likely to be the real meaning of the Mādhyamika proposition that *Prajñāpāramitā* knows no knowing. Here we are tempted to hazard the opinion that, if at all, only the pure Void can be the object of pure knowing.

It is significant in this regard that, when the Mādhyamika proceeds to found a philosophy upon such ultimate experience, he leaves no doubt that he does not believe in a noumenon subjacent to phenomena. Likewise, the Buddha's experience of *Nirvāṇa* also proved to him wholly incommunicable and tended to drive him into quietude, but, when it came to giving it some expression or other with a view to compassionately letting his disciples share the extraordinary experience, he appeared to explain it in terms of nihility, in terms of culmination of a process of nihilation of the self, or rather the ego, in terms of permanent death beyond all possibility of survival in any form whatsoever designating this state as *Nirvāṇa.*

It would not be out of place here to refer to a debate in China between Kamalaśīla, a disciple and commentator of Śāntarakṣita, the founder of the Yogācāra-Svātantrika-Mādhyamika school, and an anonymous representative of the Chinese 'Fa-shang Mahāyāna' school, which, according to Buston, "favoured nihilistic views and did not exert themselves in the practice of virtue."[61] This school appears to be Prāsaṅgika-Mādhyamika. Now, the encounter between Kamalaśīla and the anonymous representative of the Chinese Prāsaṅgika-Mādhyamika (San-lun) school has been recorded by Buston. Kamalaśīla's animad versions on the Prāsaṅgika view of *Prajñāpāramitā* are given below: "Thou sayest that one ought not to think about anything whatsoever. But this means the negation (or rejection) of highest analytic wisdom (*shes.rab.*: *prajñā*) likewise. . . . If the mere absence of (consciousness and) recollection is regarded as sufficient, it follows that in a swoon or at the time of intoxication one comes to the state where there is no constructive thought."[62]

We feel inclined to the view that the infinite peace and tranquillity and the consequent bliss and beatitude, ecstasy and felicity, attendant upon the highest stage of Samādhi and that, too, without the accompaniment of a known process of knowing, is the chief factor which is at the root of the peculiar conception of *Prajñāpāramitā* and which accounts for the consuming passion displayed by the Mādhyamika philosophers in their love for *Śūnyatā*. Indeed, Jalāl ud-Dīn Rūmī, the greatest Sūfī poet, appears to have a kindred state in mind when he sings:

Man āṅ waqt kardam Khudā rā sujūd
Ki dhāt-ō ṣifāt-ī Khudā ham na būd

("I bowed to God at a time when even God's existence and attributes were not there.") According to the *Yoga-Bhāṣya* also, the *Nirbīja-Asamprajñāta-Samādhi* is characterized by objectlessness, contentlessness, supportlessness–negation-oriented (*abhāva-prāptam iva*).[63]

To sum up the discussion in this section: According to the early formative texts of Mahāyāna referred to above, all *dharmas* without exception are *Śūnya*. *Śūnyatā* is nothing over and above the *dharmas*, so that one cannot install it as the Absolute over against the *dharmas*. The highest wisdom consists in the non-apprehension of any *dharmas*, of anything whatsoever. Since there is nothing to apprehend, non-apprehension of anything can alone be the highest wisdom. Were there is something like the Absolute, apprehension of it would be said to be the highest wisdom. Hence, the question of there being an Absolute simply does not arise. Accordingly, the philosophy taught by these texts is pure and simple nihilism.

REFERENCES

1. *Apratītyasamutpanno dharmaḥ kaścin na vidyate. MŚ* 24.19.
2. *Apratītyāsthitā nāsti kadācit kenacit kvacit. CŚ* with *CŚP* 9.2.

3. *Sarvam idaṁ asatyaṁ. Lokābhāvāl lokōttaram api nāsti.* Nāgārjuna, *Bhavabhedaśāstra*, p. 21; *Sarvabhāvaś ca nāsty evaṁ loka eṣa paro 'pi ca.* Nāgārjuna, *Bhavasaṅkrānti* 4. Cp. *Udāna* 8.1.
4. *Yadīndhanam apekṣyāgnir apekṣyāgniṁ yadīndhanam,*
Katarat Pūrvaniṣpannaṁ yad apekṣyāgnir indhanam?
Yo 'pekṣya sidhyate bhāvas tam evāpekṣya sidhyati.
Yadi yo 'pekṣitavyaḥ sa sidhyatāṁ kam apekṣya kaḥ?
Yo 'pekṣya sidhyate bhāvaḥ so 'siddho 'pekṣate katham?
Athāpy apekṣate, siddhas; tv apekṣā 'sya na yujyate. MŚ 10.8, 10, 11.
5. *Yaḥ pratītyasamutpādaḥ śūnyatāṁ taṁ pracakṣmahe.*
Sā prajñaptir upādāya, pratipat saiva madhyama. MŚ 24.18. Also see *Cst.* 2.20; 3.38.
6. *Pratyayebhyaḥ samutpannaṁ notpannaṁ te subhāṣitam.*
Notpannaṁ tat svabhāvena; tasmāc chūnyaṁ pradarśitam. CSt. 3.3;
Tat tat prāpya yad utpannaṁ notpannaṁ tat svabhāvataḥ. Nāgārjuna, Yuktiṣaṣṭikā, quoted in *Murti, The Central Philosophy of Buddhism,* p. 89, fn. 2;
Yat pratītya samutpannaṁ notpannaṁ tat svabhāvataḥ.
Svabhāvena yan notpannam utpannaṁ nāma tat katham?
Advayavajrasaṅgraha, p. 25.
7. . . . *svabhāvenānutpādaḥ. MŚP* 24.18, p. 219. *Laṅkāvatārasūtra* (Gāthā 582) says, however: "All this is uncreated. But it is not that things do not exist. Things do exist, but they do so without sufficient reason, like *fata morgana*, dream, and illusion":
Anutpannam idaṁ sarvaṁ, na ca bhāvā na santi ca.
Gandharva-svapna-māyākhyā bhāvā vidyanty ahetukāḥ.
8. *Bhāvebhyah śūnyatā nānyā, na ca bhāvo 'sti tāṁ vinā.*
Tasmāt pratītyajo bhāvaḥ śūnyas pradarśitas tvayā. Ct. 3.41.
9. *Advayavajrasaṅgraha,* p. 24.
10. *Na ca śūnyatā bhāvād vyatiriktā, bhāvasyaiva tatsvabhāvatvāt. Anyathā, śūnyatāyā bhāvād vyatireke, dharmāṇāṁ niḥsvabhāvatā na syāt. BCAP* 9.34.
11. *Bhāvānāṁ niḥsvabhāvānāṁ na sattā vidyate yataḥ,*
Satīdaṁ asmin bhavatity etan naivopapadyate. MŚ 1.12.
12. *Bhāvānāṁ niḥsvabhāvānām anyathābhāvadarśanāt,*
Asvahāvo bhāvo nāsti, bhāvānāṁ śūnyatā yataḥ. Ibid., 13.3.
13. *Kasya syād anyathābhāvaḥ, svabhāvaś cen na vidyate?*
Kasya syād anyathābhāvaḥ, svabhāvo yadi vidyate?
Tasyaiva nānyathābhāvo, nāpy anyasyaiva yujyate.
Yuvā na jīryate yasmād, yasmāj jīrṇo na jīryate.
Tasya ced anyathābhāvaḥ, kṣīram eva bhaved dadhi.
Kṣīrād anyasya kasyātha dadhibhāvo bhaviṣyati? Ibid. 13.4-6.
14. *Yathā mayā, yathā svapno, gandharvanagaraṁ yathā,*
Tathotpādas, tathā sthānaṁ, tathā bhaṅga udāhṛtam. Ibid., 7.34.

Also see *ibid.*, 23.8; *CSt.* 1.15; 2.4.18, 34; 3.5, 17, 31; *Bhavasaṅkrānti* 19; *Udāna* 8.1; etc.

15. S.N. Dasgupta, *Indian Realism*, p. 79.
16. *Anādhāram idam sarvam, anādhāram prabhāṣitam. Bhavasaṅkrānti* 10.
17. *Anālambam idaṁ sarvam, anālambaṁ prabhāṣitam. Bhavasaṅkrānti-Parīkṣā* 8.
18. *Utpāda-sthiti-bhaṅgānām asiddher nāsti saṁskṛtam.*
Saṁskṛtasyāprasiddhau ca kathaṁ setsyaty asaṁskṛtam? MŚ 7.33.
19. *Avidyāmāne bhāve ca kasyābhāvo bhaviṣyati?*
Bhāvābhāvavidharmā ca bhāvābhāvam avaiti kaḥ? Ibid., 5.6.
20. *Bhāvasya ced aprasiddhir abhāvo naiva sidhyati.*
Bhāvasya hy anyathābhāvam abhāvaṁ bruvate janāḥ. Ibid., 15.5.
21. *Ibid.*, 15. 7-8.
22. *Nāgārjuna, Ratnāvalī* 1.71.
23. *Na cābhāvasya kalpitasvābhāvatayā kiñcit svarūpam asti. Na ca bhāvanivṛttirūpo 'bhāvo, nivṛtter niḥsvabhāvatvāt. Yadi ca bhāvasyaiva kaścit svabhāvaḥ syāt, tadā tatpratiṣedhātmā abhāvo 'pi syāt. Bhāvasya tu svabhāvo nāstīti pratipāditam eva. Ato na bhāvanivṛttirūpo 'bhāvo nāma kaścit. BCAP* 9.2, p. 173.
24. *Yadā na labhyate bhāvo yo nāstīti prakalpyate,*
Tadā nirāśrayo'bhāvaḥ kathaṁ tiṣṭhen mateḥ puraḥ?
Yadā na bhāvo nābhāvo mateḥ santiṣṭhate puraḥ,
Tadā 'nyavṛttyabhāvena nirālambā praśāmyati. BCA 9.34-35.
25. *Kalpitaṁ bhāvam aspṛṣṭvā tadabhāvo na gṛhyate.*
Tasmād bhāvo mṛṣā, yo hi tasyābhāvaḥ sphuṭaṁ mṛṣā. Ibid., 9.140.
26. *Vandhyāputra iti śabdamātram evaitat. Nāsyārtha upalabhate yasyārthasya bhāvatvam abhāvatvaṁ vā syād iti kuto 'nupalabhyamāna-svabhāvasya bhāvābhāvakalpanā yokṣyate? Tasmān na vandhyāputro 'bhava iti vijñeyam. MŚP* 25.8, p. 231.
27. *Kaścid yadi padārtho 'bhaviṣyat, syāt tasyāpavādād abhāvadarśanān mithyādṛṣṭiḥ. Yadā tu padārtham eva kaścin na paśyāmas, tadā kiṁ tatra muṣyate? Naiva kiñcid abhāvo bhavatīty ayukto 'yam upālambho bhavati. Atrāha—Yady abhāvadarśanam api na pratipādyate, kiṁ punar anenāgamena pratipādyata it? Ucyate—Etat tūktaṁ Bhagavatā śūnyatā-paridīpakam,* (*MŚ* 13.2). *Yad etad uktaṁ Bhagavatā tan na bhāvānam abhāvaparidīpakam. Kiṁ tarhi? Śūnyatāparidīpakaṁ svabhāvānut-pādaparidīpakam ity arthaḥ. MŚP* 13.2, p. 104.
28. *Friederich Nietzsche, Twilight of the Idols,* p. 388.
29. *BCAP* 9.2, p. 173.
30. *Na ca bhāvabhāvayor uktakrameṇāsattve pratipādite tadubhaya-saṅkīrṇātmat sambhavaty ubhayapratiṣedhasvabhāvatā vā. Bhāvāvikalpasyaiva sakalavikalpani bandhanatvāt tasmin nirākṛte sarva evāmī ekaprakāreṇa nirastā bhavantīti. Loc. cit.*
31. *Tan mṛṣā mosadharma* (sic) *yad Bhagavān ity abhāṣata*

Sarve ca moṣadharmāṇaḥ saṁskārās tena te mṛṣā. MŚ 13.2.

32. *Yady aśūnyaṁ bhavet kiñcit, syāc chūnyam iti kiñcana. Na kiñcid asty aśūnyaṁ ca, kutaḥ śūnyaṁ bhaviṣyati?* MŚ 13.7. Cp.: *Aśūnyāpekṣayā śūnyaśabdārthaparikalpanā. Yogavāsiṣṭha* 3.10.14.
33. *Śūnyatā sarvadṛṣṭīnāṁ proktā niḥsaraṇaṁ Jinaiḥ. Yeṣāṁ tu śūnyatādṛṣṭis tān asādhyān babhāṣire.* MŚ 13.8. Also see *CSt.* 2.21; 4.9.
34. *Ye tu tasyāṁ api śūnyatāyāṁ bhāvābhiniveśinas tān praty avācakā vayam . . . Yo na kiñcid api te paṇyaṁ dāsyamīty uktaḥ sa ced 'dehi bhoḥ! tad eva mahyaṁ na kiñcin nāma paṇyam' iti brūyāt sa kenopāyena śakyaḥ paṇyābhāvaḥ grāhayitum? MŚP,* 13.8, p. 108.
35. *Yadi śūnyatā nāma kaścit syāt, tadāśrayo bhāvasvabhāvaḥ syāt. Na tv evam. Iha hi śūnyatā nāmeti sarvadharmāṇāṁ sāmānyalakṣaṇam ity abhyupagamād aśūnyadharmābhāvād aśūnyataiva nāsti. Yadā cāśūnyāḥ padārthā na santi aśūnyatā ca nāsti, tadā pratipakṣa-nirapekṣatvāc chūnyatā 'pi khapuṣpamālavan nāstity avasiyatām. MŚP* 13.7, pp. 107-08. Cp. *Ratnāvalī* 2.4-5.
36. *Tatra śūnyam ucyate yat svabhāvena nāsti. MŚP* 20.18, p. 174. It is significant that *'nāsti', 'abhāva', 'asat',* etc. used in this connection are illustrated by space and the like. Here, too, it is said: *'Na hi svabhāvenāvidyamānasyākāśāder udaya-vyayau dṛṣṭau.' Loc. cit.*
37. *. . . śūnyatā sarvadharmaniḥsvabhāvatā, anupalambhayogena. BCAP* 9.54.
38. Cp. *Candrakīrti's* remark: *Ācārya-Nāgārjunasya viditāviparīta-prajñāpāramitānīteh . . . MŚP,* p. 1.
39. *Sarveṇa sarvaṁ sarvathā sarvam ātmā na vidyate nopalabhyate. Evaṁ sarvadharmā na vidyante nopalabhyante. Aṣṭarāhasrikā-Prajñāpāramitā,* p. 14.
40. *Samyaksambuddho 'pi māyopamaḥ svapnopamaḥ. Samyaksam-buddhatvam api māyopamaṁ svapnopamam. Loc. cit.*
41. *Samyaksambuddho 'py Ārya-Subhūte! māyopamaḥ svapnopama iti vadasi? Samyaksambuddhatvam api māyopamaṁ svapnopamam iti vadasi? Ibid.,* p. 20.
42. *Nirvāṇam api devaputrā! māyopamaṁ svapnopamam iti vadāmi. Kiṁ punar anyaṁ dharmam? Loc. cit.*
43. *Tad yadi, devaputrā! nirvāṇād apy anyaḥ kaścid dharmo viśiṣṭataraḥ syāt, tam apy ahaṁ māyopamaṁ svapnopamam iti vadeyam. Loc. cit.*
44. *Rūpaṁ rūpeṇa śūnyam. Yā ca rūpaśūnyatā tad rūpam. Na cānyatra rūpāc chūnyatā. Rūpam eva śūnyatā, śūnyam eva rūpam. Vedanā vedanayā śūnyā. Yā ca vedanāśūnyatā na sā vedanā. Na cānyatra vedanāyāh śūnyatā. Vedanaiva śūnyatā. Śūnyataiva vedanā. . . Śatasāhasrikā-Prajñāpāramitā,* I, p. 554.
45. Murti, p. 228.

46. *Yo 'nupalambhaḥ sarvadharmānāṁ sā prajñāpāramitety ucyate. Yadā na bhavati sañjñā, mamajñā, prajñaptir, vyavahāras, tadā prajñāramitety ucyate. Aṣṭasāhasrikā-Prajñāpāramitā,* p. 89.
47. *Na cānyatra dhātvāyatanebhyaḥ prajñāpāramitā 'vaboddhavyā. Tat kasya hetoḥ? Skandhadhātvāyatanam eva Subhūte! śūnyaṁ, viviktaṁ, śāntam iti hi prajñāpāramitā. . . Loc. cit.*
48. *Yatra na kaścid abhisambuddhayate. Ibid.*, p. 156.
49. *Śūnyatvād Bhagavan! sarvadharmāṇāṁ na sa kaścid dharmaḥ saṁvidyate yo dharmaḥ śakyo 'bhisamboddhum. Tathā hi Bhagavan! sarvadharmāḥ śūnyaḥ. Yasyāpi Bhagavan! dharmasya prahāṇāya dharmo deśyate so 'pi dharmo na saṁvidyate. Evaṁ yaś cābhīsambudhyetānuttarāṁ samyaksambodhiṁ, yaś cābhisam-boddhavyaṁ, yaś ca jānīyat, yac ca jñatavyaṁ, sarvam ete dharmāḥ śūnyāḥ. Ibid.*, pp. 156-57.
50. See, for example, *Śatasāhasrikā-Prajñāpāramitā,* I, pp. 192-93.
51. *Sarvam etan nāmamātraṁ sanjñāmātre pratiṣṭitam.*
Abhidhānāt pṛthagbhūtam abhidheyaṁ na vidyate.
Yena yena hi namna vai yo yo dharmo 'bhilapyate.
Nāsau saṁvidyate tatra—dharmāṇāṁ sā hi dharmatā.
Nāmnā hi nāmatā śūnyā, nāmnā nāma na vidyate.
Anāmakāḥ sarvadharmā nāmnā tu paridīpitāḥ.
Ime dharmā asantaś ca kalpanāyāḥ samuddhitāḥ. Bhavasaṅkrānti Sūtra, 5-6.
52. . . . *vitathā ime sarvadharmā, asanta ime sarvadharmā, viṭhapitā ime sarvadharmā, māyopamā ime sarvadharmāḥ, svapnopamā ime sarvadharmā, nirmitopamā ime sarvadharmā, udakacandropmā ime sarvadharmā iti vistaraḥ. Āryaratnakūṭasūtra,* quoted in *MŚP* 1.3, p. 17.
53. *Śūnyatā sarvadṛṣṭīnāṁ proktā niḥsaraṇaṁ Jinaiḥ.*
Yeṣāṁ tu śunyatādṛṣṭis tān asādhyān babhāṣire.
Sarvadṛṣṭiprahānāya yaḥ saddharmam adeśayat
Anukampāṁ upādāya taṁ namasyāmi Gautamam. MŚ 13.8; 27.30.
54. *Paramārtho hy āryāṇaṁ tūṣṇīmbhāvaḥ. MŚP* 1.3, p. 19.
55. *MŚ* 1.2; 25-24.
56. *Sarvopalambhopaśamaḥ prapañcopaśamaḥ śivaḥ, Ibid.*, 25.24. *Yo 'nupalambhaḥ sarvadharmāṇāṁ sā prajñāpāramitety ucyate. Yadā na bhavati sañjñā, mamajñā, prajñaptir, vyavahāras, tadā prajñāpāramitety ucyate. Aṣṭasāhasrikā-Prajñāpāramitā,* p. 89.
57. *MŚP* 18.9, p. 159.
58. *Richard H. Robinson, Early Mādhyamika in India and China,* pp. 213-14.
59. *MŚP* 18.9, p. 159.
60. Robinson, p. 307.
61. Buston, *Chos. 'byung.*, fasc.142b, quoted in Nathan Katz, 'An Appraisal of the Svātantrika-Prāsaṅgika Debates'. *Philosophy: East and*

West, 26, No. 3, July 1976, p. 263.

62. Buston, *Chos.*, *'byung.*, fasc. 142a sq., quoted in Katz, *ibid.*, p. 264.

63. *Virāmapratyayo nirvastuka ālambanīkriyate, sa cārthaśūnyaḥ, Tadabhyāsapūrvaṁ cittaṁ nirālambanam abhāvaprāptam ive bhavatīty eṣa nirbījaḥ samādhir asamprajñātaḥ. Yogā-Bhāṣya, Samādhi-Pāda* 18, p. 56.

CHAPTER 8

The Mādhyamika Dialectic and its Significance

The Mādhyamika dialectic is destructive of metaphysics and all that it implies and leads to cessation of all thought. It has its roots in the utterances of the Buddha. Let us begin with him.

From Bypassing Metaphysics through its Outright Rejection to its Total Transcendence

We have seen, in chapters 1 and 5, that the Buddha would not talk about certain fundamental metaphysical questions, the *avyākṛtas* to be precise, adjudging them irrelevant to spiritual life. His attitude did not amount, however, to rejection of metaphysics; it meant just bypassing it with a view to concentrating upon spiritual discipline without frittering away energy.

We have also seen that the Buddha is, more often than not, inclined to repudiating dogmas (*diṭṭhis*).

Despite all this, however, he is found engaged in controversies centring round such metaphysical issues, off and on. Which means that he had no great hate for metaphysics, nor that he looked upon it as entirely useless.

The Mādhyamika Rejects Metaphysics

The Mādhyamika starts with rejection of metaphysics and ends with total transcendence of metaphysics, true to his Absolute Nihilism.

His method is called *Prasaṅga* (*reductio ad absurdum*). He takes up the Buddhist realists' categories one by one and reduces them to absurdity by subjecting them to a rigorous logico-linguistic test.

In Indian philosophy in general, art of debate *(kathā)* is threefold: *vāda* (*bonafide* exchange of thought), *jalpa* (disputation for victory), and *vitaṇḍā* (refutation-mania/propensity to refutation without taking any position whatever).[1] They can be termed discussion, disputation, and wrangling, respectively. Of these, the first is considered good, the second bad, and the third worse. All the same, Akṣapāda is prepared to justify the use of even the bad and the worse with a view to guarding and defending the truth where it is otherwise at stake, even as the hedge of thorny branches is put up to protect sprouting seeds.[2]

Sometimes, the Mādhyamika is ridiculed as a mere wrangler, a *vitaṇḍā-vādin.* But there is a difference between his *Prasaṅga* and Akṣapāda's *vitaṇḍā. Vitaṇḍā* is merely procedural, without any philosophical presuppositions or commitments; whereas *Prasaṅga* has a well-defined philosophical basis. *Prasaṅga* is a studied repudiation of everything whatsoever, including the objects of knowledge, the means of knowledge, in fact knowledge itself, without commitment to anything whatsoever. The wrangler loves polemics and dodges commitment, while the Mādhyamika feels driven or rather condemned to polemics for others and rules out the very possibility of any commitment on his part. It will be clear as we proceed.

Introduction of the method of *reductio ad absurdum,* the dialectical method, is credited to Zeno of Elea (490-430 B.C.). His argumentation based on a chain of *reductiones ad absurdum,* or refutation by reduction to impossibility, is to the effect that the adversary's position is riddled with contradictions and hence untenable. He differs from the Mādhyamika, however, insofar as he has a position of his own to establish or defend. He was a monist of a sort.

There are two radically different, mutually opposed, and apparently equally forceful attitudes to existence. According to one attitude, existence is rational, meaningful; according to the other, it is irrational, meaningless. Thereby, the whole of world-thought is divisible into the rationalistic, meaningful concept of existence on one hand and the irrationalistic, meaningless concept of existence on the other. In the West, Schopenhauer, Nietzsche, and Eduard vön Hartmann may be taken to be irrationalistic in this sense, to some extent or other. In fact Godless existentialists in general, such as Albert Camus, Unamuno, and Sartre, too, may be said to fall under this category. Bertrand Russell displays a kindred mood in *A Free Man's Worship.* We dare say, Marx the dialectician is a rationalist, while Marx the materialist displays, along with other materialists, a marked but unacknowledged tendency towards irrationalism. In this respect, existentialism, materialism, and atheism partake of a common way of thought. "Existentialism", says Sartre, "is nothing but an attempt to draw the full conclusions from a consistently atheistic position".[3] Although atheist, as is evident from his *Risālah fi 'l-Mawjūd,*[4] Umar Khayyām stands out as a confirmed irrationalist in his *Rubā'iyyāt.* In India, leaving the ancient Lokāyata alone, about which we possess so little information, Jayarāśi Bhaṭṭa is a Lokāyata of the eighth century with a clearly irrationalistic outlook on existence. To us, the Mādhyamika's position is unmistakable, so far as his philosophy goes. It is Nihilism, breathing a clearly irrationalistic spirit. According to it, there is no rhyme or reason for things to exist, wherefore they are essenceless, void.

The Mādhyamika's method is to examine the various modes of being countenanced by common sense and philosophies in general and to repudiate all of them by showing that they lack law, lack logic, and hence are a chaos rather than a cosmos. This is surely a chaotic or irrationalistic conception of reality. Hegel, who is in a way the most thoroughgoing rationalist ever born and whose cosmic or rationalistic conception of reality can perhaps never be surpassed, declares, "What is rational is actual and what is actual is rational."[5] The Mādhyamika is prepared to grant this dictum to start with, that only the rational can be actual, real; but his finding is that there is nothing rational, from which premise he concludes that there is nothing real. In sum, Hegel takes it that the actual is rational; the Mādhyamika, that the apparently actual is the irrational, and hence at bottom unactual, unreal.

The chaotic or irrationalistic conception of whatever be the case leads to outright rejection of metaphysics. All science, all metaphysics, proceeds on the tacit assumption that existence is law-governed at bottom and is amenable to reason and logic, which is the first casualty at the hands of the Mādhyamika.

And the outright rejection of metaphysics in its turn leads to total transcendence of metaphysics, *sarva-dṛṣṭi-prahāṇa* (abandonment/elimination of all metaphysical views/speculations). This stage of thinking may be designated as the stage of thesislessness, about which more in the sequel.

An Omnibus Five-Member Dialectic

Unlike the Hegelian dialectic, which has three moments or stages—thesis, antithesis, and synthesis, as Karl Marx would have it[6]—, the Mādhyamika dialectic tends to have five moments (*koṭis*)—thesis, antithesis, synthesis, anti-synthesis, and super-synthesis. The well-known dialectical formula of Hegel, modelled on the three-beat rhythm, is (1) being, (2) nothing, and (3) becoming; that of the Mādhyamika,

1. being (*sat*)
2. nothing (*asat*)
3. both (*ubhaya/sad-asat/sad-asad-ubhaya/tad-ubhaya-saṅkīrṇātmatā*),
4. neither (*an-ubhaya/na san nāsat/ubhaya-pratiṣedha-svabhāvatā*), and
5. quietude/silence (*tūṣṇīṁbhāva*),[7] non-apprehension, cessation of thought and speech (*an-upalambha*),[8] the inexpressible (*prapañcopaśama*),[9] the essenceless (*niḥsvabhāva*), or beyond-the-four-moments (*catuṣkoṭi-vinirmukta*).[10]

The fundamental difference between the Hegelian and the Mādhyamika dialectic is that, while the former affirms the reality of all the three moments of his dialectic, the third constituting a higher reality comprehending the other two moments, the Mādhyamika denies the reality of his first four moments, letting the fifth moment alone for consideration in the next sentence. His reality, or rather his apology for one, is beyond the four moments. This beyond-the-four-moment category must not be construed, however, to mean a fifth moment along the lines of the fifth moment (*pañcama-koṭi*) predicated of the Brahman, as *pañcamakoṭi-mātra,* by Śrīharṣa and certain other Advaitins.[11] The word *śūnyatā,* which is often used to denote the second moment of 'nothing', is also used to denote this so-called fifth moment.[12] However, this moment is not found mentioned as such in Mādhyamika literature. This is our innovation offered here to throw the Mādhyamika standpoint into bold relief. Of course, the basis of the innovation is not lacking in Mādhyamika literature. There are numerous references therein to the four categories and their repudiation, directly or indirectly.[13] Besides, Nāgārjuna openly admits: "Not that only suffering has none of the four modes of being. The external entities, too, have none of the four modes."[14] Candrakīrti avers that "only four are the *dṛṣṭis* (views/theses)".[15]

That things are existent is the thesis; that they are non-existent is the antithesis; that they are both existent and non-existent is the synthesis; that they are neither existent nor non-existent is the anti-synthesis; and that they are none of these is the super-synthesis. The first four moments constitute the expressible (*prapañca*), while the fifth moment is the inexpressible (*prapañcopaśama*).

Nihilistic Significance of the Dialectic

There are philosophers of being who maintain that the ultimate reality is of the nature of Being. There is also at least one philosophy of nothing, that of Harivarman, maintaining that the ultimate reality is of the nature of nothing. Jainism is the philosophy of being-cum-nothing, so to speak. Skeptics like Sañjaya Belaṭṭhiputta and Pyrrho expressed there inability to say whether the ultimate reality was being, nothing, or both. That it is neither being, nor nothing, nor both would be the fourth alternative. The Mādhyamika system maintains that the real has to be devoid of all these four categories. Taking his cue from him, Śrīharṣa regards the Brahman as belonging to a fifth category, as shown above.

Again, the Mādhyamika rejects the four categories of reason, the four lemmas of the tetralemma (*catuskoṭi*)—being, nothing, both, and neither. Since the tetralemma exhausts all possible categories of reason, the question of there being a fifth lemma, a fifth category, simply should not arise. The tetralemma, says Candrakīrti, is a graduated or ranked course of higher instruction for different grades or ranks of disciples (*vineya-jana*). The sequence (*ānupūrvī*) of the graduated teaching is indicated by Nāgārjuna thus:[16]

1. All is genuine/real (*sarvaṁ tathyam*)
2. All is spurious/unreal (*na vā tathyam*)
3. All is both genuine/real and spurious/unreal (*tathyaṁ cā-tathyam eva ca*)
4. All is neither genuine/real nor spurious/unreal (*naivātathyaṁ naiva tathyam*).

Candrakīrti, in his comments on it, purports to say that the first teaching is meant for worldlings or the laity, the second for the select few, the third for the advanced, and the fourth for the most advanced. He adds that the final teaching, at the level of the fourth lemma, is that phenomena are neither real nor unreal, even as the son of a barren woman is neither white nor black.[17] The suggestion is clear, that it is all void and does not admit of any predication whatsoever, including that of reality and unreality, being and non-being. The negation of non-being is not a prelude to, nor does it presuppose or involve, the position of some kind of Absolute but simply to bring into relief the fact that, as a Chinese Mādhyamika text says, phenomena are "Like a phantom man who is not inexistent, but merely not a real man."[18] In fact, as Kumārajīva explains, "the tetralemma is a piece of therapeutic dialectic, not a piece of physics,"[19] is, as it were, a pedagogical device rather than an ontological scheme. In the tetralemma, each later view is introduced with a view to purging the mind of the earlier view. At the fourth level, all the views stand negated and *Śūnyatā* is the result. But, if *Śunyatā* itself lingers in the mind as a view, the position will be impossible. Candrakīrti quotes the Lord as teaching that the purgative taken for purging the bowels must come out with the foreign matter causing disease and that, if it lingers in the bowels, it will only add to the ailment.[20]

The position as stated by Candrakīrti is that, since there is no subject, there can be no predicate whatever, positive or negative. A monk with diseased eyes or in the dark thinks he sees hairs in his alms-bowl, where they are simply not. As a matter of fact, he does not see them for the simple reason that they are not there. When he is told so, he negates the hairs. On the other hand, a man with undiseased eyes does not have to affirm or deny them, for the simple reason that they are not there and that he has no thoughts of them.[21] Again, as one suspects having taken poison, even though one has not taken poison, and faints, so the people at large are given to imagining being and non-being and have to suffer on that account.[22] Therefore, *Śūnyatā* transcends negation and yet is not position or affirmation of any kind. It is, indeed, the very acme of negation, where negation is so complete that it ceases to be negation.

Five stages are discernible in the Mādhyamika's treatment of the ultimate truth. First, things are shown to be essentially chaotic and hence non-existent. Then, secondly, non-existence, too, is demonstrated to be false, together with things. That is to say, both being and non-being come to be rejected as false. In the first stage, *Śūnyatā* is presented as non-being; in the second, it is adjudged beyond both being and non-being. Thirdly, even *Śūnyatā* is rejected on the ground of there being no non-*Śūnya*, and essencelessness (*niḥsvabhāvatā*) is established. Fourthly, the doctrine of non-apprehension (*anupalambha*) or *aprāptatva*[23] is set forth. Finally, transcendence of all metaphysics is the result.

One is bound to arrive at the conclusion, after a scrutiny of the hybrid and seemingly conflicting utterances of the Mādhyamikas, that being and non-being are the only really fundamental positions, the rest enjoying just a derivate status. Yes, 'is' and 'is-not' are the only positions worth the name that one can possibly take with regard to ultimate reality. The other hypotheses are only semantic ones. Strictly speaking, the ontological issue is between the first two hypotheses only. And, believe it or not, the Mādhyamika adheres to the hypothesis of non-being to the last. In effect, his seeming objection to non-being is directed not towards non-being as such but towards styling it as non-being. Non-being cannot be thought of save as opposed to being, and, he argues, if there is no being, how can there be—or, what is the same thing, how can anything be styled as—non-being? At bottom, both the Satyasiddhi and the Mādhyamika schools appear to hold the same position.

The Mādhyamika's denial of negative reality, non-being, would acquire greater significance if we recall that the Nyāya-Vaiśeṣika accords full ontological status to non-being, terming it a category, a *padārtha.* In Buddhism, too, a negative category is recognized, as a *pratiṣedha-dharma* (negative entity), as distinguished from a *sādhanā-dharma* (positive entity). An example of the one is space (*ākāśa),* the knowledge of which depends upon negation of everything else (*pratigha-sparśa*), and an example of the other, jar, etc., whose knowledge is due to direct encounter without obstruction. Therefore, according to both the Nyāya-Vaiśeṣika and Buddhism, negation, non-being, is not wholly unreal but a veritable reality, a 'negative fact', to use Russell's expression.[23] And, since the Mādhyamika cannot countenance any kind of reality, be it ever so negative, it would be preposterous to characterize his negation of everything as his 'reality'.

Unlike the Nyāya-Vaiśeṣika tradition but very like Raghunātha Śiromaṇi the Navya-Naiyāyika, the Mādhyamika seems to maintain that his negation of negation is not position but another negation.[24] But he does not seem to call in question what the Naiyāyika would term absolute non-being/absolute negation (*atyantābhava*) and what he seems to put as absolute birthlessness (*atyantānutpāda*). He denies, of course, the negative counterpart of an entity, but that kind of negation he would like to define, to follow Robinson, "as an absence in the place where the existent would have been if it had been present, or in the place where the existent was before it became inexistent."[25]

Harivarman's Void is said to be merely an antithetic Void, whereas the Mādhyamika's Void is called the synthetic Void.[26] That is to say, the first Void supervenes upon the stage of antithesis, whereas the other Void supervenes at the very end of the dialectic, viz., at the stage of synthesis. But we have shown the Mādhyamika dialectic to be a five-member dialectic. We, therefore, maintain that his Void is the supersynthetic Void.

Accordingly, the Mādhyamika's *Śūnya* is not nothing but what Hegel would like to call Pure Nothing. Hegel's even Pure Being becomes identical with his Pure Nothing; otherwise it is bound to remain a determinate being in some measure or other. All determination is negation, that is, all predication is negation. That is why the Mādhyamika is led ultimately to reject the *Śūnyatā* view, too. All viewing is determination.

The Logico-Linguistic Dilemma

We had an occasion to note in chapter 4 that the Madhyamikas themselves refer to the Nihilistic interpretation of their outlook without demur, that the whole of Nāgārjuna's *Vigrahavyāvartanī* accords tacit approval to the critics ascription of Nihilism to him, and that Bhāvaviveka and Āryadeva follow suit. The imaginary critic in the *Vigrahavyāvartanī* raises the issue that, if all is void, the Mādhyamika's proposition that all is void is itself void and that, therefore, all is not void.[27] If, on the other hand, the said proposition is not void, all remains unvoid.[28] Nāgārjuna appears to fail to face the self-criticism squarely. He gives us the impression of sidetracking the whole issue. He contends that the voidity of his proposition lends support to the proposition that all is void.[29] He purports to say that all is void just like his void contention that all is void. He proceeds to adduce a queer argument in this behalf. He says that phantom men and women created by magicians and thaumaturgists appear to behave like real men and women. Through the magician's tricks, a phantom man prohibits another phantom man from a certain course of action. Both of them are unreal, and yet there is prohibition and its effect. Likewise, there is nothing out of the way in the use of an unreal argument to show the unreality of all.[30] Then he asserts that, as a matter of fact, he has no thesis of his own to establish, not even a negative one like the voidity of all.[31] And this for the simple reason that he finds nothing to affirm or deny.[32] Thus, he seems to bring home to his critic the purely provisional nature of his proposition that all is void, purely a make-believe resorted to lead the wayfarer to a state of dumbness as regards his ultimate truth. And the ultimate truth posited by him is universal, ineffable Void.

There are some who try metalinguistically to defend the Mādhyamika and to help him wriggle out of the self-referential situation he appears to have been caught in. Writes A.K. Chatterjee, "The language that the Mādhyamika speaks is metalanguage. . . . The Mādhyamika philosophy is therefore correspondingly a philosophy of a higher order, and is characterizable only as metaphilosophy."[33] Of course, there is object-language, which is language of the first order. There is meta-language, language about object-language, which is language of the second order. Language about meta-language is language of the third order. And so on. Hence, such followers of Carnap and Russell argue, when the Mādhyamika says that all is void, his proposition that all is void does not fall within the ambit of the all. Here as elsewhere, he speaks meta-language, not the (object-)language that he analyzes. And that way he does not fall into the trap of his critic.

But, as a young, promising scholar points out, "If Nāgārjuna does not speak the language that he analyzes, then he would be credited with a thesis of his own."[34] He adds that Nāgārjuna "advocates the extreme form of *prasajya-pratiṣedha* type of negation where commitment aspect is zero."[35] This is true: Nāgārjuna seems to purport to maintain that all is void, *including this sentence itself.* But can the commitment aspect ever be zero? Is it possible really to negate everything real and possible? Emphatically no. There is a kernel of truth in the metalinguistic interpreter's stand, though he confuses the issue, as too much emphasis on language by the philosophers often tends to. Though the Mādhyamika claims to negate everything whatsoever, without exception, he fails miserably to do away with the human consciousness which witnesses the negation. This is the secret of the fact that all may be void but the proposition or rather the awareness that all is void cannot be void. Witness consciousness eludes the grasp of everything that we think, say, or do. This marks the triumph of Advaita Vedānta over the Mādhyamika's universal Nihilism.

Total Transcendence of Metaphysics

The Mādhyamika system is all negation, linguistically as well as metaphysically speaking. It is a thesisless system, so to speak. We have already noted that its thesislessness springs from a consciousness of absolute void and that its thesis of thesislessness, as it were, is nothing but absolute nihilism in disguise. It has no categories of its own. It examines the categories posited by others with a view to showing up their hollowness and self-contradictory character. Candrakīrti writes: "We do not postulate the non-being of it. What then?

We simply repudiate the being conceived by others. Likewise, we do not postulate its being. What then? We simply repudiate the non-being of it as conceived by others."[36]

The Mādhyamika brooks no views, for the simple reason that there is nothing for him to view. His *Śūnya* is comparable to the *tuccha/alīka* of Advaita Vedānta as also to *Atyantābhāva* of the Naiyāyaika, which are illustrated by the son of a barren woman, sky flower, and the like, so that *Śūnyavāda* can be termed as *Alīkavāda* as well. *Śūnya* is absolute negation (*nirviśeṣa nañа*), pure and simple. Absolute negation is so inexpressible, however, that one who tries to use it is bound to render himself ridiculous. Nevertheless, the Mādhyamika is condemned to use language to express it, for "One who criticises the use of language to express absolute, contentless negation (*nirviṣaya nañа*) is given the lie by his own language; otherwise how on earth can he communicate with others?"[37]

Henri Bergson thinks that absolute nothing is absolute nonsense, but that absolute vacuity is a possible concept. According to him, as also according to many of our contemporaries, nothing or non-being is a second order concept. As Bergson would have it, "An affirmative proposition expresses a judgment on an object; a negative proposition expresses a judgment on a judgment. *Negation, therefore, differs from affirmation properly so called in that it is an affirmation of the second degree; it affirms something of an affirmation which itself affirms something of an object.*"[38] (Italics in the original) We have reason to disagree. 'Nothing'/non-being may be a second order concept, a second degree affirmation, in the sense that it presupposes the possible or actual being of something. What Bergson forgets is that strictly speaking, it is not non-being but perception/awareness of non-being which is dependent upon perception of some object, even as all perception depends upon light. Hence non-being is very much of a fact.

The position is different, however, so far as universal, all-embracing absolute non-being is concerned. As shown above, witness consciousness is always there to give the lie to the concept. Witness consciousness is a matter of every-moment experience, self-conscious or otherwise. But the Mādhyamika is out to belie all experience (*anubhava*). Writes Candrakīrti: "If one argues, 'it is our experience', that, too, is illogical. Experience itself is false (*mṛṣā*), because it is experience, like the experience of double moon by the diseased eye."[39]

This is nothing short of idle logic-chopping. If the Mādhyamika has no position and discards all experience, he must not take part in the debate amongst philosophers, must not be a party to it, must keep aloof from it like an onlooker. But he does choose to enter the debate. Perhaps he wants to assert his reason for not taking part in the controversy; perhaps, again, he finds the debaters to be arguing a false case, in which case he must acknowledge that he has a criterion of truth and falsehood. Then his disclaimer of all positions becomes pointless.

REFERENCES

1. *NS* 1.2.1-3.
2. *Ibid.*, 4.2.50.
3. Jean-Paul Sartre, *Existentialism and Humanism*, p. 56.
4. 'Umar Khayyām, *Risālah fi 'l-Mawjūd*, in Sayyid Sulaymān Nadwī, *Khayyām*, throughout.
5. G.W.F. Hegel, *Philosophy of Right*, p. 10. Also see his *Logic* (smaller). For elucidation of the dictum, see Harsh Narain, *Evolution of Dialectic in Western Thought*, pp. 34-35.
6. Genesis of the Hegel legend of thesis-antithesis-synthesis is ascribable to Karl Marx, vide Harsh Narain, *ibid.*, pp. 39-40.
7. *MŚP* 1.3, p. 19.
8. *MŚ* 25.24; *BCAP* 9.45, 54.
9. *MŚP* 1.2.
10. *Na san, nāsan, na sadasan, na cāpy anubhayātmakam. Catuṣkoṭi-vinirmuktaṁ tattvaṁ Mādhyamikā viduh. Advayavajrasaṇgraha*, pp. 19, 46, 54, 57.
11. Śrīharṣa, *Naiṣadhīyacarita* 13.53. Cp. Appaya Dīkṣita, *Siddhāntaleśasaṅgraha* 4.6. We shall recur to this concept of fifth moment in the sequel, *vis-á-vis Avidyā*.
12. Cp., for example, *MŚ* 13.8.

13. See *MŚ* 1.3; 18.8; 22.11. Also see:
Sad, asat, sadasac ceti, nobhayaṁ ceti ca kramaḥ.
Eṣa prayojyo vidvadbhir ekatvādiṣu nityaśaḥ. *CS* 14.21;
Vidhānaṁ, pratiṣedhaś ca, tāv eva sahitau punaḥ,
Pratiṣedhaṁ tayor eva sarvathā nāvagacchati.
Abhisamayālaṅkārāloka, p. 300.
14. *MŚ* 12.10.
15. *MŚP* 27.2.
16. *Sarvam tathyaṁ, na vā tathyaṁ, tathyaṁ, cātathyam eva ca,*
Nai vātathyaṁ naiva tathyaṁ etad Buddhānuśāsanam. *MŚ* 18.8.
17. *MŚP, ad ibid.*
18. Richard H. Robinson, *Early Mādhyamika in India and China,* (1967), p. 141.
19. *Ibid.*, p. 109.
20. *MŚP* 13.8.
21. *Ibid.*, 15.11; 18.16; etc. Especially: *Yathā timiraprabhāvāt taimirikaḥ sarvam ākāśadeśaṁ keśoṇḍukamaṇḍitam itastato mukhaṁ vikṣipan napi paśyati, tathā kurvantam aveksya ataimirikaḥ kim ayaṁ karotīti tatsamīpam upasṛtya tadupalabdhakeśapraṇihitalocano 'pi na ke- śākṛtim upalabhate, nāpi tatkeśādhikaraṇān bhāvābhāvaviśeṣān parikalpayati. Yadā punar asau taimirikaḥ ataimirikāya svābhiprāyaṁ prakāśayati—keśān iha paśyāmīti-, tadā tadvikalpāpasāraṇāya tasmai yathābhūtam asau bravīti—nātre keśāḥ santīti. Taimirikopalabihānu-rodhena pratiṣedhaparam eva vacanam āha. Na ca tena tathā pratipādayatā, 'pi kasyacit pratiṣedhaḥ kṛto bhavati vidhānaṁ vā. Tac ca keśānāṁ tattvaṁ yad ataimirikaḥ paśyati tan na taimirikaḥ. BCAP* 9.2, p. 176.
22. *Yatha śaṅkitena viṣasañjña abhyupeti*
No cāpi koṣtha gantu āviṣṭa papadyate,
Evam eva bālu, 'pagato ....
......jāyi mriyate sadā abhūto. Iti. Quoted in *MŚP* 25.3, p. 229.
23. Bertrand Russell, *The Philosophy of Logical Atomism,* in his *Logic and Knowledge,* p. 211, for example.
24. Cp.: *'Na abhāvasya abhāva iti bhāvarūpatayaiva iyam iti vaktavyam, abhāvasya tuccharūpasya abhāvāntaram api tuccharūpam eveti hi vaksyate.*
Abhinavagupta, *Īśvarapratyabhi jñāvivṛtivimarśinī,* p. 63.
25. Robinson, p. 53.
26. Takakusu, p. 78.
27. *Sarveśāṁ bhāvānaṁ sarvatra na vidyate svabhāvās cet,*
Tvadvacanam asvabhavaṁ, na nivartayitum svabhāvamalam. *VV* 1.
28. *Atha sasvabhāvam etad vākyaṁ, hatā pratijñā te.*
Vaiṣamikatvaṁ tasmin, viśeṣahetuś ca vaktavyaḥ. Ibid., 2.
29. *Hetupratyayasāmagryāṁ pṛthagbhāve 'pi madvaco na yadi, Nanu śūnyatvaṁ siddhaṁ bhāvānam asvabhāvatvat. Ibid.,* 21.
30. *Nirmitako nirmitakaṁ māyāpuruṣaḥ svamāyayā sṛṣṭam Pratiṣedhayate*

yadvat, pratiṣedho 'yaṁ tathaiva syāt. Ibid., 23.

31. *Yadi kācana pratijñā tatra syād eṣa me bhaved doṣaḥ. Nāsti ca mama pratijñā, tasmān naivāsti me doṣaḥ. Ibid.*, 29.
32. *Yadi kiñcid upalabheyaṁ, pravartayeyaṁ nivartayeyaṁ vā Pratyakṣādibhir arthais, tadabhāvān me 'nupālambhaḥ. Ibid.*, 30.
33. A.K. Chatterjee, *Facets of Buddhist Thought,* p. 30.
34. Arvind Kumar Rai, "Non-Tenability of Metalanguage in the Context of the Paradox of Nāgārjuna's Dialectic", *Amalā Prajñā,* N.H. Samtani & H.S. Prasad, eds., *P.V. Bapat Vol.*, p. 344.
35. *Loc. cit.*
36. . . . . *na vayam asyasattvaṁ pratipādayāmah. Kiṁ tarhi? paraparikalpitaṁ sattvam asya nirākurmaḥ. Evaṁ na vayam asya sattvaṁ pratipādayāmaḥ. Kiṁ tarhi? paraparikalpitam asattvam asya apākurmaḥ. MŚP* 20.3. Cp. *Na khalv āryāḥ lokasaṁvyavahāreṇapapattiṁ varṇayanti, kin tu lokata eva yā prasiddhopapattis tāṁ paravabodharthaṁ abhyupetya tayaiva lokaṁ bodhayanti. Ibid.*, 1.3, p. 19.
37. *Naño nirviṣayasyasya na prayoga iti bruvan Paribhūtaḥ svavācaiva, paraṁ vā bodhayet katham? Jñānaśrīmitra, Sākārasiddhiśāstra, in Jñanaśrīmītra-nibandhavalī,* p. 482.
38. Henri Bergson, *Creative Evolution,* p. 313.
39. *Athāpi syāt—anubhava eṣo 'smākam—iti, etad apy ayuktam. Yasmād anubhava eva mṛṣā, anubhavatvāt, taimirikadvicandrādyanubhavavad iti. Tataś cānubhavasyāpi sādhyasamatvāt. . . . MŚP* 1.3, p. 20.

CHAPTER 9

Nihilism and Absolutism

It is wrong to suppose that the Mādhyamika characterizes as void only *dharmas* and not the ineffable Absolute. Buddhism, the Mādhyamika system not excepted, analyzes the whole of reality into *dharmas*, which are of two kinds, conditioned and unconditioned, *saṁskṛta* and *asaṁskṛta,* and the ineffable Absolute must, if at all, take its place somewhere in the list of the *dharmas*. To the Buddhists of all persuasion, there is nothing higher than *Nirvāṇa,* which is a *dharma,* an unconditioned (*asaṁskṛta) dharma.* Besides, the Mādhyamika seeks to reconcile the Buddha's *dharma*-positing with nihilistic, *dharma*-denying sermons by declaring the former as of a secondary or empirical import and the latter as of primary or absolute import.[1] Indeed, there are suggestions in the Buddha himself that the latter is a higher teaching than the former.[2]

'Tattva', Dharmatā, Tathatā, Bhūtakoṭi

Murti sets much store by the Mādhyamikas' statements about *'Tattva', Dharmatā, Tathatā, Bhūtakoṭi,* and the like. He writes: "The *Tattva,* however, is accepted by the Mādhyamika as the Reality of all things (*dharmāṇām dharmatā*), their essential nature (*prakṛtir dharmāṇām*). It is uniform and universal, neither decreasing nor increasing, neither originating nor decaying. The Absolute alone is in itself (*akṛtrima svabhāva*). The Absolute is that intrinsic form in which things would appear to the clear vision of an Ārya (realized saint) free from ignorance."[3] Nāgārjuna defines *Tattva*, literally Reality, as follows: "Not realizable through other, calm, inexpressible through words, exempt from conceptualization, of not many meanings—this is the definitive of *tattva*."[4] Likewise, he defines *Svabhāva*, Self-Being, in the same vein: "Self-Being is inartificial and irrelative to other (being)."[5] The absolutistic interpreter places undue reliance on such utterances of the Mādhyamikas. He seems to be oblivious of Candrakīrti's gloss thereon, to the effect that the first definition is purely pragmatical (*vyavahārasatya*)[6] and that both the definitions imply that, in the ultimate analysis, nothing positive but only non-origination (*an-utpāda*) can, if at all, be called *Tattva* or *Svabhāva*.[7] We have already quoted Candrakīrti's example of a man with diseased eyes who sees hair, etc. where they are not and where a man with normal eyes sees no such thing.[8]

Besides, the Mādhyamika makes no secret of the facts that he has no thesis of his own to propound and that he simply employs the theses and logical device of his opponents themselves with a view to facing them with the difficulties arising out of the latter's own logic.[9] So, if the Mādhyamika proposes a definition of *Tattva* or *Svabhāva*, it does not mean that he has a thesis to propound or defend; it simply means that *Tattva* or *Svabhāva*, if there was one as the realist believes, should be such. After all, ordinary mortals have to be taught even extraordinary truths in their own language, for the simple reason that they can understand only ordinary language.[10]

In a letter addressed to the present writer in reaction to his paper, "Śūnyavāda: A Reinterpretation",[11] Dr. Jacques May once proposed that absolute negation might be treated as the 'reality' of the Mādhyamika, adding immediately, however, that "this reality, being intrinsically negation, exists only in so far it is negated. As soon as you state it, it vanishes as a reality. Therefore, *tūṣṇīmbhāva* [silence]." Unaffected by the proposal as the merits of the case sought to be made out by us remains, to be sure, it is difficult to accept it on technical grounds. Designating negation as reality would be foreign to the Mādhyamika vocabulary for two reasons: first, it will turn *Śunyavāda* into a *dṛṣṭi* so stoutly opposed by the Mādhyamika and, second, the definition of reality quoted above does not cover negation. Once it is realized that the Mādhyamika's is a no-reality attitude, it becomes difficult to foist a reality upon him, be the reality ever so negative. In fact, it is simply a semantical question whether *Śūnyatā* should be called a reality, a substitute for reality, or a negation of reality. So long as it is held to be absolute Void, designations used for it do not matter much.

Mādhyamika philosophy is characterized and distinguished by a no-reality attitude. It would be a sheer travesty of truth to import into it a belief in some kind of reality like the Absolute. It categorically repudiates the notion of an Absolute (*apratītyasamutpanna-dharma*),[12] of the unconditioned (*asaṁskṛta*),[13] of the other world (*paraloka*).[14]

It is true that Nāgārjuna appears to argue as if he believed in so many laws of thought and being, so many truths. He wields logic as skilfully as others, as though he were demonstrating that at least logic contained the whole truth and that it was an exception to the theory of total, absolute Nihility propounded by him. At first sight, it appears that for him the law assumed in his argumentation is unquestionably true and real and that it is not a non-entity, not an illusion. But the actual position is that he employs popular notions to refute popular theses, thereby trying to demonstrate that our notions of things are self-contradictory. It is not that he really believes, for example, that what is self-subsistent alone can cause another. He simply means to say that on the realist's own logic what does not exist cannot make others exist. So, when he defines *Tattva* or *Svabhāva*, he does not mean to suggest that there is a reality conforming to his definition. What he does mean to suggest is that it follows from the realist's own way of thinking that reality, if there were a reality, should be such.

Indeed, Candrakīrti makes a categorical statement in this

direction, which should settle the matter once for all. He states a possible objection against the Mādhyamika's thesis thus: If the Mādhyamika has no thesis of his own, he is far from justified in propounding the thesis that things are caused not by themselves, nor by other things, nor by both, nor by neither. To this Candrakīrti's reply is that the thesis in question is, as a matter of fact, not a Mādhyamika thesis at all and that the Mādhyamika's method is to meet the realist on the latter's own ground by facing him with the difficulties arising out of the latter's own logic.[15]

Moreover, it can also be shown that Nāgārjuna's definitions of *Tattva* and *Svabhāva* are fully applicable to his Void. Murti remarks: "*Tattva* as *Dharmatā* or *Bhūtakoṭi* is accepted by the Mādhyamika as the underlying ground of phenomena."[16] But the question is, what is there to warrant the assumption that *Tattva, Dharmatā,* and *Bhūtakoṭi* cannot be identified with the Void? Nāgārjuna avers: "On cessation of the object of consciousness, the object of speech ceases to exist. For *Dharmatā* is, like *Nirvāṇa,* uncaused and imperishable."[17] Candrakīrti's explanation is: "*Dharmatā* is the essence of *dharma,* the nature of *dharma,* which neither originates nor perishes, like *Nirvāṇa.*"[18] Giving an alternative explanation, he writes that in this verse Nāgārjuna explains the proposition, made in an earlier verse,[19] that all speech (*prapañca*) ceases in *Śūnyatā*: ". . . how then can speech cease to exist in *Śūnyatā*? The reply is, on cessation of the object of speech, etc. . . ."[20]

In another connection, Candrakīrti tries to give a third, clearer definition of *Dharmatā* in these words: "What is this *Dharmatā*? The character (*svabhāva*) of *Dharma.* What is this character? Nature (*prakṛti*). What is this nature? It is what is this *Śūnyatā.* What is this *Śūnyatā*? Essencelessness (*naiḥsvābhāvya*). What is this essencelessness? Suchness (*Tathatā*). What is this suchness? So-being (*tathābhāva*), changelessness, everlastingness.[21] Lest someone should be misled by the word 'everlastingness', Candrakīrti adds that, being irrelative and inartificial, only the non-origination of things is called their nature.[22] He also suggests that this non-origination is identical with non-being.[23] It is significant that, in explanation of the verse quoted at reference 19 ante, Candrakīrti makes it perfectly clear that "*Śūnyatā* itself is called *Nirvāṇa* on account of its being characterized by the cessation of all speech."[24]

Besides in another work, Nāgārjuna has made the significant remark that *Dharmatā* is *Śūnya,* like space.[25] In fact, according to him, all essence is like space.[26] As a matter of fact, as indicated in the *Advayavairasaṅgraha,*[27] *Dharmatā* is nothing else than *dharmas,* which are at bottom *Śūnya,* nothing.

The Absolutist interpreter of *Śūnyavāda* tends to make much of its concept of *Dharmatā,* as well as *Tathatā.* We have seen that *Dharmatā* is nothing mysterious like an Absolute and that it is but another name for *Śūnyatā,* or Void. Let us now examine the concept of *Tathatā.*

We have seen how Candrakīrti uses '*Dharmatā*' and '*Tathatā*', viz., interchangeably. Bhavaviveka's observations on the nature of *Tathatā* will, however, be found decisive. Writes he: "If it be contended that the *Tathatā,* although it is foreign to words (*abhilāpa, -vyavahāra-vivikta)* is nevertheless a reality (*tattva*): in that case, the expression *Tathatā* refers only to the *Ātman* of the Tīrthikas [non-Buddhists] under another name. Just as the *Tathatā,* although it is a reality, is nevertheless, from the point of view of exact truth, beyond the concepts of being and not-being, it is the same with *Ātman.* The Tīrthikas think that the *Ātman,* which is real, omnipresent, eternal, agent, enjoyer, is nevertheless foreign to every concept (beyond the pale of conceptions). As it transcends the domain of words, and as it is not the object of the dealing-with-ideas intellect (*vikalpa-buddhi*), it is said to be foreign to concepts. The doctrines of the Tīrthikas say: "The words do not go there; the thought does not realize it; therefore, it is named *Ātman.*" The *Atman* being such, is it reasonable to assert that 'the knowledge (*jñāna*) which takes the *Tathatā* as its object leads to deliverance, while the knowledge which takes the *Ātman* as its object does not?' But what is the difference between the *Tathatā* and the *Ātman,* since both are ineffable and real? It is only the *esprit de parti* (*pakṣa-grahaṇa*) that it is said."[28]

This emphatic repudiation of identity between *Tathatā* and the Absolute should set at rest all speculation about the meaning of *Tathatā. Tathatā, Dharmatā, Nirvāṇa, Śūnyatā, Bhūtakoṭi,* and such like are more or less synonymous terms in effect, used to designate the Void in various ways. It is difficult, rather impossible, to convey the true idea of the Void. But some name or other has to be given to it to make discourse possible. This exigency of discourse is responsible for the invention or employment of the aforesaid terms, be they ever so imperfect. Candrakīrti remarks that, though the fire is essenceless, it has to be spoken of as an entity, and some essence has to be superimposed upon it just to guard against the auditor's being frightened.[29] *Dharmatā* etc. are terms born of such superimposition.[30]

Being is positive reality and non-being is negative reality, and the Mādhyamika will not recognize any reality whatsoever, positive or negative, much less the Absolute. According to him, all being is characterized by and is subject to birth, decay, and death,[31] and is invariably other-dependent and relative (*pratītya-samutpanna*).[32] And to him non-being is nothing but other-being/alter-being (*anyathābhāva*).[33] Therefore, both being and non-being, positive and negative reality, are essenceless, *Śūnya.* It would be pertinent to point out, however, that it is being-opposing non-being, relative non-being, only which is characterizable on the Mādhyamika view as other-being/alter-being. Absolute non-being/negation/*Śūnya* involves no opposition to being, as we have already noticed.

The Mādhyamika is a repudiator of being and non-being, but what is seldom appreciated is the fact that, in repudiation of being and non-being, he tends generally to take up for examination only relative being and non-being. There are rare exceptions, of course, such as Āryadeva's refutation of eternal being (*nitya*) in chapter IX of his *Catuḥśataka*;[34] but exceptions prove the rule. Well, the Mādhyamika repudiates being on the ground that, owing its origin to another being, it cannot subsist in its own right and that, since the other being, too, depends for its subsistence on a third being, the third on a fourth being, the fourth on a fifth being, and so on, there is no self-subsistent being whatever. On his view, if at all, all being is caused being, hence relative being, contingent being. There is no uncaused, uncontingent, self-dependent being, viz., being *per se.* There is no being apart from relative or contingent being. The argument sounds faultless so far as it goes, but it does not appear to go far enough. The consensus of the philosophies of being is that being is essentially uncaused. They may or may not be right, but they cannot be judged this way or that without due examination. The Mādhyamika would rejoin, however, that such examination is already completed in Hīnayāna.

There can be three positions with regard to reality: That the reals are all caused, that they exist in their own right without being caused, and that they never have been. It is the third alternative that finds favour with the Mādhyamika. Says the *Laṅkāvatāra-Sūtra:* "non-existent as space, horn of hare, and the son of a barren woman are and yet are spoken of. Same is the case with things."[35] Candrakīrti observes: 'Son of a barren woman' is nothing but a sound, pure and simple. It has no referent, which could be existent or non-existent. How can existence or non-existence be predicated of something of the nature of non-apprehension? Therefore, son of a barren woman cannot be treated as non-existent."[36]

Meaning of Absolute

What does the absolutist interpreter of Mādhyamika philosophy mean by the term Absolute? So far as we can see, any meaning of the term will remain incomplete, rather vacuous, without conception of it as the one self-subsistent, self-grounded Real constituting the ground and goal of existence. The Absolute has to exist and be true in its own right and at the same time support everything that is the case. On the other hand, by the relative is meant what has to derive from and thereby be subservient and subordinate to the Absolute. The relative is grounded in the Absolute.

Even roughly speaking, the Mādhyamika's *Śūnya/Śūnyatā* is antipodally opposed to an Absolute: it is, as it were, the very *meaning* of what passes for the relative, obviating the necessity of assuming a ground thereof. The Mādhyamika will be the last to countenance anything like this. He is out to show that phenomena are noumenonless, groundless, essenceless, and hence illusory, *Śūnya.* Indeed, if non-Buddhist thought as well as Buddhist idealism is noumenalist and early Buddhism is, excretions apart, phenomenalist, Mādhyamika thought is illusionistic. This being the case, Mādhyamika philosophy is at the farthest removed from Absolutism. In fact, the very method of the Mādhyamika is to demonstrate that all phenomena are noumenonless-groundless, hence essenceless-absoluteless, and hence illusory, irrational, *Śūnya.* That is why Bhāvaviveka castigates those who call the *Tathatā* a reality (*tattva*), ineffable, and beyond the pale of conceptions like the *Ātman* of the non-Buddhists, as we have already seen.

The Absolute may well be characterized, if it must be, as Full/Perfect (*Pūrṇa*), as against *Śūnya* which is all Empty, Vacuous. Says the Upaniṣad:

Pūrṇam adaḥ, pūrṇam idaṁ; pūrṇāt pūrṇam ud-acyate.
Pūrṇasya pūrṇam ādāya pūrṇam evāvaśiṣyate.

In R.E. Hume's translation, the verse reads as under:

The yon is fulness, fulness this.
From fulness fulness doth proceed.
Withdrawing fulness' fulness off,
E'en fulness then itself remains.

Will the Mādhyamika endorse it? Far from it. He would like rather to rephrase it as under, substituting *'śūnya'* for *'pūrṇa'* wherever it occurs:

Śūnyam adaḥ, śūnyam idaṁ; śūnyāc chūnyam ud-acyate.
Śūnyasya śūnyam ādāya śūnyam evāvaśiṣyate.

Indeed, a similar juxtaposition between *'śunya'* and *'pūrṇa'* is found in the *Uttara-Gītā* ascribed to *Gauḍapāda:*

ṙdhva-śūnyam, adhaḥ-śūnyaṁ, madhya-śūnyaṁ yadātmakam,
Sarva-śūnyaṁ sa Ātmeti samādhisthasya lakṣaṇam.
ṙdhva-pūrṇam, adaḥ-pūrṇaṁ, madhya-pūrṇaṁ yadātmakam,
Sarva-pūrṇaṁ sa Ātmeti samādhisthasya lakṣaṇam.[37]

The Mādhyamika will surely retort with the remark, ascribed by Candrakīrti to the Buddha:

Śūnyam ādhyātmikaṁ paśya, paśya śūnyaṁ bahirgatam.
Na vidyate so 'pi kaścid yo bhāvayati śūnyatām.[38]

(Look upon the inner world as Void, look upon the external world as Void. Even that one does not exist who imagines *Śūnyatā* (Voidness).

The *Maitreyī-Upaniṣad* also juxtaposes '*Pūrṇa*' to '*Śūnya*' thus:

Antaḥ-pūrṇo, bahiḥ-pūrṇaḥ, pūrṇa-kumbha ivāmbare.
Antaḥ-śūnyo, bahiḥ-sūnyaḥ, sūnya-kumbha ivāmbare.[39]

It must be noted, however, that the later Upaniṣads have developed the trait of using *Śūnya* in such contexts as synonymous with *Pūrṇa* or the *Brahman,* like the *Uttara-Gītā* and the *Yogavāsiṣṭha.*

Śūnyaṁ vai Paraṁ Brahma. . . .[40]
Śūnyātmā, sūkṣmarūpātmā, viśvātmā, viśvahīnakaḥ[41]
Śūnyāśūnyaprabhāvo 'smi śobhanāśobhano 'smy aham[42]
Śūnyaṁ na saṅketaḥ Parameśvara-sattā.[43]

Nihilism and Advaitism

There are quite a few apparently close similarities, parallels, and correspondences between Mādhyamika philosophy and Advaitism, which seem to have conspired to lead many a modern scholar to an Absolutistic interpretation of the former. We would, therefore, do well to examine these similarities and the like in right earnest.

Above, we have had occasion to notice the four categories (being, etc.) under which the Mādhyamika chooses to order his subject matter for examination. In fact, he has one more quadritype scheme of categories for the purpose, which is: first, things cannot come into being of themselves (*svataḥ*); second, they cannot come into being through another (*parataḥ*); third, they cannot come into being in both ways combined (*dvābhyām*); and, fourth, they cannot come into being without a cause (*ahetutaḥ*).[44] Of the two schemes the first, as we have seen, dates back to pre-Buddhaic times. It sometimes oversteps the frontiers of the Mādhyamika and reaches Vijñānavāda as well as Advaitism. So, Haribhadra, the author of *Abhisamayālaṅkārāloka,* as well as Asaṅga mention it approvingly.[45] We shall advert to Advaitism in the sequel. The second scheme is typically Mādhyamika. Nāgārjuna contends that it holds good not only in the case of suffering but in the case of the external objects as well.[46] On the basis of the first scheme, Candrakīrti remarks that the categories are four only.[47]

Now, Advaitism may also be said to postulate four categories; first, the transcendental category (*paramārtha*) that is the *Brahman,*[48] second, the empirical category (*vyavahāra*) that is the world;[49] third, the illusory reality (*pratibhāsa*) like rope, snake, etc.;[50] and, fourth, pure nothing (*tuccha, alīka, nityabādhita),*[51] like the horn of a hare, son of a barren woman, sky-flower, etc. Of these, the first is called '*sat*' (being), the next two '*sad-asad-vilakṣaṇa*' (neither-being-nor-non-being), and the last '*asat*' (non-being). *Sat* is the *Brahman; sad-asad-vilakṣaṇa, Māyā/Avidyā,*[52] and *asat* is nonentity pure and simple.

There is a confusion in regard to the Advaitic concept of *Māyā*, however. Śaṅkara, the commentator of the *Māṇḍūkya-Kārikā/Āgamaśāstra,* characterizes *Māyā* sometimes as *asat,* non-existent.[53] Śaṅkara, the commentator of the *Bhagavad-Gītā,* characterizes it as *tamas,* of the nature of darkness.[54] According to the *Śvetāśvatara-Upaniṣad, Māyā* is *Prakṛti,*[55] and according to the *Gītā, Prakṛti* is of two kinds, the inconscient (*aparā*) and the conscient (*parā*)/individual soul (*jīva*).[56] Śaṅkara describes *Māyā* as inexpressible/imponderable (*anirvacanīyā*) in the sense that it neither is nor is-not (*tattvānyatvābhyām anirvacanīyā*).[57] The *Saura-Purāṇa* says that *Māyā* is something which neither is, nor is-not, nor both is and is-not.[58] Śaṅkara, the author of *Pañcīkaraṇa* and *Tattvopadeśa,* also says that it is inexpressible in the sense that it neither is, nor is-not, nor both is and is-not (*na san, nāsan, nāpi sad-asat.*)[59] It means that it belongs to a fourth category of neither-is nor is-not nor-both. According to Vācaspati Miśra in the *Brahmatattvasamīkṣā,* quoted by Ānandabodha in the *Pramāṇamālā, Avidyā* is beyond the four categories.[60]

According to Avaitins like Ānandabodha, removal of *Māyā* (*Māyā-nivṛtti*) is beyond all the aforesaid four categories and belongs to an unspecified fifth category (*Pañcamī vidhā*),[61] obviously because, from the very nature of the case, it has to transcend *Māyā,* the fourth category. Some of the Advaitins appear, however, to take *Māyā,* too, beyond the fourth category. Thus, says Sureśvara, the distinguishing feature of *Māyā/Avidyā* is the incapacity of withstanding the blow of the standards of valid knowledge (*mānāghātāsahiṣṇutva*).[62] Vidyāraṇya's version of presumably this very statement replaces "the incapacity of withstanding the blow of the standards of valid knowledge" by "the incapacity of withstanding the touch of the standards of valid knowledge" (*mānayogāsahiṣṇutva*) at one place[63] and by "the incapacity of withstanding [the might of] thought" (*vicārāsahiṣṇutva*) at another.[64] Such statements do serve to take *Māyā/Avidyā* out of the purview of the tetralogy of the categories, or even of a fifth category for that matter. In fact, Ānandajñāna goes the farthest in this direction when he construes inexpressibility to mean negation of all categories of thought and speech, all concepts and words.[65] And the Mādhyamika's *Śūnyatā* is exactly like that.

Now about the *Brahman*. According to an Upaniṣad, the *Brahman* simply 'is' (*sat*).[66] Certain scriptures call It "being-non-being" (*sad-asat*).[67] Another Upaniṣad seeks to describe It as "not this", (*neti*), "not this" (*neti*),[68] which means that It belongs to the fourth category of neither being nor non-being. The *Śrīmad-Bhāgavata* calls It "the All" (*aśeṣa*) and yet "pure Negation" (*niṣedha-śeṣa*).[69] Gauḍapāda's *Bhagavat* (the Lord, the Buddha) is also beyond the four categories.[70] Śaṅkara's *Brahman* is undefined (*anirukta*), for a particular alone, being a modification (*vikāra*), is definable.[71] The *Gītā* has sometimes to acknowledge that the *Brahman* neither is nor is-not (*na san nāsat*),[72] which, too, attracts the fourth category. Sometimes, again, the *Gītā* describes It as what is, is not, as also is beyond both (*sad-asat tatparaṁ yat*).[73] This statement is an extension of the one placing It under the third category.

Śrīharṣa characterizes the *Brahman* as belonging exclusively to the fifth category (*pañcama-koṭi-mātra*).[74] Which seems clearly to identify the *Brahman* with the Mādhyamika's *Śūnyatā* beyond the four categories (*catuṣkoṭi-vinirmukta*). The clearest statement, however, serving seemingly to identify the *Brahman* and *Śūnyatā* is the one quoted by Śaṅkara from some inextant Vedic-Upaniṣadic text (*Śruti*). Bāṣkali asks Bādhva: What is the *Brahman/Ātman*? Bādhva kept silent (*tūṣṇīm babhūva*). This happened twice. Asked thrice, Bādhva said, "I do reply, but thou dost not understand: The Ātman is all silence" (*Upaśānto 'yam Ātmā*).[75] Here one is bound to hark to Candrakīrti's characterization of the Ultimate Truth (*paramārtha*) as silence (*tūṣṇīmbhāva*).[76] And silence appears to be the ultimate meaning of such Upaniṣadic utterances as "the Brahman transcends thought and speech" (*yato vāco nivartante, aprāpya manasā saha*).[77] "It is other than the known and the unknown" (*anyad eva tad viditād atho aviditād adhi*),[78] and, in fact, even "not this, not this" (*neti neti*).[79]

A story more or less similar to that of Bāṣkali and Bādhva is told in Mahāyāna tradition as well: Bodhisattva Vimalakīrti once asked a host of Bodhisattvas led by Mañjuśrī to say how to enter into the *Dharma* of non-duality. Some replied, Birth and Death are two, but *Dharma* itself is unborn and deathless. Those who understand it enter into the *Dharma* of non-duality. Some said, *Saṁsāra* and *Nirvāṇa* are two, but, when we discover the ultimate nature, *Saṁsāra* vanishes from our consciousness and there is neither bondage nor release, neither birth nor death. By thus realizing, we enter into the *Dharma* of non-duality. Others said, Ignorance and Enlightenment are two. Those who enter into the thought of sameness are beyond both. This thought is entering into the *Dharma* of non-duality. Others said, Longing for *Nirvāṇa* and Shunning *Saṁsāra* are two. Go beyond both the relative terms. And you will enter into the *Dharma* of non-duality. Mañjuśrī said, To know that which is worldless, wordless, signless, incognizable, and beyond question and answer—to know that is to enter into the *Dharma* of non-duality. Asked by Mañjuśrī to tell his own view, Vimalakīrti kept silent and uttered not a word. Mañjuśrī exclaimed, Well done, Well done. The *Dharma* of non-duality is truly above letters and words.[80] Suzuki also refers to a Chinese Buddhist who after prolonged meditation suddenly realized that "The very instant you say that it is something (or nothing), you miss the mark."[81]

Likewise, St. Augustine remarks: "God is not even to be called ineffable, for to say this is to make an assertion about him." And the great Persian Poet 'Urfī Shīrāzī: "The frontiers of thy beauty cannot be known by reason. And this statement, too, is circumscribed by the limits of my reason!":

Ḥadd-i ḥusn-ī tu ba-idrāk na shāyad dānist.
W' īṅ sukhan nīz ba-andāzah-i idrāk-i man ast.

Well, from the foregoing discussion, it transpires that *Māyā/Avidyā,* the cessation of *Māyā/Avidyā* (*Māyā-Nivṛtti*), as well as the *Brahman*—all the three—lie beyond the four categories stated above and may thereby, at first sight, be said to be the Advaitic counterparts of the Mādhyamika *Śūnyatā,* which, too, is such, as we have seen. That way, to be sure, they all become identical with *Śūnyatā.* This goes to account for identification of the *Brahman* and *Śūnyatā* in the *Yogavāsiṣṭha*[82] and certain later Upaniṣads.

The modern Advaitin may welcome the identity so established between the *Brahman* and *Śūnyatā,* in the sanguine hope of Vedāntizing the Mādhyamika. He may also not demur to the talk of identity of the *Brahman* and the cessation of *Māyā/Avidyā.* But he will be the last to entertain the thought of identifying the *Brahman* and *Māyā/Avidyā.*[83] It is strange, however, that not only he but even Śaṅkara and his followers do not seem to visualize the problem of keeping the *Brahman, Māyā/Avidyā,* and *Māyā/Avidyā-Nivṛtti* apart.[84]

If Advaitism is taken at its face value, it will appear to hold out the promise and possibility of what may be called a three-tier teaching: first, the lower (*apara*), determinate (*saguṇa*) *Brahman,*[85] such as the Brahman of the nature of the mind (*manomaya*), having the body of vital breaths (*prāṇa-śarīra*), luminous (*bhā-rūpa*), etc.;[86] second, the higher (*para*), indeterminate (*nir-guṇa*) *Brahman* beyond name and form etc.;[87] and, third, the higher than the highest (*parāt-para*) *Brahman,* which is the cessation of all the phenomena.

As a matter of fact, a three-tier teaching is suggested by some of the leading Śaṅkarites, too. For instance, the theory of pre-existent effect (*satkāryavāda*) is treated as belonging to the lowest level of truth;[88] theory of illusory effect (*vivartavāda*) to a higher level and yet approximating to empirical truth (*vyavahāra*);[89] and theory of no-causation (*ajātivāda*), to the highest level.[90] Likewise, Vidyāraṇya sets out three approaches to *Māyā*:[91]

1. In the last analysis guided by the highest knowledge

yielded by the *Śruti, Māyā* is pure nothing (*tucchā/nityanivṛttā*).

2. Logically speaking, *Māyā* is inexpressible in the sense of belonging to neither of the categories of being and non-being. It is not being, for it ceases (*bādhanāt*). It is not nothing, for it is apprehended (*vibhātatvāt*).
3. Empirically speaking, it is real (*vāstavī*).

Now, we are inclined to believe that the gulf between the *Brahman* and *Śūnyatā* is basically unbridgeable and that Advaitism and the Mādhyamika can never meet.

There must be some real difference between the inexpressibility of the *Brahman* and that of *Śūnyatā*. And the difference is not far to seek. In the *Kaṭha-Upaniṣad* it is clearly stated, after describing the *Brahman* as beyond thought and speech, that it can be apprehended only as 'is' (*astīty evopalabdhavyaḥ*).[92] This makes all the difference between the two thought-systems. In no circumstances will the Mādhyamika be prepared to ascribe isness to *Śūnyatā*.

In this connection, we would crave the indulgence of our readers for a brief reference to Immanuel Kant, who, I believe, fares equally well in a similar situation. His noumena or things-in-themselves are beyond the categories, which according to his scheme include reality and negation on one hand and existence and non-existence on the other. It means that noumena are neither existent nor non-existent, neither real nor unreal. Is it not tantamount to dispensing with them altogether? Kant's reply would be in the negative, notwithstanding the fact that he is led to postulate them as a 'problematic' concept whose objective reality is unknowable, which is not self-contradictory, which cannot be said to be possible or impossible, which all the same is indispensable to thought.[93] The noumena do have to be admitted to exist for postulation, but with a difference. There are two kinds of existence, so to speak, categorial existence and transcategorial existence, and "the existence here referred to is not a category."[94] The same formula may be said to apply to the Advaitin's *Brahman*. The *Brahman* is (*asti*), but transcategorially. Thus, the *Brahman* is the *Brahman* and *Śūnyatā* is *Śūnyatā*, and never the twain can meet. The Mādhyamika knows no transcategorial being.

Incidentally, Kant's position seems to involve a contradiction. In another work, he has the temerity to proclaim, to our utter consternation, that such categories as substance, causality, etc. do apply to the noumena,[95] thereby undoing all that was sought to be done by the first critique. We confess we do not know how to deal with such Kant.

REFERENCES

1. *MŚP* 1.3, p. 13; 15.11 p. 120.
2. See *MN*, I, 22 (Alagaddūpama-Sutta), pp. 179-80, where *dharmas* are likened to a raft to be left off after crossing the stream. Cp. "My propositions are elucidatory in this way: he who understands me finally recognizes them as senseless, when he has climbed out through them, on them, over them. . . ." Ludwig Wittgenstein, *Tractatus Logico-Philosophicus*, 6.54.
3. Murti, p. 235.
4. *Aparapratyayaṁ, śāntaṁ, prapañcair aprapañcitam, Nirvikalpam anānārtham—etat tattvasya lakṣaṇam. MŚ* 18.9.
5. *Akṛtrimaḥ svabhāvo hi nirapeksaḥ paratra ca. Ibid.*, 15.2. Cp. *Cst.* 3.35-39, 42.
6. *Kiṁlakṣaṇaṁ punas tattvam yasyaitā deśanāvatārārtham upadiśante Bhagavantaḥ? Uktam etad asmābhiḥ, 'nivṛttam abhidhātavyaṁ nivṛtte cittagocare' (MŚ* 18.7) *iti. Yadā caitad evaṁ, tadā kim aparaṁ pṛcchyate? Yady apy evaṁ, tathā 'pi vyavahāra-satyānurodhena laukikatathyādyabhyupagamavat tasyāpi samāropato lakṣaṇam ucyatām iti. Tad ucyate—'aparapratyayaṁ śāntaṁ. . . .' MŚP* 18.9, p. 158.
7. *Paramārthatas tathatā dharmadhātuḥ atyantājātis ca. . . . Paramārthato 'tyantānutpādatvāt sarvadharmāṇām iti. Tad evam anānārthatā tattvasya lakṣaṇam veditavyaṁ, śūnyataikarasatvāt. Ibid.*, pp. 159-60. *Sarvathā 'nutpāda eva hy agnyādīnām paranirapekṣatvād akṛtrimatvat svabhava ity ucyate. Ibid.*, 15.2, p. 116.
8. *MŚ* 18.9.
9. *Yadi kaścin niścayo nāmāsmākaṁ syāt, sa pramāṇajo vā syād apramāṇajo vā. Na tv asti. . . . Yady evaṁ niścayo nāsti sarvataḥ, kathaṁ punar idaṁ niścitarūpaṁ vākyam upalabhate bhavatāṁ—'na svato, nāpi parato, na dvābhyāṁ, nāpy ahetutah' bhāvā bhavanti' iti? Ucyate—Niścitam idaṁ vākyaṁ lokasya svaprasiddhyaivopapattyā, nāryāṇām. . . Yadi hy āryā*

upapattiṁ na varṇayanti, kena khalv idānīṁ paramārthaṁ lokaṁ bodhayisyanti? Na khalv āryā lokasaṁvyavahāreṇopapattiṁ varṇayanti, kin tu lokata eva yā prasiddhopapattis tāṁ parāvabodhārtham abhyupetya tayaiva lokam bodhayanti. Ibid., 1.3, p. 19.

10. *Nānyayā bhāṣayā mlecchaḥ śakyo grāhayituṁ yathā, Na laukikam ṛte lokaḥ śakyo grāhayituṁ tathā.* CŚ 8.9.
11. Harsh Narain, 'Śūnyavāda: A Reinterpretation', *Philosophy: East and West*, XIII, 4 (January, 1964).
12. *Apratītyasamutpanno dharmaḥ kaścin na vidyate Yasmāt, tasmād aśūnyo hi dharmaḥ kaścin na vidyate.* MŚ 24.19.
13. *Utpāda-sthiti-bhaṅgānām asiddher nāsti saṁskṛtam. Saṁskṛtasyaprasiddhau ca kathaṁ setsyaty asaṁskṛtam?* Ibid., 7.33.
14. *Lokābhāvāl lokottaram api nāsti. Sarvabhāvaś ca nāsty evaṁ loka eva paro 'pi ca. Bhavabhedaśāstra*, p. 21.
15. See n. 9, *supra*.
16. Murti, p. 237.
17. *Nivṛttam abhidhātavyaṁ nivṛtte cittagocare. Anutpannā 'niruddhā hi nirvāṇam iva dharmatā.* MŚ 18.7.
18. *Anutpannā 'niruddhā nirvāṇam iva dharmatā dharmasvabhāvaḥ dharmaprakṛtiḥ vyavasthāpitā.* MŚP 18.7, p. 155.
19. *Karmakleśakṣayān mokṣaḥ, karmakleśa vikalpataḥ. Te prapañcāt prapañcas tu śūnyatāyāṁ nirudhyate.* MŚ 18.5.
20. *Atha vā ayam anyaḥ pūrvapakṣaḥ—yad uktaṁ 'prapañcaḥ śūnyatāyāṁ nirudhyate'* (MŚ 18.5) *iti, kathaṁ punaḥ prapañcasya śūnyatāyāṁ nirodhaḥ? Ucyate—yasmān nivṛttam abhidhātavyam ityādih...* MŚP 18.7, p. 155.
21. *Atha keyaṁ dharmānāṁ dharmatā? Dharmānāṁ svabhāvaḥ. Ko 'yam svabhāvaḥ? Prakṛtiḥ. Kā ceyaṁ prakṛtiḥ? Yeyaṁ śūnyatā. Keyaṁ śūnyatā? Naiḥsvābhāvyam. Kim idaṁ naiḥsvābhāvyam? Tathatā. Keyaṁ tathatā? Tathābhāvo 'vikāritvaṁ sadaiva sthāyitā. Sarvathā 'nutpāda eva hy agnyādīnāṁ paranirapekṣatvād akṛtrimatvāt svabhāva ity ucyate.* Ibid., 15.2, p. 116.
22. *Sarvathā 'nupāda eva hy agnyādīnāṁ paranirapekṣatvād akṛtrimatvāt svabhāva ity ucyate.* Loc. cit.
23. *Sa caiṣa bhāvānāṁ anutpādātmakaḥ svabhāvaḥ akiñcittyena abhāvamātratvāt svabhāva ity ucyate.* Loc. cit.
24. *Śūnyataiva sarvaprapañcanivṛttilakṣaṇatvāñ nirvāṇam ity ucyate.* Ibid., 18.5, p. 150.
25. *Dharmatā hi nabhas tulyā....* Bhavasaṅkrānti, st. 2.
26. *Sarvaḥsvabhāvaḥ khasamaḥ...* Ibid., st. 3. Cp. BCA 9.155.
27. *Advayavajrasaṅgraha*, p. 44.
28. See Louis de La Vallee-Poussin, 'The Mādhyamika and the Tathatā', *Indian Historical Quarterly*, IX, 1 (March, 1933), pp. 30-31.

Bhavaviveka's work quoted from is mentioned by La Vallee-Poussin as *Jewel in Hand* or *Gem in Hand.*

29. *Kiṁ khalv agnes tad itthaṁ svarūpam asti? Na tad asti na cāpi nāsti svarūpataḥ. Yady apy evaṁ, tathā 'pi śrotṛṇām uttrāsaparivarjanārthaṁ saṁvṛtya samāropya tad astīti brūmaḥ. MŚP* 15.2, p. 115.
30. *Ibid.*, p. 116.
31. *Bhāvas tāvan na nirvāṇaṁ jarāmaraṇalakṣaṇam.*
Prasajyetāstibhāvo hi na jarāmaraṇaṁ vinā. MS 25.4.
32. *Apratītyasamutpanno dharmaḥ kaścin na vidyate.*
Yasmāt, tasmād aśūnyo hi dharmaḥ kaścin na vidyate. Ibid., 24.19.
33. *Bhāvasya ced aprasiddhir abhāvo naiva sidhyati.*
Bhāvasya hy anyathābhāvam abhāvaṁ bruvate janāḥ. Ibid., 15.5; *Avidyamāne bhāve ca kasyābhāvo bhaviṣyati? Ibid.*, 5.6.
34. *Sarvaṁ kāryārtham utpannaṁ, tena nityaṁ na vidyate. CŚ* 9.1.
35. *Ākāśaṁ, śaśaśṛṅgaṁ ca, vandhyāyaḥ putra eva ca*
Asanto hy abhilapyante, tatha bhāveṣu kalpanā. LS 2.164.
36. *Vandhyāputra iti sabdamātram evaitat Nāsyārtha upalabhyate yasyārthasya bhāvatvam abhāvatvaṁ vā syād iti. Kutaḥ anabhilapyamānasvabhāvanya bhāvābhāvakalpanā yokṣyate? Tasmān na vandhyaputra abhava iti vijñeyam. MŚP* 25.8, p. 231.
37. Gauḍapāda, *Uttara-Gītā* 1.35, 37-38.
38. Quoted as an utterance of the *Bhagavat* (Lord, Buddha) in *MŚP* 18.3, p. 148.
39. *Naitreyī-Upaniṣad* 2.27.
40. *Gaṇeśapūrvatāpinī-Upaniṣad* 3.1.
41. *Tejobindu-Upaniṣad* 4.43.
42. *Maitreyī-Upaniṣad* 3.5.
43. *Nirvāṇa-Upaniṣad.*
44. *MŚ* 1.3.
45. Haribhadra, *Abhisamayālaṅkārāloka* 6.1.
46. *MŚ* 12.10.
47. *MŚP* 27.2, p. 249.
48. Śaṅkara, *Śārīrakā-Bhāṣya* 2.17, 14, 22; 2.2.10.
49. *Ibid.*, 1.1.5; 2.1.14; 2.2.29.
50. Śaṅkara, *Bhagavadgītā-Bhāṣya* 1.6.
51. Śaṅkara, *Māṇḍūkyakārikā-Bhāṣya* 1.6.
52. Śaṅkara, *Śārīraka-Bhāṣya* 1.1.5; 1.4.3; 2.1.14.
53. *Māṇḍūkya-Kārikā* 1.7; 4.58.
54. Śaṅkara, *Bhagavadgītā-Bhāṣya* 13.2.
55. *Śvetāśvatara-Upaniṣad* 4.10.
56. *Gītā* 7.4-5.
57. See n. 45, *supra.*
58. *Saura-Purāṇa* 11.28.
59. Śaṅkara, *Pañcīkaraṇa*, p. 2; *Tattvopadeśa* 52-53.

60. Writes Ānandabodha: *Ata evoktam Ācārya-Vācaspatinā Brahmatattvasamī-kṣāyām—sadasadubhayānubhayādiprakārair anirvacaniyatvam eva hy avidyāya avidyātvam iti.*
    Lakshmipuram Srinivasachar, *Darśanodaya*, p. 132.
61. Appaya Dīkṣita, *Siddhāntaleśasaṅgraha*, p. 516; Ānandabodha, *Nyāyamakaranda*, p. 352.
62. *Avidyāyā avidyātva idam eva tu lakṣaṇam—Mānāghātāsahiṣṇutvam asādharaṇam iṣyate.*
    Sureśvara, *Bṛhadaranyakopaniṣad-Bhāṣya-Vārtika*, otherwise known as *Sambandha-Vārtika*, 181.
63. *Avidyāyā avidyātvam idam evātra lakṣaṇam—Mānayogāsahi ṣṇutvam asādharaṇam iṣyate.*
    Vidyāraṇya, *Bṛhadāraṇyaka-Vārtika-Sāra* 117.
64. *Avidyāyā avidyātvam idam evātra lakṣaṇam—Vad vicārāsahiṣṇutvam, anyathā vastu sā bhavet. Aho dhārṣṭyam avidyāyā! na kaścid ativartate—Pramāṇam vastv anādṛtya paramātmeva tiṣṭhati.*
    Vidyāraṇya. *Vivaraṇaprameyasaṅgraha*. p. 176.
65. *Yena yena prakāreṇa paro nirvaktum icchati Tena tenātmnā 'yogas tadanirvācyatā matā.*
    Ānandajñāna, *Tarkasaṅgraha*, p. 136.
66. *Sad eva somyedam agra āsīd ekam evādvitīyam.*
    Chāndogya-Upaniṣad 6.2.1.
67. *Gītā* 9.19.
68. *Bṛhadāraṇyaka-Upaniṣad* 4.4.22.
69. *Sa vai na devāsura-martya-tiryaṅ, na strī, na ṣaṇḍho, na puman, na jantuḥ, Nāyaṁ guṇaḥ, karma, na san, na cāsan—niṣedhaseṣo jayatad aśeṣaḥ. Śrīmad-Bhāgavata* 8.3.24.
70. *Koṭyaś catasra etās tu grahair yāsāṁ sadā "vṛtaḥ. Bhagavān ābhir aspṛṣṭo, yena dṛṣṭaḥ sa sarvadṛk.*
    Gauḍapāda, *Māṇḍukyakārika-Bhāṣya* 4.83-84.
71. *Viśeṣo hi nirucyate, viśeṣaś ca vikāraḥ. Avikāraṁ ca Brahma,... tasmād aniruktam.* Śaṅkara, *Taittirīya-Upaniṣad-Bhāṣya* 2.7.1, p. 178.
72. *Gītā* 13.12; 11.37.
73. *Ibid.*, 11.37.
74. Śrīharṣa, *Naiṣadhīyacarita* 13.35.
75. Śaṅkara, *Śārīraka-Bhāṣya* 3.2.17, p. 644.
76. *MŚP* 1.3.19.
77. *Kena-Upaniṣad* 2.4.1.
78. *Ibid.*, 1.3.
79. *Bṛhadaraṇyaka-Upaniṣad* 4.4.22.
80. Suzuki, *Outline of Mahayana Buddhism*, pp. 106-7.
81. *Ibid.*, p.105, fn. 1.

82. *Yaḥ śūnyavādināṁ śūnyo, bhāsako yo 'rktejasām,*
Vaktā, mantā, ṛtaṁ bhoktā, draṣṭā, kartā sadaiva saḥ. Yogavāsiṣṭha 3.5.7.

83. *Yuṣmadasmatpratyayagocarayor viṣayaviṣayiṇos tamaḥprakāśavadvirud-dhasvabhavāyor itaretarabhāvānupapattau siddhāyām taddharmānām api sutarām itaretarabhāvānupapattiḥ.* Śaṅkara, *Śārīraka-Bhāṣya*, opening words.

84. Cp.: *Yaḥ śūnyavādinaḥ śūnyaṁ tad eva Brahma māyinaḥ.*
Na hi lakṣaṇabhedo 'sti nirviśesatvatas tayoḥ.
Madhva Brahmasūtra-Anuvyākhyāna 2.2.29.

85. Śaṅkara, *Śārīraka-Bhāṣya* 4.3.7-14, pp. 879-89.

86. *Chāndogya-Upaniṣad* 3.14.2.

87. Śaṅkara, *Śārīraka-Bhāṣya* 4.3.7-14, pp. 879-89.

88. See, for instance, Śaṅkara, *Bhagavadgītā-Bhāṣya*, ch. 13, introductory remarks.

89. *Bālān prati vivarto 'yaṁ, Brahmanaḥ sakalaṁ jagat.*
Avivartitam ānandam āsthitah kṛtinaḥ sadā.
Prakāśānanda, *Vedāntasiddhāntamuktāvalī* 67, p. 275.

90. See, for instance, Gauḍapāda, *Māṇḍūkyakārika* 4.21.

91. *Nāsad āsīd' vibhātatvān, 'no sad asic' ca bādhanāt,*
Vidyadṛṣṭyā śrutaṁ 'tucchaṁ' tasya nityanivṛttitāḥ.
Tucchā, 'nirvacaniyā ca, vāstavī cety asau tridha.
Jñeyā māyā tribhir bodhaih srauta-yauktika-laukikaih. Vidyāraṇya, *Pancadaśī* 6.129-130.

92. *Kaṭha-Upaniṣad* 2.3.13.

93. Immanuel Kant, *Critique of Pure Reason,* pp. 271ff., 292ff.

94. *Ibid.*, p. 378, fn.

95. Kant, *Prolegomena to Any Future Metaphysics,* p. 107.

CHAPTER 10

Résumé and Review

We have almost reached the end of our enquiry. Before winding it up, however, we would do well to have a short retrospect and review.

The Buddha was primarily a Nirvāṇa-teacher rather than a philosopher. His practical or rather praxiological approach is illustrated by his emphasis on egolessness and deliverance from the conceit of 'I' and 'mine'. In the process, he is led to rather overemphasize impermanence of all things without any enduring substratum or residue whatsoever. His realism transpired to be pregnant with idealism oriented towards Nihilism on the one hand and absolutism on the other. Idealism leads to solipsism, scepticism, or nihilism on the one hand and absolutism on the other. His theory of universal impermanence made short work of realism and quickened the process of its metamorphosis. This trend of thought found its culmination in Nihilism at the hands of the Mādhyamika in Mahāyāna and Harivarman in Hīnayāna. In fact, sometimes the Pāli canon itself is found to show nihilistic trends, as we have seen earlier.

The Nihilistic interpretation of Mādhyamika philosophy seems to be tacitly assumed to be impossible on the ground that Nihilism itself is impossible, that Nihilism is a figment of imagination rather than a fact in the history of philosophy, and that it is impossible to think of philosopher worth the name maintaining Nihilism seriously. Accordingly, the common tendency today is to interpret Mādhyamika philosophy in such a way that it becomes a variety of idealism or even critical realism. If the position were so simple, Vasubandhu would not have started as a Vaibhāṣika and ended as a Vijñānavādin; Diṅnāga and Dharmakīrti would not have had to accept Vijñānavāda Paramārthically and Sautrāntika philosophy empirically; and non-absolutists (including Buddhist) would not have directed their criticism against the Mādhyamika on the score of Nihilism rather than of Absolutism.

Whatever they may think or say as religious devotees or mystics, the Mādhyamikas have been found in this work to be thoroughgoing Nihilists as philosophers. Candrakīrti ascribes the following to the Lord (*Bhagavat*):

> *Śūnyaṁ ādhyātmikaṁ paśya, paśya śūnyaṁ behirgatam.*
> *Na vidyate-so 'pi kaścid yo bhāvayati śūnyatām.*[1]
>
> ('See *Śūnya* inside yourself, see *Śūnya* outside. None, too, exists who visualizes *Śūnyatā*.')

It is evident that the Mādhyamika's *Śūnyatā* is another name for unreality. Yet he thinks that it is better to avoid the expression as a synonym for the term. The reason is purely semantic. Candrakīrti says that a monk with diseased eyes thinks he sees hairs in his almsbowl, even though they are simply not there. Somebody detects his mistake and tells him that there are no such hairs. Thus the man with diseased eyes is led to negate the hairs conceptually constructed by him. Since, however, they are actually not there at all, there has in fact been neither affirmation nor negation.[2] Again, "son of a barren woman" is a mere word without a referent. Hence it is preposterous to predicate existence or non-existence about it.[3]

The clearest statement of the Nihilistic view of *Śūnyatā* is this: Exasperated at those who are out to give a positivistic twist to *Śūnyatā*, Candrakīrti contends that he does not know how to deal with one who, told that there is no money, insists upon getting the very no-money.[4] Compare the comic nonsense in the play on the term 'Nobody' in the well-known passage of *Alice Through the Looking-Glass:*

> ' "I see nobody on the road", said Alice.
> "I only wish *I* had such eyes", the king remarked in a fretful tone.
> "To be able to see Nobody. And at the same distance too!" '[5]

Indeed, the Nihilistic interpretation of Mādhyamika philosophy cannot be lightly dismissed with the remark that the Mādhyamika's use of *'Śūnyatā'* is mere rhetoric and that, otherwise, he is an Absolutist. But, if the *Prajñāpāramitā* and other canonical Mādhyamika texts use rhetoric or metaphor, Nāgārjuna is there to unravel the mystery; and, if Nāgārjuna, too, begins to talk in rhetoric/metaphor, Candrakīrti is there to come to our help; but, if Candrakīrti, too, has nothing but rhetoric/metaphor for us, we are doomed. Urdu poet Jamīl Maẓharī's meaningful couplet is:

> *Ḥaqīqateṅ jab hoṅ isti 'ārah 'ilāmateṅ hoṅgī mu 'tabar kyā*
> ("If realities themselves turn out to be metaphors/ figurative, who will give credence to symbols?")

In that case, to be sure, "Everything is only a metaphor; there is only poetry."[6]

To our mind, Mādhyamika philosophy is beautifully summed up in Candrakīrti's epigram: "The accomplished saints do not at all find anything which could be false or true" (*Naiva tv āryāḥ kṛtakāryāḥ kiñcid upalabhante yan mṛṣā vā a-mṛṣā vā syāt*).[7] And our own Sanskrit couplet:

> *Prasajyapratiṣedhātmaṁ Śūnyaṁ Mādhyamikasya tu*
> *Śūnyīkṛtyāstināstitve svayaṁ Śūnyībhavaty aho!*

("The Mādhyamika's *Śūnya* is of the nature of pure negation, which, lo! nullifying all being and non-being, stands self-nullified.")

Well, there are three broad but well-defined levels discernible in Mādhyamika thought: religion, philosophy, and mysticism. As a practitioner of religion, the Mādhyamika is a believer, worshipper, and realist like other practitioners of religion. As a philosopher, he is an all-destroyer. In his dialectical philosophy, being is the first casualty. When, after the demise of being, non-being rushes in, it, too, goes to pieces. There follows the Mādhyamika's proclamation that the same fate awaits being-cum-nonbeing and neither-being-nor-nonbeing as well, if they aspire to be the heirs to being and non-being. Thus, as an iconoclast of being, the Mādhyamika is a negativist or nihilist, blank phenomenalist or illusionist; as an iconoclast of non-being in addition, an irrationalist and illusionist; and, as a repudiator of being-cum-nonbeing and neither-being-nor-nonbeing, into the bargain, an Asolute Nihilist and a quietist. His philosophy gives way to or culminates in mysticism, the known form of which is Quiescence, a common symbol of both Absolute Nihilism and Absolutist Mysticism, even though they are poles apart. Quiescence or Quietude supervenes upon cessation of all viewing, actual or possible. Indeed, the Mādhyamika thought as such is the most thoroughgoing Nihilism the world has ever known: it is absolute illusionism and absolute irrationalism, Absolute Nihilism and absolute Quietism; it is *Śūnyavāda.*

With the Mādhyamika, *Śūnyatā* sometimes appears to be a consuming passion, at any rate in the canonical texts. How to account for such ardour for the Void? We may hazard the opinion that, in the state of trance ecstasy, he must be feeling well relaxed and relieved from tension to which his whole code of conduct based on celibacy and renunciation would keep him exposed. But this is an experiential ground which even angels fear to tread.

Prajñākaramati discusses an interesting question as to the *raison de'être* of the beneficent Bodhisattvas involving themselves in such activities as alms-giving, etc., which are, according to the Mādhyamika, *Śūnya,* false. His reply is that they do so spontaneously, involuntarily, or unpremeditatedly (*avicārataḥ*).[8] If he held any other view of *Śūnyatā* than as void, his spontaneous reply would be that, his *Śūnyatā* not being identifiable with the Void, the objection was pointless.

Some are inclined to the view that the Mādhyamika's emphasis on Nihilism springs from his extra concern for attainment of renunciation, and that, otherwise, his Void need not be taken seriously. But this interpretation is demonstrably false. Āryadeva has raised the issue and answered it unequivocally: "It is not that the non-*Śūnya* is shown to be *Śūnya* simply by the desire to attain *Nirvāṇa;* for the Buddhas do not describe *Nirvāṇa* as attainable through false vision."[9] Candrakīrti comments: "Are these objects non-*Śūnya* but shown to be *Śūnya* for the attainment of renunciation? Or are they demonstrated to be *Śūnya* in their very nature? It is said in reply [here he quotes the above stanza of Āryadeva and goes on] ". . . ., entities are known to be *Śūnya* in their very nature."[10]

The Mādhyamika's method is something like this. He first seeks to show that all is relative, hence chaotic, hence essenceless, and hence void. Lest undiscerning people should erect his void into a positive reality like the *Brahman* of the Vedānta or the Absolute of Hegel or Bradley, he later refuses to admit even the void, contending that the void can be there only when there is a non-void. This leads him to affirm the doctrine of non-apprehension, ending in the rejection of all metaphysics. "In the first instance," says Nāgārjuna, "all is declared imaginary and thereafter imagination itself is dismissed as false."[11] Elsewhere, he says that even the conception by which *Śūnyatā* comes to be conceived is itself *Śūnya.*[12] Śāntideva writes in the same vein: "By contemplation on *Śūnyatā,* conception of being vanishes. By contemplation on the idea that there is nothing whatever, that, too, vanishes afterwards."[13]

Is *Śūnyavāda*, or rather the Mādhyamika's thesis of thesislessness, so to speak, tantamount to admission of failure on his part to fathom the mystery of the ultimate reality?

His tone does not disclose any defeatist mentality.[14] He does not seem to regret the fact that he is not in a position to talk about the real. He does know, but cannot express. He believes in the Void, pure and simple. But he is not in a position to explain to others what the state of affairs would be like in the absence of all that we can perceive or conceive as real, or, for that matter, even unreal. Language can operate only in the realm of being. Where there is absolutely nothing whatever, its operation is bound to come to a standstill.

The last difficulty in giving credence to the nihilistic interpretation of the Mādhyamika's standpoint is the religious fervour shown by him as a Mahāyānist. If all is void, how can this fervour be explained? The best course for a Nihilist would be to be unruffled by emotions and sentiments, rather than to be so devoted to the Buddha as to erect him into a veritable Godhead. The reason, though slightly difficult to appreciate, is not far to seek. The Mādhyamika does not present a much greater problem on this score than the Advaitin, who claims not only substantiality but veritable identity with the Absolute and declares the world to be illusory, but, nevertheless, does not lag behind others in his devotion to gods and goddesses. As a matter of fact, they both share the common Indian trait of dichotomizing truth into the ultimate and the immediate, in effect wholly discontinuous with each other. While contemplating the ultimate truth, the Mādhyamika is led to consider everything as illusory and void and goes to the extent of declaring the Tathāgata himself, the supreme object of his devotion, to be nothing better than the void. But, while contemplating the immediate/empirical truth, he distinguishes between his gods and their devotees and behaves as if he were as much of a realist as others.[15] Indeed, Indians have seldom been able to reconcile the empirical with the ultimate, and one need not be surprised if the Mādhyamika fares no better.

Before closing our account of Mādhyamika philosophy, it would be interesting to make a passing reference to a difficulty, pointed out by A.B. Keith, which besets *Śūnyavāda*. Writes Keith: "Whence, however, comes this illusion which appears in the form of the world of spirit and matter? If illusion persists in its generation of things that are void, how can it be made to desist from this evil habit?"[16] The Mādhyamika is inclined to believe that illusion is like the Advaitin's *Māyā*, beginningless but not endless, that it will end when enlightenment dawns culminating in *Nirvāṇa*,[17] which is itself illusory, though. There is no reason why the illusory objects filling the illusory world should commit suicide instead of continuing their illusory existence. The position is complicated and the difficulty accentuated by the Prāsaṅgika school of Buddhapālita and Candrakīrti, Śāntideva and Prajñākaramati, who seem to maintain that the world has neither noumenal nor phenomenal existence. On this issue, Bhāvaviveka seems to differ from them, inasmuch as he allows a phenomenal being to the world."[18] Let us leave it as an *Avyākṛta*, as an imponderable.

REFERENCES

1. *MŚP* 18.3, p. 148.
2. *Ibid.*, 15.11, p. 120; 18.6, p. 153; etc.
3. *Ibid.*, 25.8, p. 231.
4. *Ibid.*, 13.8, p. 108.
5. Quoted in Milton K. Munitz, *The Mystery of Existence*, p. 148.
6. Norman O. Brown, *Love's Body*, concluding sentence of the book.
7. *MŚP* 1.3, p. 14.
8. *Nanu yadi niḥsvabhāvāḥ sarvabhāva it vastutattvaṁ, kathaṁ tarhi sarvasattvasamuddharaṇāśayena dānādiṣu sambhāraparipūraṇārthaṁ tattvavedinām api bodhisattvānāṁ pravṛttiḥ? Teṣām api niḥsvabhāvatvāt. Ity ata āha—kāryārtham avicārataḥ' iti. Kāryaṁ sādhyam, upādeyaṁ, phalam ucyate. Tadarthaṁ tannimittam. Avicārātaḥ avicāreṇaiva tadhetau pravartanāt. Tathābhūteṣv api tatra idampratyayatāniyamasya vidyamānatvāt na hetuphalabhāvasya virodhaḥ. BCAP* 9.4, p. 179.
9. *Nāśūnyaṁ śūnyavad dṛṣṭaṁ nirvāṇaṁ me bhavatv iti.*
   Mithyādṛṣṭer na nirvāṇaṁ varṇayanti tathāgatāḥ. CŚ 8.7.
10. *Kiṁ punar ime padārthā aśūnyā eva vairāgyārthaṁ śūnyavad dṛṣyante, atha prakṛtyaiva śūnyā iti vyapadiśyante? Ucyate—Nāśūnyam śūnyavad....'*

Bhāvāḥ śūnyāḥ svabhāvenety adhigamyate. CŚV, ad ibid.

11. *Kalpanāmātram ity asmāt sarve dharmāḥ prakāśitāḥ. Kalpanā 'py asatī proktā yayā śūnyaṁ vikalpyate. CST.* 3.34.
12. *Kalpanā sā 'pi śūnyeyaṁ yayā śūnyeti kalpitāḥ. Bhavasaṅkrānti-Parikathā* 12.
13. *Śūnyatāvāsanādhānād dhīyate bhāvavāsanā. Kiñcin nāstīti cābhyāsāt sā 'pi paścāt prahīyate. BCA* 9.33.
14. *Yadi kaścin niścayo nāmāsmākaṁ syāt, sa pramānajo vā syād apramāṇajo vā. Na tv asti. Kiṁ kāraṇam? Ihāniścayasambhave sati, syāt tatpratipakṣas, tadapekso niścayaḥ. Yadā tv aniścaya eva tāvad asmākaṁ nāsti, tadā kutas tadviruddho niścayaḥ syāt? MŚP* 1.3, p. 19.
15. *Yathā prākṛtalokena yogiloko na bādhate. Bādhyante dhīviśeṣeṇa yogino 'py uttarottaraiḥ. Cittavi-śuddhi-prakaraṇa* 83.
16. A.B. Keith, *Buddhist Philosophy in India and Ceylon,* p. 240.
17. *Ibid.*, pp. 240-41. Also see:
    Yathā bījasya dṛṣṭo 'nto, na cādis tasya vidyate, Tathā kāraṇavaikalyāj janmano 'pi na sambhavaḥ. CŚ 8.25.
    Sometimes, however, it is urged that illusion is contingent upon and caused by will (*saṅkalpa*): *Avidyā 'pi bhikṣavaḥ! sahetukā, sapratyayā, sanidānā. Kaś ca bhikṣavo! 'vidyāyā hetuḥ. Ayoniśo bhikṣvo! manaskaro 'vidāyā hetuḥ. Āvilo mohajo manaskāro bhikṣavo! 'vidyāyā hetuḥ. Ity ataḥ avidya saṅkalpaprabhavā bhavati. Pratītyasamutpāda-Sūtra,* quoted in *MŚP* 23.1, p. 197.
18. Keith, pp. 240-41.

Abbreviations

AN — *Aṅguttara-Nikāya,* Bhikkhu Jagadisa Kassapa, ed. (Nalanda: Pali Publication Board, 1960).

BCA — *Bodhicaryāvatāra* by Śantideva, with *BCAP,* P.L. Vaidya, ed. (Varanasi: Pali Publication Board, 1960).

BCAP — *Bodhicaryāvatara-Pañjikā* by Prajñākaramati, see *BCA.*

CŚ — *Catuḥśataka* by Āryadeva, with Candrakīrti's *Vṛtti* (Nagpur, 1971); Vidhushekhara Bhattacharya, ed. (Visva Bharati, 1931).

CŚV — *Catuḥśataka-Vṛtti* by Candrakīrti, see *CŚ.*

Cst. — *Catuḥstava* by Nāgārjuna, Prabhubhai Patel ed., *Indian Historical Quarterly,* VIII, 2 (June, 1932), 316-31; 4 (December, 1932), 689-705.

DN — *Dīgha-Nikāya,* Bhikkhu Jagadisa Kassapa, ed. (Nalanda: Pali Publication Board, 1958).

LS — *Laṅkāvatāra-Sūtra,* see under the full form.

MN — *Majjhima-Nikāya,* Bhikkhu Jagadisa Kassapa, ed. (Nalanda: Pali Publication Board, 1958).

MŚ — *Madhyamakaśāstra* by Nāgārjuna, with *MŚP VV,* and *Ratnāvalī,* P.L. Vaidya, ed. (Darbhanga: Mithila Research Institute, 1960).

MŚP — *Madhyamakaśāstra-Prasannapadāvṛtti* by Candrakīrti, see *MŚ.*

SN — *Saṁyutta-Nikāya,* Bhikkhu Jagadisa Kassapa, ed. (Nalanda: Pali Publication Board, 1959).

Sn. — *Suttanipāta,* see *Dhammapada.*

TS — *Tattvasaṅgraha* by Śāntaraksita, with Kamalaśīla's *Pañjikā,* P.L. Vaidya, ed. (Darbhanga: Mithila Research Institute, 1960).

TSP — *Tattvasaṅgraha-Pañjikā* by Kamalaśīla, see *TS.*

VV — *Vigrahavyāvartanī* by Nāgārjuna, see *MŚ.*

Bibliography

Abhidhammatthasaṅgaha by Anuruddha, Bhadanta Revatadhamma and Rama Shankar Tripathi, eds. and trs. (Varanasi: Varanaseya Sanskrit Vishwavidyalaya, 1967).

Abhidharmadīpa, with *Vibhāṣāprabhāvṛtti,* Padmanabh S. Jaini, ed. (Patna: Kashi Prasad Jayaswal Research Institute, 1977).

Abhidharmakośa, by Vasubandhu, with Yaśomitra's *Sphuṭārthāvyākhyā,* Swami Dwarikadas Shastri, ed. (Varanasi: Bauddha-Bharati, 1972).

Abhidharmakośa-Sphuṭārthā of Yaśomitra, see *Abhidharmakośa.*

Abhidharmāmṛta by Ghoṣaka, Shanti Bhikshu Shastri, resto. from the Chinese (Visva-Bharati, 1953).

Abhisamayālaṅkārāloka by Haribhadra, see *Aṣṭasāhasrikā-Prajñāpāramitā.*

Advayavajrasaṅgraha, Haraprasad Shastri, ed., Gaekwad's Oriental Series, XL (Baroda: Oriental Institute, 1927).

Āgamaśāstra of Gauḍapāda, The Vidhushekhara Bhattacharya, ed. (Calcutta University, 1943).

Anyayogavyavacchedadvātriṁśikā by Hemacandra, with Malliṣeṇa Sūri's *Syādvādamañjarī,* A.B. Dhruva, ed., Bombay Sanskrit and Prakrit Series, LXXXIII (Pune: Bhandarkar Research Institute, 1933).

Aṣṭādhyayī by Pāṇini, with Patañjali's *Mahābhāṣya,* Kātyāyana's *Vārtika,* Kaiyaṭa's *Mahābhāṣya-Pradīpa,* Nāgeśa Bhaṭṭa's *Uddyota,* and Vaidyanātha's *Chāyā* (Delhi etc.: Motilal Banarsidass, 1967).

Aṣṭasāhasrikā-Prajñāpāramitā, with Maitreyanātha' *Abhisamayālaṅkāra-Kārikā,* Haribhadra's *Abhisamayā-*

laṅkārāloka, Diṅnāga's *Prajñāpāramitā-Piṇḍārtha,* and Nāgārjuna's *Prajñāpāramitā-Stuti,* P.L. Vaidya, ed., Buddhist Sanskrit Texts, No. 4 (Darbhanga: Mithila Research Institute, 1960).

Aurobindo, Sri: *The Life Divine,* I (2nd ed., Calcutta: Arya Publishing House, 1943).

Bergson, Henri: *Creative Evolution,* Arthur Mitchell, tr. (New York: Modern Library, n.d.)

Bhagavad-Gītā (Gorakhpur: Gita Press).

Bhagavadgītā-Bhāṣya by Śaṅkara (Gorakhpur: Gita Press).

Bhavabhedaśāstra (third recension of *Bhavasaṅkrānti-śāstra* of Nāgārjuna), see *Bhavasaṅkrānti-Sūtra.*

Bhavasaṅkrānti (first recension of Nāgārjuna's *Bhavasaṅkrānti-śāstra*) see *Bhavasaṅkrānti-Sūtra.*

Bhavasaṅkrānti-parikathā (second recension of Nāgārjuna's *Bhavasaṅkrānti-śāstra*), see *Bhavasaṅkrānti-śūtra.*

Bhavasaṅkrānti-sūtra, restored with Nāgārjuna's *Bhavasaṅkrānti-śāstra* in three recensions, entitled *Bhavasaṅkrānti, Bhavasaṅkrānti-parikathā,* and *Bhavabhe-daśastra,* with Maitreyanātha's commentary from Tibetan and Chinese by N. Aiyaswami Sastri (Adyar: Adyar Library, 1938).

Brahmabindu-Upaniṣad, in the compilation of 120 Upaniṣads under the title *Īśādiviṁśottaraśatopaniṣadaḥ* (Bombay: Nirnaya-Sagar Press).

Brhadāraṇyaka-Upaniṣad, see the Upaniṣadic compilation.

Bṛhadāraṇyakopaniṣad-Bhāṣya by Śaṅkara (Gorakhpur: Gita Press).

Brhadāraṇyakopaniṣad-Bhāṣya-Vārtika, also known as *Sambandha-Vārtika,* by Sureśvara, with Ānandagiri's *Śāstraprakāśikā,* Kashinath Shastri Agashe, ed. (2nd ed., Poona: Anandasrama, 1937).

Bṛhadāraṇyakabhāṣyavārtika-Sāra by Vidyāraṇya, (Varanasi: Acyuta Granthamala, 1999 Anno Vik.).

Catuḥśataka by Āryadeva, with Candrakīrti's *Vṛtti* (Nagpur:

Alok Prakashan, 1971).

Chāndogya-Upaniṣad (Gorakhpur: Gita Press).

Chatterjee, A.K.: *Facets of Buddhist Thought* (Calcutta: Sanskrit College, 1975).

Cittaviśuddhiprakaraṇa, Prabhubhai Patel, ed. (Santiniketan: Visva-Bharati, 1949).

Conze, Edward: *Thirty Years of Buddhist Studies* (London: George Allen & Unwin, 1962).

Darśanodaya by Lakshmipuram Srinivasachar (Mysore: Govt. Branch Press, 1933).

Dasgupta, S.N.: *Indian Idealism* (Cambridge University Press, 1933).

de Bary, Wm. Theodore: *The Buddhist Tradition* (ed.), (New York: Modern Library, 1969).

De Jong, J.W., "Emptiness", *Journal of Indian Philosophy,* 2 (1972), 7-15.

Dhammapada, with *Khuddakapāṭha, Udāna, Itivuttaka,* and *Sutta-nipāta,* Bhikkhu Jagadisa Kassapa, ed. (Nalanda: Pali Publication Board, 1959).

Gaṇeśapūrvatāpinī-Upaniṣad, vide compilation referred to above.

Guṇakāraṇḍavyūha-Sūtra, in *Mahāyāna-Sūtra-Saṅgraha,* Vol. I, P.L. Vaidya, ed. (Darbhanga: Mithila Research Institute, 1961).

Hastavālaprakaraṇa by Āryadeva, F.W. Thomas & H. Ui, eds., *JRAS,* 1918, pp. 277, 281.

Hegel, G.W.F.: *Philosophy of Right,* T.M. Knox, tr. (Oxford: Clarendon Press, 1942).

Īśvarapratyabhijñāvivṛtivimarśinī by Abhinavagupta, Mukunda Ram Shastri, ed., Kashmir Series of Texts and Studies, No. XXII (Bombay: Nirnaya Sagar Press, 1918, 1927).

Itivuttaka, see *Dhammapada.*

Jātaka (Nalanda: Pali Publication Board).

Jayatilleke, K.N.: *Early Buddhist Theory of Knowledge* (Delhi etc.: Motilal Banarsidass, 1980 reprint).

——*Facets of Buddhist Thought* (Kandy: Buddhist Publications Society, 1971).

Kant, Immanuel: *Critique of Pure Reason* (3rd reprint of 2nd ed., London: Macmillan & Co.; New York: St. Martin's Press, 1956).

——*Prolegomena to Any Future Metaphysics,* L.W.Beck, tr. and ed., (New York: Indianapolis, 1950).

Karatalaratna by Bhāvaviveka, restored from Huen Tsang's Chinese version by N. Aiyaswami Sastri (Santiniketan: Visva-Bharti, 1949).

Kathāvatthu, Bhikkhu Jagadisa Kagsapa, ed. (Nalanda: Pali Publication Board, 1961)

Kaṭha-Upaniṣad, see the compilition referred to above.

Katz, Nathan: 'An Appraisal of the Sautrāntika-Prāsaṅgika Debate', *Philosophy East and West,* 26, 3 (July, 1976), 253-67.

Keith, A.B.: *Buddhist Philosophy in India and Ceylon* (Oxford: Clarendon Press, 1923).

Kena-Upaniṣad, see the compilation referred to above.

Khayyām, 'Umar: *Risālah fi 'l-Mawjūd,* in Sayyid Sulayman Nadwi, *Khayyām* (Azamgarh: Dāru 'l-Musannifin, 1932).

Kimura, Ryukan: *A Historical Study of the Terms Hīnayāna and Mahāyāna and the Origin of Mahāyāna Buddhism* (Patna: Indological Book Corporation, 1978).

Laṅkāvatāra-Sūtra, P.L.Vaidya, ed. (Darbhanga: Mithila Research Institute, 1963).

La Vallèe-Poussin, Louis de: 'The Mādhyamika and the Tathatā', *Indian Historical Quarterly,* IX, 1 (March, 1933).

Lida, Shotaro: *Reason and Emptiness* (Tokyo: The Hokuseido Press, 1980).

(The) *Madhyamakaśāstram* of Nāgārjuna, with his *Akutobhayā*, Buddhapālita's *Madhyamakavṛtti* Bhāvaviveka's *Prajñāpradīpavṛtti*, and Candrakīrti's *Prasannapadāvṛtti*, critically reconstructed from the Tibetan by Raghunatha Pandeya (Delhi etc. : Motilal Banarsidass, 1988, 1989).

Madhyāntavibhāgabhāṣya-Ṭīkā by Sthiramati, with Maitreyanātha's Kārikās and Vasubandhu's *Bhāṣya*, Ramchandra Pandeya, ed. (Delhi etc.: Motilal Banarsidass, 1971).

Madhyāntavibhāgaśāstra-Kārikā by Maitreyanātha, see *Madhyānta-vibhāgabhāṣya-Ṭīkā*.

Mahābhāṣya-Pradīpa by Kaiyaṭa, see *Aṣṭādhyāyī*.

Mahāvagga, Bhikkhu Jagadisa Kassapa ed., (Nalanda: Pali Publication Board).

Mahāyāna-Śraddhotpādaśāstra by Aśvaghoṣa, Timothy Richard, tr. from Paramārtha's Chinese version, Alan Hull Walton, ed. (London: Charles Skilton Ltd., 1961).

Mahāyānasūtrālaṅkāra by Asaṅga, S. Bagchi (Darbhanga: Mithila Research Institute, 1970).

Maitri-Upaniṣad, see the compilation referred to above.

Māṇḍūkyā-Kārikā/Āgamaśāstra by Gauḍapāda (Gorakhpur: Gita Press).

Māṇḍūkyakārikā-Bhāṣya by Śaṅkara, *Māṇḍukya-Kārikā* edition.

Milindapañha, Bombay University Series.

Mīmāṁsāślokavārtika by Kumārila, with Pārthasārathi Miśra's *Nyāyaratnākara*, Dwarikadas Shastri, ed. (Varanasi: Tara Publications, 1978).

Munitz, Milton K.: *The Mystery of Existence* (New York: Appleton Century Crafts, Division of Meredith Publishing Company, 1965).

Murti, T.R.V.: 'Buddhism and *Śūnyatā*, The Nava-Nalanda Mahavihara Publication, Vol. IV, C.S. Upasak and C.S. Prasad, eds. (Nalanda 1979, pp. 94-116).

——*The Central Philosophy of Buddhism* (London: George Allen & Unwin, 1955).

Naiṣadhīyacarita by Śrīharṣa (Varanasi: Chowkhamba Sanskrit

Series Office, 1954).

Narain, Harsh: *Evolution of Dialectic in Western Thought* (Varanasi: Motilal Banarsidass, 1973).

——"Feasibility of a Dialogue between Hinduism and Islam", *Islam and the Modern Age,* VI, 4 (November, 1975), pp. 57-85.

——"The Nature of Mādhyamika Thought", *Mādhyamika Dialectic and the Philosophy of Nāgārjuna,* S. Rinpoche, ed., The Dalai Lama Tibetan Indology Studies, Vol. I (Sarnath: Central Institute of Higher Tibetan Studies, 1977), pp. 175-96.

——'Nihilism and Advaitism', *Prajñāloka: Journal of the Nāgārjuna Buddhist Foundation,* Special Inaugural Number (January & April, 1979), pp. 25-32.

——'Śūnyavāda: A Reinterpretation', *Philosophy East and West,* XIII, 4 (January, 1964), pp. 311-38.

Narendradeva, *Bauddha-Dharma-Darśana* (2nd ed, Patna: Bihar Rāshtrabhāṣā Pariṣad, 1971).

Nietzsche, Friedrich: *Twilight of the Idols,* quoted in D.J.O 'Connor, *A Critical History of Philosophy* (3rd printing, New York: Free Press, 1968), p. 388.

Nyāyamakaranda by Anandabodha (Varanasi: Chowkhamba Sanskrit Series).

Nyāyamañjari by Jayanta Bhaṭṭa (Varanasi: Chowkhamba Sanskrit Series, 1936)

Nyāya-Sūtra, with Vātsyāyana's *Nyāya-Bhāṣya* (Poona: Oriental Book Agency, 1939).

Nyāyavārtikatātparyatīkāpariśuddhi by Udayana, Vindhyesvariprasada Dvivedin and Lakshman Shastri Dravida, eds., with Vardhamana's *Nyāyanibandhaprakāśa* (Varanasi, CSS, 1924).

Pañcadaśī by Vidyāraṇya, with Rāmakṛṣṇa's *Vyākhyā* (7th ed., Bombay: Nirnaya Sagar Press, 1949).

Pañcīkaraṇa by Śaṅkara, with six commentaries (Bombay: Gujarati Printing Press, 1930).

Pande, G.C.: *Studies in the Origins of Buddhism* (3rd ed., Delhi: Motilal Banarsidass, 1983).

Pandeya, R.C.: 'The Mādhyamika Philosophy: A New Approach', *Philosophy: East and West,* XIV, 5 (April, 1964).

Paṭisambhidāmagga, Bhikkhu Jagadisa Kassapa, ed. (Nalanda: Pali Publication Board, 1960).

Prajñāpāramitā-Stuti by Nāgārjuna, see *Aṣṭasāhasrikā-Prajñāpāramitā.*

Pramāṇavārtika by Dharmakīrti, with Manorathanandin's *Vṛtti,* Dwarikadas Shastri, ed. (Varanasi: Bauddha Bharati, 1968).

Pramāṇavārtika-Bhāṣya by Prajñākaragupta, Tibetan Sanskrit Works Series, Vol. I.

Prameyakamalamārtaṇḍa, with Māṇikyanandin's *Parīkṣāmukhasūtra,* Mahendrakumar Shastri, ed. (2nd ed., Bombay: Nirnaya Sagar Press, 1941).

Rai, Arvind Kumar: 'Non-tenability of Metalanguage in the Context of the Paradox of Nāgārjuna's Dialectic', *Amalā Prajñā,* N.H. Samtani and H.S. Prasad, eds., *P.V. Bapat Volume,* Indian Books Centre, Delhi, 1989.

Ramnan, K. Venkata: *Nāgārjuna's Philosophy as Presented in the Mahāprajñāpāramitāśāstra* (Rutland, Vermont-Tokyo: Charles E. Tuttle Co. for the Harvard-Yenching Institute, Cambridge-Massachusettes, 1966).

Ratnāvalī by Nāgārjuna, see *MŚ.*

Robinson, Richard H.: *Early Mādhyamika in India and China* (Madison, Milwaukee, and London: University of Wisconsin Press, 1967).

Ṣaḍdarśanasamuccaya by Rājaśekhara Sūri (Ahore, 1943).

Sākārasiddhisaṅgrahasūtra by Jñānaśrīmitra, in *Jñānaśrīmitranibandhāvalī,* Anantalal Thakur, ed., Tibetan Sanskrit Works Series, Vol. V (2nd ed., Patna: Kashi Prasad Jayaswal Research Institute, 1987).

Sākārasiddhiśāstra, See *Jñānaśrīmitranibandhāvalī.*

Sambandhavārtika, See *Bṛhadāraṇyakopaniṣad-Bhāṣya-Vārtika.*

Shalya, Yash Deva: *Nāgārjuna-kṛta Madhyamakaśāstra aur*

Vigrahavyāvartanī (New Delhi: Indian Council of Philosophical Research, 1990).

Sāṅkhyapravacana-Bhāṣya by Vijñānabhikṣu, with *Sāṅkhyapravacana-Sūtra* (3rd ed., Calcutta: Vacaspatya Press, 1936).

Śārīrakabhāṣya by Śaṅkara, with *Brahmasūtra,* with Govindānanda's *Ratnaprabhā,* Vācaspati Miśra's *Bhāmati,* and Ānandagiri's *Nyāyanirṇaya* (3rd ed., Bombay: Nirnaya Sagar Press, 1914).

Sartre, Jean-Paul: *Existentialism and Humanism,* Philip Mairet, tr. (7th reprint, London: Methuen & Co., 1965).

Sarvasiddhāntasaṅgraha by Śaṅkara, M. Rangacharya, ed. (Madras: Govt. Press, 1909).

Sarvadarśanasaṅgraha by Mādhava, Vasudeva Sastri Abhyankara, ed. (BORI, 1924).

Sarvāstivāda-Pañcavastukaśāstra, N. Aiyaswami Sastri, resto. from the Chinese, *Visva-Bharati Annals,* X

Śatasāhasrikā-Prajñāpāramitā, Pratapachandra Ghosa, Part I, N.S. No. 1006 (BI, 1902).

Satyasiddhiśāstra, N. Aiyaswami Sastri, resto. from the Chinese, GOS, No. 159 (Baroda: Oriental Institute, 1975).

Saundarananda by Aśvaghoṣa (4th ed., Delhi: Motilal Banarsidass, 2031 Anno Vik.).

Saura-Purāṇa (2nd ed., Anandashram, 1924).

Sharma, C.D.: *A Critical Survey of Indian Philosophy* (Delhi: Motilal Banarsidass, 1964).

Siddhāntaleśasaṅgraha by Appaya Dīkṣita (2nd ed., Varanasi: Achyuta Granthamala, 2011 Anno Vik.).

Śrībhāṣya by Rāmānuja, Vasudeva Sastri Abhyankara, ed., Bombay Sanskrit and Prakrit Series (Bombay, 1914).

Śrīmad-Bhāgavata (Gorakhpur: Gita Press).

Stcherbatsky, F.Th.: *The Conception of Buddhist Nirvāṇa* (Leningrad, 1927).

Streng, Frederick J.: *Emptiness* (Nashville: New York: Abingdon Press, 1967).

Suzuki, D.T.: *On Indian Mahāyāna Buddhism,* Edward

Conze, ed. (New York: etc.: Tharper & Row, 1968).

Śvetāśvatara-Upaniṣad, see the compilation referred to above.

Syādvādamañjarī by Maliṣeṇa, see *Anyayogavy avacchedad-vātiṁśikā Taittiriya-Upaniṣad,* see the compilation referred to above.

Taittirīyopaniṣad-Bhāṣya by Śaṅkara (Gorakhpur: Gita Press).

Takakusu, Junjiro: *The Essentials of Buddhist Philosophy,* Wingtsit Chan and Charles E. Moore, eds. (Bombay, etc.: Asia Publishing House, 1956).

Tantravārtika by Kumārila Bhaṭṭa, with *Mīmāṁsā Sūtra,* Śabara's *Mīmāṁsā-Bhāṣya,* (Poona: Anandashram, 1953, 1970, and so on).

Tarkasaṅgraha by Ānandajñāna, T.M. Tripathi, ed., GOS, No. 111 (Baroda: Central Library, 1917).

Tattvopadeśa by Śaṅkara, in *Prakaraṇapañcaka* (Varanasi: Achyuta Granthamala, 1990, Anno Vik.).

Tattvopaplavasiṁha by Jayarāśi Bhaṭṭa, Sukhlal Sanghavi and Rasiklal C. Parikh, eds., GOS, No. LXXXVII (Baroda: Oriental Institute, 1940).

Tejobindu-Upaniṣad, see the compilation referred to above.

Therīgāthā, Bhikkhu Jagadisa Kassapa, ed (Nalanda: Pali Publication Board).

Triṁśikā-Bhāṣya by Sthiramati, with Vasubandhu's *Triṁsikā-Vijñaptimātratasiddhi,* Thubtan Chogdub and Ramashankara Tripathi, eds. and tr. (Varanasi: Varanaseya Sanskrit Vishva-Vidyalaya, 1972).

Tripathi, Bhagirathaprasada: ' "*Śune Kukkurāya Hitam" iti Śūnyam', Sārasvatī Suṣamā,* XXIV, 2 (Bhādrapada, 2026, Anno. Vik.).

Tucci, Giuseppe (ed.), *Pre-Diṅnāga Buddhist Texts on Logic from Chinese Sources,* GOS, No. XLIX (Baroda: Oriental Institute, 1929).

Udāna, see *Dhammapada.*

Uttara-Gītā by Gauḍapāda, with auto-commentary (Shriranga: Shri Vanivilas Press, 1926).

Vaidalya-Sūtra by Nāgārjuna, Sempa Dorje, recons. and tr. from the Tibetan (Varanasi: Tibetan-Hindi Centre, 1974).

Vedāntasiddhāntamuktāvalī by Prakāśānanda, with Jivananda Vidyasagara's *Vyākhyā* (3rd ed., Calcutta: Vachaspatya Press, 1935).

Vibhāṣāprabhāvṛtti, see *Abhidharmadīpa*.

Visuddhimagga by Buddhaghoṣa, with Bhadantacariya Dhammapala's *Paramatthamañjūsātikā*, Revatadhamma, ed. (Varanasi: Varanaseya Sanskrit Vishvavidyalaya, 1972), Vol. III.

Vivaraṇaprameyasaṅgraha by Vidyāraṇya (Varanasi: Achyuta Granthamala, 1996 Anno Vik.).

Vivekavilāsa by Jinadatta Sūri, Jhumakalal Rataria, ed. (Belganj, Agra: Saraswati Granthamala Office, 1976 Anno Vik.).

von Glasenapp, Helmuth: *Buddhism—A Non-Theistic Religion*, Irmgard Schloegl (London: George Allen & Unwin, 1970).

Yogabhāṣya, with *Yoga-Sūtra* of Patañjali, and four glosses, etc., under the title *Sāṅga-Yogadarśana* (Varanasi: CSS, 1935).

Yogavāsiṣṭha, wiih Ānandabodha's *Tātparyaprakāśa* (Varanasi: Achyuta Granthamala, 2033, Anno. Vik.).

Index

A Free Man's Worship, 109
Abhāva-Śūnyatā, 78
Abhidharmadīpa, 56
Abhidharmakośa, 41
Abhidharmakośa-Bhāṣya, 41
Ābhidharmika, 3
Abhisamayālaṅkāra, 37
Abhisamayālaṅkārāloka, 132
abhūta-parikalpa, 79
absence (*avidyamānatā*), 35
Absolute, 37, 86, 87, 96, 100, 123, 130
Absolute (*apratītyasamutpanna-dharma*), 125
absolute birthlessness (*atyantānutpāda*), 115
Absolute Brahman, 53
absolute negation (*atyantābhava*), 115
absolute negation (*nirviśeṣa naña*), 118
Absolute Nihilism, 3, 31, 33, 49, 57, 58, 107, 146
Absolute Nihilist, 146
Absolute of Hegel, 147
Absolute Reality, 51
absolute Śūnyatā, 97
Absolute Void, 62
Absolutism, 1, 11, 33, 36, 37, 40, 41, 49, 52, 95, 143, 144
Absolutist, 145
Absolutist Mysticism, 146
Absolutistic interpretation, 53
Absolutistic monism, 3
abstract (*vivikta*), 96
acintya, 37
Ādi-Buddha, 40
advaita, 52
Advaita Vedānta, 1, 52, 89, 117, 118
Advaitin(s), 35, 36, 111, 136, 148
Advaitin's Brahman, 138
Advaitin's *Māyā,* 149
Advaitism, 35, 36, 132, 137
advaya, 52
Advayavairasaṅgraha, 127
Advayavajra, 31, 88
Aggañña-Sutta, 27
Aggi-Vacchagotta-Sutta, 24
agnīndhana, 32
ajātivāda, 136
ākāśa, 114
ākāsānañcāya-tana-saññā, 74
ākiñcaññāyatana-saññā, 74
akkhaṇas (*khandhas*), 16
Akṣapāda, 108
Akutobhayā, 2
Ālayavijñāna, 37
Albert Camus, 109
Alice Through the Looking-Glass, 145
Alīka, 62
Alīkavāda, 118
All is nothing, 70
allegorical, 7
All-Enlightened One (*Samyak-Sambuddha*), 95
All-Enlightened-One-Hood, 95
All-Enlightenment, 96, 97
all-knowing (*sarvajñatā*), 98
Amarāvikkhepikā, 70
amṛta, 67
analytic zeroism, 54
Ānanda, 18, 38, 40
Ānandabodha, 133
Ānandajñāna, 134
Ānanda-Sutta, 25
Anātman, 78
Anattā (soullessness), 77
Anatta-Pariyāya, 25
Aṅguttara-Nikāya, 76
anicca, 11
Anicca-Sutta, 24
Animitta, 76, 78
animittacetosamādhi, 74
Animitta-Samādhi, 76
Anispanna-svabhāvatā, 79
anitya, 42
annihilation, 13
antithetic Void, 115
an-ubhaya, 110
Anupada-Sutta, 24
anupalambha, 98

anyathābhāva, 128
Apara-Accharāsaṅghātā - Vagga, 26
Appaṇihita, 76
Appaṇihita-Samādhi, 76
apprehension (*upalambha*), 35
aprāptatva, 114
apratītya-samutpanna, 86
arañña-saññā, 74
Arhat, 38
Arthur Schopenhauer, 4
Ārya, 123
Āryadeva, 3, 31, 52, 58, 69, 116, 128, 147
Āryasammtīyas, 41
Ārya-Sandhinirmocana-Sūtra, 37, 45
Asaṅga, 37, 46, 56, 79, 80, 82, 83, 132
asaṅkhata/asaṁskṛta, 90
Asaṅkhata-Saṁyutta, 26, 27
Asat, 67, 68
Asat-Kārya, 68
Assutavā-Sutta, 24
Aṣṭādhyāyī, 25
Āstika, 17
Aśūnya, 56
Aśvaghoṣa, 37, 78, 79, 83
Atadbhāva-Śūnyatā, 78, 79
Ātānāṭiya-Sutta, 26
atheism, 14
Ātma-dṛṣṭi (soul-view), 78
Ātman, 16, 32, 41, 127, 128, 130
Ātmīya-dṛṣṭi (view of things concerning the soul), 78
attā, 15, 17, 42
attainment (*pratilambha*), 35
attainment of Nibbāna., 43
Aṭṭhaka-Vagga, 24
atthattā'ti, 18
Atyantābhāva, 1, 118
Avalokiteśvara, 40
avayavas, 68
Avyākata-Saṁyutta, 25
avyākṛtas, 107, 149
avyākṛtāstivādin, 56
awareness (*viññāṇa*), 96
ayoga-śūnyatā, 56

Bādhva, 134, 135
Bahuśrutīya school, 29
Bahuśrutīyas, 29
bāhyārtha-śūnyatā, 81
Bāla-Vagga, 24
Bapat, P.V., 121
bases (*dhātus*), 96
Bāṣkali, 134, 135
being (*bhāva*), 32
being (*sat*), 110
being a modification (*vikāra*), 134
being-non-being (*sad-asat*), 134
Bergson, Henri, 118, 121
beyond both *(sad-asat tatparaṁ yat*), 134
beyond-the-four-moments (*catuṣkoṭi-vinirmukta*), 110
Bhaddaji-Sutta, 26
Bhagavad-Gītā, 20, 133
Bhagavadgītā-Bhāṣya, 25
Bhagavat, 134
Bhaṭṭa, Jayanta, 36, 46
Bhaṭṭa, Jayarāsī, 4, 5, 69, 71, 109
bhāvanānu-palambha, 35
Bhāvaviveka, 1, 2, 57, 65, 115, 130, 149
Bhūtakoṭi, 78, 126, 128
blank phenomenalism, 50, 89
bliss (*sukha*), 37
Bodhi *charyāvatāra*, 2, 52
Bodhi-Chitta, 52
Bodhisattva Vimalakīrti, 135
Bodhisattvas, 146
body (*kāyā*), 16
Bradley, 147
Brahma-*bhūta*, 23
Brahma-*yāna*, 24
Brahmajāla-Sutta, 26
Brahman, 20, 21, 23, 35, 38, 73, 131, 136, 137
Brahman (*Brahma-patta*), 23
Brahman of the Vedānta, 147
Brahmanimantanika-Sutta, 25
Brahmatattvasamīkṣā, 133
brahmodya, 56
Brāhmaṇa(s), 38, 39
Brown, Norman O., 149
Buddha, 8, 9, 10, 12, 13, 14, 15, 16, 17, 18, 19, 20, 21, 34, 38, 39, 40, 43, 44, 59, 61, 62, 73, 74, 75, 90, 91, 93, 97, 107, 123, 131, 143, 148
Buddha, a dualist, 11
Buddha, a phenomenalist, 11
Buddhaghoṣa, 12, 41, 76, 77, 82
Buddhahood, 41
Buddhapālita, 1, 2, 149

Buddhas, 7, 19, 29, 42, 70
Buddha's *Dharma-kāya*, 37
Buddha's statements, 7
Buddha's theses of egolessness, 88
Buddhism, 16, 17, 29, 31, 32, 36, 41, 42, 44, 55, 63, 73, 81, 89, 90, 114, 123
Buddhism and *Śūnyatā*, 51
Buddhism, Chinese, 50
Buddhism, Japanese, 50
Buddhism, Tibetan, 50
Buddhist idealism, 37
Buddhist Mind, 43
Buddhist Saṅgha, 29
Buddhist schools, 44
Buddhologist, 15, 19, 51
Burnouf, 49
Buston, 99, 105

Candrakīrti, 1, 2, 4, 13, 14, 33, 58, 59, 60, 61, 62, 75, 87, 91, 94, 98, 111, 112, 113, 117, 119, 124, 125, 126, 127, 128, 129, 131, 132, 134, 144, 145, 147, 149
Carnap, 117
Cārvāka, 15, 17, 20
Catuḥśataka, 3, 58, 129
Catuḥstava, 2
catukoṭika, 77
catuṣkoṭi, 14
causal efficiency (*arthakriyākāritva*), 12
causality (*pratyaya*), 32
Central Philosophy of Buddhism, 51
cessation of *Māyā/Avidyā (Māyā-Nivṛtti)*, 136
cetiya, 21
Chāndogya-Upaniṣad, 67, 68
changeless (*dhruva*), 37
character (*svabhāva*), 126
Chatterjee, A.K., 54, 63, 116, 121
Chinese San-lun school of Buddhism, 53
Cittamātratā, 37
citta-pracāra, 98
Cittaviśuddhi-prakaraṇa, 52
conceptual thinking (*vikalpa*), 98
conditioned (*saṅkhata/saṁskṛta*), 32, 90
conscient (*parā*), 133
Constructive ideation, 79, 80
contemplation (*bhāvanā*), 35
contentless negation (*nirviṣaya naña*), 118
conventional truth (*saṁvṛti-satya*), 33
Conze, Edward, 63
Cūla-Mālukya-Sutta, 24, 25
Cūla-Saccaka-Sutta, 24, 25
Cūla-Suññatā-Sutta, 73, 76

Dakṣiṇāmūrti-Stotra, 36
Dasabala-Sutta, 27
Dasgupta, S.N., 49, 63, 89, 102
Dasuttara-Sutta, 26
definable, 134
de Jong, J.W., 63
Destructed Nihilism, 4, 29
determinate (*saguṇa*) Brahman, 136
determinate negation, 94
Devadaha-Sutta, 26
Dhamma(s), 12, 13, 23, 77
Dhamma-yāna, 24
Dhammacakkapavattana-Sutta, 27
Dharmadhātu, 78
dharma-hood, 97
Dharmakāya, 40, 80
Dharmakīrti, 17, 25, 39, 47, 144
Dharma-nairātmya, 78, 89
Dharma of non-duality, 135
dharma-positing, 123
dharma, saṁskṛta, 123
Dharma-śūnyatā, 78, 30
dharmas, 30, 74, 123
dharmas, *asaṁskṛta*, 123
Dharmatā, 126, 127, 128
dhātus, and *āyatanas*, 16
dhātus, elements, 11
Dhātuvibhaṅga, 25
Dhātuvibhaṅga-Sutta, 25, 26
Dīghanakha, 70, 75
Dīghanakha-Sutta, 24
Diṅnāga, 42, 144
Docetism, 36, 40
doctrine of beginningless and endless pure mind, 41
doctrine of non-apprehension, 147
doctrine of universal relativity, 86
dogma (*diṭṭhīnāṁ*), 14
dogmas (*diṭṭhis*), 107
doubt (*vikalpa*), 42
duḥkha, 9
Duka-Nipāta, 26
Dutiya-Metta-Sutta, 26

Dutiya-Nānākaraṇa-Sutta, 26

Eduard vön Hartmann, 4, 109
ego (*pudgala-nairātmya*), 89
elements (*dharmas*), 86
Enlightened Ones, 39
enlightenment, 41
enlightenment (*bodhi*), 35
equivocal, 7
essence, 32
essence (*svabhāva*), 32
essenceless (*niḥsvabhāva*), 110
essencelessness, 114
Essencelessness (*naiḥsvābhāvya*), 126
essencelessness (*niḥsvabhāvatva*), 35
essencelessness of all dharmas, 44
eternal (*nicca/sassata*), 24
eternal being (*nitya*), 129
eternalism, 20, 43, 44
Eternalism (*sassata-vāda*), 14
Exalted One, 39
experience (*anubhava*), 119
expressible (*prapañca*), 111
expression (*prapañcopaśama*), 98
extinction (*nirodha-satya*), 29

Fa-shang Mahāyāna school, 99
false (*mṛṣā*), 119
final deliverance (*śānta*), 11
first sermon, 44
five dharmas, 75
formless consciousness (*sva-saṁvitti*), 98
four categories of intellect (*chatuṣkoṭi-vinirmukta*), 52
four categories of reason, 112
four-cornered, 77
Four-Cornered Negation, 70
Four Noble Truths, 7, 19, 34, 58, 59, 60, 61
Four Noble Truths (*ariya saccāni*), 9

Gauḍapāda, 46, 55, 74, 81, 131, 134, 140, 142
Ghoṣaka, 78, 82
gifts (*bali-patiggāhikā*), 21
Gijjhakūta hills at Rājagaha (Gṛdhrakūṭa hills), 44
Gītā, 67, 68
God [*Issara*], 20
God, the Creator, 38
Godhead, 148
Greek metaphysics, 43

Haribhadra, 132, 140
Harivarman, 4, 29, 30, 31, 39, 45, 47, 77, 78, 82, 91, 111, 115, 143
Harsh Narain, 47, 119, 139
Hegel, G.W.F., 109, 110, 115, 119
Hegelian dialectic, 110, 111
Hemacandra, 64
higher than the highest (*parāt-para*) Brahman, 136
Hīnayāna, 5, 129, 143
Hīnayāna Buddhism, 77
human consciousness, 117
Hume, R.E., 130
Hwa-yāna, 40

Idealism, 11, 36, 81
Idealism-cum-Absolutism, 45
idealist theory of contentless consciousness (*sva-saṁvitti*), 42
idle dialectic, 56
ignorance (*avidyā*), 35
imperishable (*a-mosadhamma*), 22
imperishable (*a-vipariṇāma-dhamma*), 24
impermanence (*anicca*), 77
impression (*saṁskāra*), 96
impurities (*āsavas*), 76
incomprehensible (*an-upalabbhiyamāna*), 40
inconscient (*aparā*), 133
independent reality, 50
indescribable (*prapañcopaśama*), 94
indeterminate (*nirguṇa*) Brahman, 136
indeterminate negation, 94
individual (*puggala*), 13
individual soul (*attā*), 85
ineffable, 37
inexpressible, 137
inexpressible (*prapañcopaśama*), 110, 111
Isipattana Migadāva (*Sārnāth*), 44
Islam, 39
Itivuttaka, 22

Jacobi, H., 49

Jaini, Padmanabhas., 65
Jainism, 112
Jalāl ud-Dīn Rūmī, 100
jalpa, 108
Jamīl Maẓharī, 145
Jāṇussoṇi-Sutta, 24
Jāṇussoṇibrāhmaṇa-Sutta, 27
Jātaka, 25
Jayatilleke, K.N., 20, 25
Jñānaśrīmitra, 31, 46, 56, 65
Jojitsu (*satyasiddhi*), 29

kāla, 32
Kāmabhū-Sutta, 24
Kamalaśīla, 2, 99
Kandaraka-Sutta, 27
Kant, Immanne, 137, 138, 142
Karl Marx, 109, 110, 119
karma-kāraka, 32
karma-phala, 32
kathā, 108
Kathāvatthu, 24, 27, 74
Kaṭha-Upaniṣad, 137
Kātyāyana, 90
Kayyaṭa, 69
Keith, A.B., 49, 149, 150
Kern, H., 49
Kevaṭṭa-Sutta, 25, 26
Khandha theory, 17
Khandha-Saṁyutta, 24
khandhas, aggregates, 11
Kimura, 47
Kolika-Sutta, 24
Koṭis, 92, 110
kṣaṇa-vāda, 12
kṣaṇabhaṅga-vāda, 12
Kṣatriyas, 38
Kumārajīva, 29, 113
Kumārila, 39, 47, 64

lakkhaṇas (*khandhas*), 16
Lakshmipuram Srinivasachar, 141
Laṅkāvatāra-Sūtra, 31, 37, 41, 42, 58, 129
law of discontinuous continuity (*pratītya-samutpāpa*), 89
limited negation (*paryudāsa*), 80
logico-linguistic test, 108
Lokāyata, 4, 109
Lokāyata Negativism, 69
Lokāyata philosopher, 69
Lokāyata schools, 5, 13
Lokāyatika-Sutta, 24
Lord (*Bhagavat*), 144
Lord of the gods (*devātideva*), 38
Louis de La Vallée-Poussin, 51, 139, 140
Ludwig Wittgenstein, 138

Mādhava, 64
Mādhyamaka-Śāstra, 2, 33, 58, 93
Mādhyamika, 29, 31, 32, 33, 35, 36, 37, 42, 44, 51, 52, 56, 62, 70, 73, 75, 80, 81, 85, 86, 87, 88, 89, 90, 91, 92, 93, 94, 95, 97, 98, 99, 100, 108, 109, 110, 111, 112, 113, 115, 116, 117, 118, 119, 123, 126, 128, 129, 130, 131, 132, 134, 137, 147, 148, 149
— dialectic, 107, 110, 111, 115
— literature, 111
— Nihilism, 2
— philosophy, 4, 49, 54, 59, 76, 116, 143, 144, 145, 148
— school, 5, 32, 33
— Śūnyatā, 136
— system, 1
— texts, 145
— thought, 146
Mādhyamikas, 14, 31, 45, 69, 124, 144
Mādhyamika's treatment of the ultimate truth, 113
Mādhyamika's *Śūnya*, 1, 115, 145
Mādhyamika's Śūnyatā, 53, 54
Mādhyamika's Void, 115
Mādhyamikālaṅkāra-Kārikā, 57
Mādhyamikavṛtti, 2
Mādhyamikologists, 67
Magga-Saṁyutta, 27
Mahābhāṣya, 25
Mahā-Brahman, 38
Mahāmoggalāna, 75
Mahānidāna-Sutta, 24
Mahāparinibbāna-Sutta, 26
Mahāsamaya-Sutta, 26
Mahāsāṅghikas, 8, 29, 41
Mahāvagga, 16, 26, 27
Mahāvagga, Bhesajja Khandhaka, 26
Mahāyāna, 1, 5, 20, 29, 32, 37, 40, 41, 50, 53, 100, 143
— Buddhism, 76, 78

— doctrines, 3
— *Sūtras*, 37, 79, 95, 97
— tradition, 135
Mahāyāna-Parinirvāṇa-Sūtra, 41
Mahāyāna-śraddhotpādaśāstra, 37, 79
Mahāyānist(s), 33, 148
Maitreyanātha, 36, 37, 78, 79, 82, 83
Maitreyī-Upaniṣad, 131
Majjhima-Nikāya, 73, 76
Mallisena, 64
Māṇḍūkya-Kārikā/Āgamaśāstra, 133
Mañjuśrī, 135
manussa-saññā, 74
materialism, 18
matter (*skandha*), 32
May, Jacques, 124
Māyā, 133
Māyā/Avidyā, 136
Māyā-nivṛtti, 133
metaphilosophy, 54
metaphysical Absolutism, 51
metaphysical speculations, 43
metaphysical systems, 10
metaphysical view of existence, 9
metaphysics, 9, 10, 11, 14, 43, 75, 107, 110
Middle Path, 60
Moggalāna-Sutta, 25
Mokṣa, 36, 52
momentarians (*kṣaṇabhaṅgavādins*), 31
monism, 49
mudrās, Seals, 9
Muḥammad, 43
Munitz, Milton K., 149
Murti, T.V.R., 3, 50, 51, 62, 65, 66, 96, 104, 123, 126, 139

Nagara-Sutta, 24
Nāgasena, 76, 82
Nāgārjuna, 1, 3, 4, 30, 32, 33, 34, 37, 40, 46, 47, 58, 59, 60, 61, 62, 66, 69, 74, 86, 87, 88, 89, 90, 93, 95, 96, 111, 112, 116, 117, 124, 126, 127, 132, 145, 147
Nāgārjunakṛta *Madhyamakaśāstra aur Vigrahavyāvartani*, 50
Nāgārjuna's refutation, 50
Nāgārjuna's *Vigrahvyāvartani*, 57
Nagarjunikond, 29
Naiḥsvābhāvya (essencelessness), 78
Nairātmya, 79
— (soullessness), 78
— (substancelessness), 79
— interpretation of Buddhism, 63
Nairātmya/Śūnyatā, 78
Naiyāyika, 36, 69, 115, 118
Narendra Deva, 47
Nāstika, 17, 42
Nathan Katz, 105
natthattā, 18
Navya-Naiyāyika, 115
negation, 117
Negative Absolute, 86
nēum, 18
nevasaññānāsaññāyatana-saññā, 74
Neyārtha-Sūtra, 14
Neyattha-Sutta, 14
Nibbāna, 8, 9, 10, 13, 14, 16, 19, 20, 22, 23, 43, 75, 88
Nibbāna/Nirvāṇa, 7, 14, 17
Nidāna-Saṁyutta, 24, 27
Nietzsche, 91, 109
nihilationism, 18, 20, 43, 44
Nihilationism (*uccheda-vāda*), 14
nihilationist (*vaināśika*), 42
Nihilism, 1, 3, 4, 11, 13, 30, 44, 45, 57, 67, 75, 81, 109, 115, 117, 132, 143, 144, 146, 147
Nihilism, absolute, 1
Nihilist, 32, 148
Nihilistic interpretation of the Mādhyamika system, 96
nihilistic scholasticism, 49
Nihilistic Śūnyavādins, 75
Niḥsvabhāvatā, 76, 114
Niḥsvabhāvatā (essencelessness), 79
Nikāyas, 16
nirākāra-buddhi, 4
niranvaya-vināśa, 68
nir-attā, 10, 42
Nirbīja-Asamprajñāta-Samādhi, 100
Nirguṇa-Brahman, 19, 40
Nirmāṇa-kāya, 40
nirodha, 30
Nirvāṇa, 29, 32, 36, 40, 53, 59, 80, 95, 99, 126, 128, 135, 147, 149
Nirvāṇa-teacher, 143
niṣprapañca, 50
Nītārtha-Sūtra, 14
Nītattha-Sutta, 14

Nityanivṛtti, 62
no-soul (*anattā*), 15
Noble Eightfold Path, 10
Noble Truths, 32
non-apprehension (*an-upalambha*), 35, 114
non-being (*abhāva*), 32, 56, 60
non-birth (*anutpāda*), 30
non-conceptual knowing (*nirvikalpaka*), 98
non-duration, 11
non-origination by nature (*svabhāvenānutpādaḥ*), 87
non-substantiality (*anattā*), 11
non-Śūnya real, 94
non-Śūnyatā, 94
not this", (*neti*), "not this" (*neti*), 134
nothing (*asat*), 110
noumena, 11
Nyāya, 42
Nyāya epistemology, 69
Nyāya-Sūtra, 68, 69
Nyāya-Vaiśeṣika, 68, 114, 115

oblations (*bali*), 22
one door (*eka-dvāraṁ*), 39
ontological nihilism, 4
other-being, 128

Pacceka-sambuddha, 38
padārtha, 114
Pāli, 21
Pāli Buddhism, 76, 85
Pāli canon, 15, 16, 38, 40, 45, 70, 73, 75, 76, 77, 87, 143
Pañcīkaraṇa, 133
pañcama-koṭi, 111
pañcamakoṭi-mātra, 111
Pande, G.C., 25
Pandeya, 55
Pandeya, R.C., 54, 63
Pāṇini, 25
para-loka, 17
paramānuttarā suññatā, 74
paramārtha, 69
Paramārthatā, 78
Paramattha-Sacca, 14
Paratantra-Svabhāva, 78
Pārāyana-Sutta, 26, 27
Pārāyana-Vagga, 24
Parikalpita-Svabhāva, 78
parinibbāna, 29
Parinibbāna/Nibbāna, 38
Pariniṣpanna, 80
parisuddha-paramānuttara-suññatā, 74
Patañjali, 25, 69
Paṭhama-Mahānāma-Sutta, 26
Paṭhama-Metta-Sutta, 26
Paṭhama-Nānākaraṇa-Sutta, 26
Paṭhama-Tathāgata-Acchariya-Sutta, 26
pathavī-saññā, 74
Paṭiccasamuppāda, 10
Paṭisambhidāmagga, 76
perception (*cakṣurādīndriya*), 32
perception (*saṁjñā*), 96
Perfect (*Pūrṇa*), 130
perishable (*mosa-dhamma*), 22
permanent (*dhuva*), 24
Pheṇapiṇḍūpama-Sutta, 24
phenomena, 11
pilgrimage of four holy places, 38
Prabhācandra, 64
pragmatical (*vyavahārasatya*), 124
Prajñākaragupta, 39
Prajñākaramati, 2, 88, 90, 92, 146, 149
Prajñāpāramitā, 3, 33, 87, 95, 96, 97, 98, 99, 100, 145
— Sūtras, 45
Prakṛti, 133
Pramāṇamālā, 133
pramāṇas, 69
Pramāṇavārtika, 25
prapañca, 97, 126
Prasad, H.S., 121
prasajya-pratiṣedha, 117
Prasaṅga, 2, 108
Prasaṅga (*reductio ad absurdum*), 107
Prāsaṅgika-Mādhyamika., 99
Prāsaṅgika school, 2, 3, 149
Prāsaṅgikas, 2
Prasannapadā, 2
pratigha-sparśa, 114
Pratilambhānupalambha, 35
pratiṣedha-dharma, 114
Pratītya-samutpāda, 3, 32, 35, 60, 61, 62, 87
pratītya-samutpanna, 86, 128
pratyakṣā-palāpinam, 69
presence (*vidyamānatā*), 35
pudgala, 41

Pudgala-nairātmya, 78, 85
pudgala-śūnyatā, 85, 89
Puggalavādins, 41
Pure Being, 115
Pure Consciousness, 52, 78
pure nihilism, 49, 55
Pure Nothing, 115
pure nothing (*tucchā*), 137
pure Void, 58
pūrṇa, 131
Pūrva-Mīmāṁsā, 39
Pūrva-Mīmāṁsakas, 89
pūrva-pakṣa, 69
Pyrrho, 112

qualified (*rāga-rakta*), 32
Quiescence, 146
quiescent (*śānta*), 96
Quietude, 146

Raghunātha Śiromaṇi, 115
Rai, Arvind Kumar, 121
Rājaśekhara, 4
Rāmānuja, 64
Ratnāvalī, 2, 52
real (*vāstavī*), 137
Realism, 11, 29, 44, 45
realist theory of object-directed
consciousness, 42
reality (*tattva*), 127, 130
reductio ad absurdum, 108
relation, 32
relative being (*upādāya prajñapti*), 87
relics (*sarīra-pūjaṁ*), 38
rest (*gatāgata*), 32
Ṛg veda, 67
Rhys Davids, 17
Risālah fi 'l-Mawjūd, 109
Robinson, Richard H., 115, 120
Rubā'iyyāt, 109
rūpa, form, 11
Russell, Bertrand, 109, 114, 117, 120
Ryukan Kimura, 47

sabbaṁ atthi, 13
sabbaṁ me khamati, 14
sabbaṁ me na khamati, 14
sabbaṁ natthi, 14, 70
Sabbamatthīti-Kathā, 27
Sacca-Saṁyutta, 27
Saccidānanda, 40
Ṣaḍdarśanasamuccaya, 4
sādhanā-dharma, 114
Saguṇa-Brahman, 40
Sakkapañha-Sutta, 26
Śakra, 38
Samādhi, 42, 100
sāmānya-lakṣaṇa, 42
Sambandhavārtika, 25
Sambhoga-kāya, 40
Sammādiṭṭhi-Sutta, 24
Sāmmitīyas, 5
Sammuti-Sacca, 14
Sammutiñāṇa-Kathā, 24
Saṁsāra, 14, 35, 80, 135
saṁsarga, 32
saṁskāra, 32
Samtani, N.H., 121
Saṁvṛti-Satya, 14
Saṁyutta-Nikāya, 23, 75, 76
Saṅgārava-Sutta, 26
Sañjaya Belaṭṭhiputta, 112
Sañjaya Velaṭṭhiputta, 70
Śaṅkara, 15, 25, 36, 55, 64, 133, 134,
136, 140, 141, 142
Sāṅkhya, 3
Sāṅkhya-Yoga, 68
San-lun school, 99
Sanron [Mādhyamika] School, 31
Śāntarakṣita, 2, 57, 99
Śāntideva, 31, 58, 90, 147, 149
sānvaya-vināśa, 68
Sārandada-Sutta, 26
Sāriputta, 38, 39
Sartre, Zean-Paul, 109, 119
Sarvadarśanasaṅgraha, 4
sarva-dharma-sūnyatā, 29, 89
sarvadṛṣṭi-niḥsaraṇa, 80, 97
sarvadṛṣṭi-prahāṇa, 70, 94, 97, 110
Sarvasiddhāntasaṅgraha, 55
Sarvāstivādins, 12, 30, 77, 89
Sarvaśūnyatā-nirākaraṇa-Prakaraṇa, 68
Sat-Kārya, 68
Śataśāstra, 3, 58, 69
satkāryavāda, 136
sattvaśūnyatā, 30, 78
Satyasiddhi, 89, 114
Satyasiddhi school, 30, 31
Satyasiddhiśāstra, 29
Saundarananda, 79

Saura-Purāṇa, 133
Sautrāntika-Svātantrika-Mādhyamika, 2
Sautrāntika-Yogācāra, 42
Sautrāntikas, 12, 144
Sayyid Sulaymān Nadwī, 119
Schayer, S., 50, 51
Schopenhauer, 109
Seals (*mudrās*), 9
seats (*āyatanas*), 96
self (*pudgala-sūnyatā*), 29
self-abnegation, 43
self-effacement, 43
sense-data (*dhammas*), 13
sequence (*ānupūrvī*), 112
sequence (*purvāparakoṭī*), 32
sermons, dharma-denying, 123
Shāntideva, 52
Sharma, C.D., 50, 52, 63
silence (*tūṣṇīṁbhāva*), 14, 44, 98, 110, 134
silence/dumbness, 97
skandhas, 30, 96
So-being (*tathābhāva*), 126
soteriological nihilism, 4
soteriology, 10
soul (*attā*), 10, 16
soullessness (*anattā*), 85
soullessness (*Nairātmya-vādinaḥ*), 42
speech (*an-upalambha*), 110
spiritual life, 10
Sri Aurobindo, 53, 63
Śrīharṣa, 111, 112, 134, 141
Śrīmad-Bhāgavata, 134
Śruti, 134
Śruti, Māyā, 137
St. Augustine, 135
Stcherbatsky, F. Th., 11, 50, 51, 63
Sthiramati, 56, 79, 80, 81, 83
Streng, Frederick J., 54, 63
stūpas, 38
Subhūti, 95, 96, 97
Suchness (*Tathatā*), 126
śuddha Mādhyamika, 56
suffering (*duḥkha*), 32, 77
Sukhāvatī-vyūha, 40
Sunīdhavassakāra-Vatthu, 26
Suñña, 75
Suñña/Suññatā, 74
Suñña/Śūnya, 73
suññaṁ Brahma-vimānam, 73
Suññatā, 76, 77, 85
Suññatā-Samādhi, 76
Suññatā/Śūnyatā, 73
suññatā-vihāra, 73
Suññatā-Vimokkha, 76
suñño loko' (the world is Suñña), 75
Śūnya, 30, 33, 35, 56, 62, 87, 96, 100, 118, 127, 128, 130, 131
Śūnya and Anātman, 77, 78
Śūnyatā, 2, 3, 30, 31, 32, 34, 35, 51, 58, 59, 60, 61, 62, 76, 78, 79, 80, 81, 85, 86, 87, 88, 91, 92, 93, 94, 95, 96, 97, 100, 111, 113, 114, 115, 125, 126, 127, 128, 130, 131, 134, 137, 138, 144, 145, 146, 147
—as Essenceless Being, 88
—as neither Being nor non-Being, 90
—as Non-Being, 89
—as Relative Being, 86
—Doctrine, 86
—of the conditioned, 97
—of the unconditioned, 97
—of Śūnyatā, 93, 97
— -svabhāva, 79
Śūnyatopādāna-Prakaraṇa, 68
Śūnyavāda, 3, 4, 31, 35, 49, 51, 52, 55, 57, 62, 67, 81, 85, 95, 118, 127, 146, 149
Super-God, 40
Sureśvara, 25, 36, 133
Svabhāva, 125, 126
Svabhāva (essence), 78
Svabhāva, Self-Being, 124
svabhāvaśūnya, 50
Svabhāva-Śūnyatā, 78, 79
svacchā parā saṁvid, 4
svalakṣaṇa, 42
Svarga, 40
Svatantrānumāna, 2
Svātantrika, 2
Svaymbhū, 40
Śvetāśvatara-Upaniṣad, 133
Suzuki, D.T., 42, 50, 51, 53, 63, 135, 141
synthetic Void, 115

Taittirīya Upaniṣad, 16, 67
Takakusu, Juñijiro, 29, 30, 45, 46, 47, 120
Tathāgata, 8, 12, 14, 17, 20, 32, 35, 36, 38, 79, 148

Tathatā, 37, 78, 127, 128, 130
Tattva, 124, 125, 126
Tattavasaṅgraha, 57
Tattvopadeśa, 133
Tattvopaplavasiṁha, 4, 69
tetralemma, 14
Tevijja-Sutta, 26
the highest wisdom, 96
the theory of origination of things, 34
theism, 14
Theo-Buddhism, 37
theory of impermanence (*anicca*), 12
theory of universal impermanence, 143
Theravāda, 20, 85
Theravādins, 12
Therīgāthā, 77
Tīrthikas (non-Buddhists), 127
Titthāyatana-Sutta, 26
total negation (*prasajya-pratiṣedha*), 80
total Nihilism, 4, 55
Total Transcendence, 107
transcendental *Śūnyatā,* 97
transcends thought and speech, 134
Trikāya-stava, 40
Triṁśikā, 80
Tripāṭhi, Bhagiratha Prasad, 78, 81
truth (*paramārtha*), 14
Tuccha, 62
Tuccha/Alīka, 1, 118
Tucci, Giaseppe, 70
Tuṣita-loka, 40
tūṣṇīṁbhāva, 97
tūṣṇīṁbhāva (silence), 124
tūum, 18

ubhaya, 110
ubhaya-pratiṣedha-svabhāvatā, 92
ubhaya-saṅkīrṇātmatā, 92
Udāna, 22, 23, 27, 101, 102
Udāyi-Sutta, 25
Ultimate Truth (*paramārtha*), 134
ultimate unsurpassable *Suññatā,* 74
Umar Khayyām, 109
Unamuno, 109
unconditioned (*a-saṁskṛta*), 32
unfree (*asvatantra*), 78
universal relativity (*pratītya-samutpāda*), 87
unrest (*dukkha*), 11
upādāya-prajñapti (relative appearance), 87
Upāli-Sutta, 27
Upaniṣads, 9, 130, 131, 134, 136
Uposatha-Sutta, 26, 27
Urfi Shīrāzī, 135
Uttara-Gītā, 131
Uttaratantra, 37

Vācaspati Miśra, 68, 133
Vacchagotta, 18
vāda, 108
Vaibhāṣika school, 56
Vaibhāṣikas, 31, 89, 144
Vaidalya-Sūtra, 69
Vaidya, P.L., 66
Vaināśika (nihilationist), 56
Vaiśeṣika, 3, 42
Vaitulika, 56
Vaitulika Ayoga-Śūnyatāvādin, 56
Vajirā-Sutta, 25
Vajjians, 21
Vajjiputtakas, 41
Vasubandhu, 25, 37, 56, 78, 80, 83
Vātsīputrīyas, 5, 41
Vedānta, 50, 55
Vedāntizers of Mādhyamika philosophy, 52
Vedāntizing the Mādhyamika, 136
Vedas, 7, 39
Vedic *Asat,* 67
Vedic-Upaniṣadic *Asat,* 53
Venerable One, 39
Vesālī, 44
Vibhāṣāprabhā-Vṛtti, 56, 78
Vidyāraṇya, 133, 136, 142
Vigrahavyāvartanī, 2, 58, 69, 115, 116
Vihāras, 36
Vijñanavādins, 45, 56, 80, 85, 144
Vijñaptimātratā, 37
Vijñānavāda, 1, 50, 52, 56, 80, 81, 89, 132, 144
vikalpa-buddhi, 127
vikalpa-jāla, 97
Viññāṇa, 16, 22, 23
viññāṇa/citta, 16
viññāṇa-sota, 16
viññāṇañ-cāyatana-saññā, 74
Visākhā, 21
Viṣṇu, 40

vitaṇḍā, 108
vitaṇḍā-vādin, 108
vivartavāda, 136
Vivekavilāsa, 4
Void, 49
void (*ākiñcanya*), 30
void (*śūnya*), 96
voidity (*śūnyatā*), 96
voidness (*śūnyatā*), 30
Vṛtti, 57
vyavahāra, 69, 136

Well-Accomplished One, 23
what is, is not, 134
whole (*avayavin*), 30
Whole of the wholes (*dharmatā* = *dharma-kāya*), 51
will (*nirīha*), 78
Witness consciousness, 119
world as pure illusion, 88
world-ruler (*rājā cakkavattī*), 38

Yama's realm, 21
Yasha Deva Shalya, 50
Yaśomitra, 78, 82
Yoga-Bhāṣya, 100
Yogavāsiṣṭha, 55, 131, 136
Yogācāra, 78
Yogācāra school of Buddhism, 55
Yogācārā-*Svātantrika-Mādhyamika*, 2, 56, 57
Yogācāra-Svātantrika-Mādhyamika school, 99
Yogācāra-*Vijñānavāda*, 36, 44, 56
Yogācāra-*Vijñānavādins*, 57
Yogācāras, 57

Zeno, 108